# *Your Baby & Toddler*

Also by Anne Marie Mueser, Ed.D.

*While Waiting*
(with George E. Verrilli, M.D., F.A.C.O.G.)

# *Your Baby & Toddler*

## A Commonsense Guide from A to Z

## Anne Marie Mueser, Ed.D.

ST. MARTIN'S GRIFFIN ⚜ NEW YORK

www.stmartins.com

Illustrations by Durell Godfrey, except where noted

Some material in this book was previously published by St. Martin's Griffin in *Welcome Baby* (1982) and *Talk & Toddle* (1983).

Library of Congress Cataloging-in-Publication Data

Mueser, Anne Marie.
    Your baby & toddler : a commonsense guide from A to Z / Anne Marie Mueser.
      p.   cm.
    ISBN 0-312-28791-7
    1. Infants—Care.   2. Toddlers—Care.   3. Child rearing.   4. Parenting.
5. Children—Health and hygiene.   I. Title.

RJ131 .M686   2002
649'.122—dc21

                                         2002069936

First Edition: December 2002

10 9 8 7 6 5 4 3 2 1

# INTRODUCTION

*Your Baby & Toddler* contains much information I wish I had known more than twenty years ago when my daughter was born and I was a new mother. The joy of the first moment I held her in my arms was instantly joined by the realization that I had a lot to learn.

Raising a child involves ongoing communication. The process is not simple, nor does it always prove to be predictable. There is no book that can provide a perfect formula that, if followed, would guarantee a smooth path. Your focus should be on your child and interaction with his or her needs.

The arrival of a new baby, even if it is not your first, is likely to bring many changes to your household. Many of the caretaking techniques you work out in response to surprises presented by your newborn in the early days will become comfortable routines as you and your baby move into the "settled baby" stage. Then, as the weeks turn into months, your infant will begin to become independently mobile, which will open up new worlds of excitement (and danger).

You will have to cope with a certain amount of conflict as your child—no longer an infant in arms—goes from being a mobile baby to toddler, and strives for independence and mastery over the various tasks of living. The toddler phase, which for most children occurs approximately between the ages of one and three, is one of the most interesting developmental periods—and also one of the most difficult, both for the child and for the caregivers. The specific suggestions in *Your Baby & Toddler* are intended to help you encourage your child in development of self control and autonomy, while at the same time providing a safe environment and appropriate limits.

*Your Baby & Toddler* supplies information and commonsense suggestions, arranged to make access to the information as easy as possible. The alphabetical format is intended to help you find what you need easily. While some sections contain information that may apply to all babies and toddlers, others are more age specific—newborn, settled baby, mobile baby, or toddler. The chart on pages ix–xvii will help you locate material that pertains to your child at each particular stage of development.

# TOPICS COVERED IN THIS BOOK

| | Newborn 0–3 mos. | Settled Baby 2 mos.–6 mos. | Mobile Baby 6 mos.–14 mos. | Toddler 1 yr.–3 yrs. |
|---|---|---|---|---|
| **A** | | | | |
| Accidents (prevention) | • | • | • | • |
| Accidents and emergencies (first aid) | • | • | • | • |
| Aggressive behavior | | | | • |
| Air quality | • | • | • | • |
| Alcoholic beverages | | | • | • |
| Allergies | • | • | • | • |
| Antibiotics | • | • | • | • |
| Apgar scale | • | | | |
| Asthma | | • | • | • |
| Attention deficit hyperactivity disorder (ADHD) | | | | • |
| Automobile safety | • | • | • | • |
| **B** | | | | |
| Baby food (commercially prepared) | | | • | • |
| Baby food (homemade) | | | • | • |
| Baby talk | | | • | • |
| Babyproofing (for a newborn) | • | | | |
| Baby-sitters | • | • | • | • |
| "Back to Sleep" | • | • | | |
| Baths (for a newborn) | • | | | |
| Baths (for an older baby or toddler) | | • | • | • |
| Beds and bedding | • | • | • | • |
| Bedtime (early or late?) | | | • | • |

| | Newborn 0–3 mos. | Settled Baby 2 mos.–6 mos. | Mobile Baby 6 mos.–14 mos. | Toddler 1 yr.–3 yrs. |
|---|:---:|:---:|:---:|:---:|
| Bedtime rituals | | | • | • |
| Bed-wetting | | | | • |
| Bibs | • | • | • | • |
| Bites (treatment) | • | • | • | • |
| Biting | | | • | • |
| Bleeding | • | • | • | • |
| Books for your child | • | • | • | • |
| Booster seats | | | • | • |
| Bottle-feeding | • | • | • | • |
| Bowel movements (newborn) | • | • | | |
| Bowel movements (older baby or toddler) | | | • | • |
| Breast-feeding | • | • | • | • |
| Breath-holding | | | • | • |
| Breathing (newborn) | • | | | |
| Breathing emergency | • | • | • | • |
| Burns and scalds | • | • | • | • |

## C

| | Newborn 0–3 mos. | Settled Baby 2 mos.–6 mos. | Mobile Baby 6 mos.–14 mos. | Toddler 1 yr.–3 yrs. |
|---|:---:|:---:|:---:|:---:|
| Candy and sweets | | | • | • |
| Carriages | • | • | | |
| Carriers (backpack) | | | • | • |
| Carriers (basket) | • | • | | |
| Carriers (front) | • | • | • | |
| Carriers (sling) | • | • | • | |
| Cereals | | | • | • |
| Challenged children | • | • | • | • |
| Changing diapers | • | • | • | • |
| Chewing (learning how) | | | • | |
| Chewing gum | | | • | • |
| Child abuse | • | • | • | • |
| Childproofing | • | • | • | • |
| Choking | • | • | • | • |

| | Newborn 0–3 mos. | Settled Baby 2 mos.–6 mos. | Mobile Baby 6 mos.–14 mos. | Toddler 1 yr.–3 yrs. |
|---|---|---|---|---|
| **M** | | | | |
| Manners | | | | • |
| Masturbation | | | • | • |
| Medications | • | • | • | • |
| Medicine cabinet (items to have) | • | • | • | • |
| Memories and milestones | • | • | • | • |
| Mobiles (for newborns) | • | | | |
| Motion sickness | • | • | • | • |
| **N** | | | | |
| Nail care (for a newborn) | • | | | |
| Naps | | | • | • |
| Navel care | • | | | |
| Neatness | | | | • |
| Nightmares | | | • | • |
| Noise (and the newborn) | • | | | |
| Nose (care of) | • | • | • | • |
| Nosebleeds | • | • | • | • |
| Nutrition | • | • | • | • |
| **O** | | | | |
| Outings for a newborn | • | | | |
| Overweight children | | | • | • |
| **P** | | | | |
| Pacifiers (for a newborn) | • | • | | |
| Pacifiers (for a mobile baby or toddler) | | | • | • |
| Pants (waterproof) | • | • | • | • |

| | Newborn 0–3 mos. | Settled Baby 2 mos.–6 mos. | Mobile Baby 6 mos.–14 mos. | Toddler 1 yr.–3 yrs. |
|---|---|---|---|---|
| Solid foods | | | • | • |
| Spanking | | | • | • |
| Strollers | | | • | • |
| Stuttering or stammering | | | | • |
| Sudden infant death syndrome (SIDS) | • | • | | |
| Sugar | | | • | • |
| Sunburn | • | • | • | • |
| Swaddling | • | | | |
| Swallowed objects | • | • | • | • |
| Swimming | | | | • |

---
**T**
---

| | | | | |
|---|---|---|---|---|
| Talking | | | • | • |
| Tantrums | | | | • |
| Teasing | | | | • |
| Teething | | | • | |
| Television | | | | • |
| Temperature (of indoor environment) | • | • | • | • |
| Temperature (taking child's) | • | • | • | • |
| Terrible twos | | | | • |
| Thrush | • | • | • | • |
| Thumb-sucking | • | • | • | • |
| Toilet training and learning | | | | • |
| Tonsils | | | | • |
| Tooth care (daily) | • | • | • | • |
| Toy safety | • | • | • | • |
| Toys | • | • | • | • |
| Travel | • | • | • | • |

---
**U**
---

| | | | | |
|---|---|---|---|---|
| Underweight children | | | • | • |

# Your Baby & Toddler

# ACCIDENTS (PREVENTION)

It's up to you to provide as safe an environment as possible for your child. Accidents involving babies and toddlers frequently occur at home, and many of these accidents could be prevented. Constant supervision is key to your child's safety. Take him with you to answer the phone or the door. If your child crawls or toddles out of sight, follow immediately. Don't leave a mobile baby or toddler alone in a room even for a moment, unless she is safely in a secure structure such as a crib or a playpen.

Remember that your child is likely to imitate your actions as he develops. That can be very appealing for behaviors such as brushing teeth or turning the pages of a magazine. That can be very dangerous, however, if what the child mimics is lighting matches, opening medication bottles, poking at fires, making tea, or adjusting the cords and controls of lamps or small appliances.

## MAKE THE SURROUNDINGS SAFER

*   Beware of places that could trap your child. Closets, freezers, refrigerators, toy chests, and similar containers can be death traps as well as enticing hiding places.
*   Make sure your child can't get locked in the bathroom or any other room in your home. A folded towel hung over the top of the bathroom door will keep a child from closing the door completely and playing with the lock.
*   Check to make sure that any furniture your child might use to pull himself up is sturdy enough to support an active toddler and secure enough not to tip over. If you are uncertain about a chair or small decorative table, for example, store it until your child is older.
*   Watch out for sharp edges and corners at your child's face level. If you can't (or prefer not to) remove the object, pad the hazardous edges for the time being.
*   Windows should have guards to prevent falls. Don't assume that your child will be unable to open a window. Don't count on her being obedient enough to stay away from a window. Make sure that window guards are strong and properly installed.
*   Beware of things your toddler can pull down from overhead. A tug on the corner of a tablecloth could pull down the entire contents of the table along with the cloth. A pull on the cord of a toaster, iron, coffee maker, or food processor could bring the appliance crashing down on a small head.
*   Unused electric outlets should be capped or covered so your child can't poke things into them. Keep the child away from outlets that are in use. If outlets can be made inaccessible by large pieces of furniture, so much the better.
*   Safety gates should be used at the top and bottom of stairs.
*   A bathroom is a dangerous place for a mobile baby or toddler to be for even a few moments without supervision. The surfaces are hard and slippery. A dive into a tub, empty or filled, could cause serious injury.
*   A toddler's fascination with the toilet can be a hazard. Although unlikely, it is possible for a young child to fall headfirst into the toilet and drown. That has been known to happen. Keep the bathroom door shut and the toilet lid down.
*   Automatic garage doors can be extremely dangerous. If you have one, make sure that

your child is safe and under control before you close the door. Never leave the transmitter where a child could get to it. Children have been known to crush themselves while playing with the controls of automatic doors. If you plan to install an automatic door, the type that stops moving when it hits an object, child, or animal along the way down is the best choice.

- Appliances such as blenders, food processors, mixers, or fans, which have moving parts that could seriously injure a child, should be left unplugged and out of reach. Keep tools, garden equipment, and sharp kitchen utensils away from a small child.
- Beware of anything that could get caught around a child's neck, such as drapery or venetian blind cords, clotheslines, and the cord of a telephone, lamp, or appliance. Such items should never be within reach of a child's crib.

## PREVENT POISONING

- Keep all poisonous household materials such as detergent, cleaning fluid, deodorizers, furniture polish, and paint where your child can't get to them. That means keep the containers completely out of reach. Don't trust safety caps to do the job. Do not store such items in kitchen baseboard cupboards unless they're under lock and key. Even so-called childproof latches are not truly childproof.
- Keep your medicine cabinet locked. Discard any substances not in current use. Never refer to medicine (even vitamins) as candy. Be careful not to leave items you use regularly (such as oral contraceptives, vitamins, aspirin, acetaminophen, or other pain relievers) out where your child could get to them.
- Your home is likely to contain many substances that are not obviously poisonous but that could, if consumed in quantity, cause serious harm to a small child. Such items include alcoholic beverages, vitamins, over-the-counter medications, and many cosmetics.
- A number of seemingly innocent-looking houseplants could, if consumed in sufficient quantity, poison a child. Philodendron, for example, is a popular houseplant because it is so easy to grow, but it could be very harmful if consumed in quantity. Mistletoe may be a romantic seasonal decoration, but it is poisonous and should be kept well out of reach. Your local poison control center may be able to provide a publication listing the common plants that are potentially dangerous.
- It is not just certain houseplants that could cause a problem. There are many outside plants that could be a problem if your child consumes them. Of course, no young child should be left unsupervised for that to happen. Obviously poison ivy, poison oak, and poison sumac should not be touched or consumed, but there are many other plants and flowers your child should not eat.

  Your child should be kept away from certain spring and summer flowers such as crocuses, daffodils, irises, or lilies of the valley. If you use them as cut flowers, put the vase where your child cannot get to it. If your landscaping includes the flowering shrub rhododendron or morning glories, keep your child away. Your local poison control center or health department may be able to provide you with a complete list of plants and shrubs used in your area that should be considered off-limits to your child.
- A mother's handbag is an enticing object. Don't keep anything in it that your toddler should not have. If you must carry medication with you, take only one day's supply at a time. Don't leave your purse where your child can freely explore.

## PREVENT DROWNING, CHOKING, SUFFOCATION, BURNS AND SCALDS

- A young child can drown in as little as two inches of water. Never leave a baby or toddler unsupervised in the bath or near a body of water, whether it be a deep puddle, pond, lake, stream, river, swimming pool, or even a wading pool.
- Prevent choking. Don't leave your child alone with a bottle or food. Keep items small enough to choke a child (marbles, coins, buttons, hard candy, etc.) out of reach. Don't use Styrofoam to serve a toddler; it can be bitten or broken into dangerously small pieces.
- Prevent suffocation. Keep plastic bags or food wrap away from children. Don't use thin plastic as a mattress cover. A small child should not use a pillow in the crib. Never place a baby to sleep facedown, or on soft bedding such as a featherbed.
- Make certain that your child does not have an opportunity to play with matches or lighters.
- Space heaters can cause serious burns as well as fires if tipped over. Keep any portable heaters and children well separated.
- Prevent scalding. If your household water is hot enough to cause a problem, either adjust the setting or make sure that your child does not have access to the faucets at any time. Be careful when using a teakettle or coffeepot. Don't set hot liquids on a surface of cloth within a child's reach.

Keeping dangerous objects out of reach may not always be easy. Make sure that a child can't move or pile things to climb to forbidden objects. Some children seem to be natural climbers and explorers. If your child is one of these, you'll have to be extra careful. Remove not only the dangerous objects but also the means to get to them.

No matter how carefully you have organized and arranged your own living space for your child's safety, keep in mind that friends and relatives may not have done the same. Be especially attentive to your mobile baby or toddler when visiting outside your home. A good rule to remember wherever you are, home or away, is, "A small child out of sight (unless sleeping soundly) is a child at risk."

# ACCIDENTS AND EMERGENCIES (FIRST AID) ⸺

Take a few minutes right now to plan how you would handle an emergency involving your newborn, mobile baby, or toddler. You may never need to use these plans, but it's helpful to be ready just in case.

Know how to summon help fast when you need it. Now is the time to look up any telephone numbers you might need in an emergency. Write the numbers here and make a copy to keep by your telephone. Fasten the list securely to the wall or on the table by the phone so the numbers don't disappear just before you need one of them. It's prudent to avoid counting on being able to remember details such as numbers in an emergency.

## EMERGENCY TELEPHONE NUMBERS

Doctor or HMO _____

Rescue squad or ambulance _____

Hospital _____

Pharmacy _____

Fire department _____

Police _____

Poison control center _____

Neighbor, relative, or friend _____

Local parent help hotline _____

Is there a general emergency number in your area, such as 911, that will connect you to an operator who will route your call to the appropriate agency? If so, write it here: _____

If possible, you might wish to program the various emergency numbers into your telephone's speed-dial system. It is useful, however, to have the numbers listed on paper as well, in case a power failure or other glitch manages to erase the telephone's memory.

Make certain that other family members, baby-sitters, or household employees know how to use these emergency numbers if necessary.

Take a course in CPR (cardiopulmonary resuscitation) and other first-aid techniques. What you learn may save the life of your child or someone else. CPR is best learned by ac-

4

tually practicing the techniques firsthand. The first-aid suggestions in this book may provide some of the information you would need in an emergency, but it's better to learn directly from trained experts if at all possible.

## EMERGENCY DIRECTIONS TO YOUR HOME

In a crisis, don't count on being able to provide clear or correct directions to your home for emergency services. Panic time is no time to be figuring out whether to take a right turn or a left, or if it's the second or third light from a main intersection.

*Now,* before the need arises, plan exactly what you would tell someone who needed to reach your home in an emergency. Write the directions down, step-by-step. Write these directions in the space below, along with your phone number. Keep them in a handy place. Your child's life could depend on it.

---

Although many 911 emergency services are supposed to be able to dispatch accurately based on your phone number alone, don't count on it. Be prepared with step-by-step directions to your home. Make sure that anyone responsible for care of your child knows how to find and use these directions in an emergency.

---

The following sections of this book provide additional information about first-aid procedures and how to respond to specific emergency situations involving your child. It would be useful to read these pages at least once before the need actually occurs.

ASTHMA, PAGE 11
BITES (animal, human, insect, snake), PAGE 28
BLEEDING, PAGE 30
BREATHING EMERGENCY, PAGE 42
BURNS AND SCALDS, PAGE 43
CHOKING, PAGE 58
CONVULSIONS (seizures), PAGE 66
CROUP, PAGE 70
ELECTRICAL SHOCK, PAGE 83
FALLS, PAGE 85
FIRE, PAGE 93
POISONING, PAGE 146

# AGGRESSIVE BEHAVIOR _____

Some aggressive behavior is normal for a toddler who is actively engaged in acquiring independence. A very young child typically lacks the understanding and the social controls to manage aggressive behavior. Adult intervention, therefore, is often necessary to keep characteristic toddler assertiveness from getting out of hand. It takes tact, energy, and lots of patience to help a toddler become a civilized, courteous human being.

A toddler may tend to treat other children as things rather than as persons. He may grab other children or push them away as the whim strikes. Such behavior is normal for the age, and children should be allowed to work things out for themselves as long as no one gets hurt. If, for example, one toddler grabs a toy and the other says *"No!"* and takes the toy back, the exchange will cause no harm and may even be a step toward learning to share. However, if a child bites or kicks, hits or pushes hard, or uses toys as clubs or missiles, then you should intervene immediately.

When it is necessary for you to intervene, the first step is to stop the child from doing whatever it is she should not be doing. Calmly but firmly say, "No, you must not kick (bite, hit, throw the toy)." At the same time, it may be necessary for you to protect and comfort the victim. Try picking up the child who needs protection in one arm while you use your other arm to restrain the child who is out of control. Do whatever seems to make the most sense, but do it quietly and firmly. Do not scream or hit. If you combat a child's aggression with more of the same, you may indeed end the immediate crisis. Striking a toddler, however, will do more to set a bad example than to teach self control and socially acceptable behavior.

To what extent, if any, should you encourage your child to stand up for his or her rights by fighting back if another child becomes aggressive? While children should be allowed to settle minor disputes through give-and-take, you should not encourage or condone violence. Never permit a child to hurt someone else, even under severe provocation. Toddlers are not yet able to think through the social consequences of their actions, so you or another caregiving adult will have to draw the line between healthy assertiveness and unacceptable aggression. (See also *Biting,* pages 29–30.)

# AIR QUALITY

Many environmental influences are beyond your control as your baby or toddler develops. What you *can* control, however, is the quality of the environment within your own home. You can make your home as healthy as possible. A good place to start is by providing an atmosphere of clean air for your child's immature respiratory system, and also for your own health.

The lungs of a newborn or toddler are still developing and growing. A household in which smoking is allowed is inevitably harmful to children. Children of smokers have an increased incidence of respiratory infections including bronchitis, pneumonia, and inner-ear infections. Infants of parents who smoke are more likely to die from sudden infant death syndrome (SIDS) than are babies of nonsmoking parents. If both parents smoke, the risks are increased. There seems to be a direct relationship between the amount of cigarettes smoked in a household and the incidence of a baby's respiratory infections. Little lungs will develop better if the air quality in the home is not degraded by tobacco smoke.

If your home contains a wood or coal stove, it's important that the device functions well with a clean chimney. There should always be a source of continuous fresh air. If you use incense in your home for recreational or ritual purposes, avoid using it in the presence of your child. Recent research has found that the smoke produced by burning incense contains cancer-causing chemicals.

# ALCOHOLIC BEVERAGES

Should you allow a small child to take a sip of wine, beer, or a cocktail? Opinions vary. Many pediatricians and psychologists would answer a firm *no* and advise against introducing a child to the taste of alcohol for any reason. Others would say that an occasional sip of a parent's drink causes no harm and avoids giving drink the special appeal of forbidden fruit.

Whatever choice you make for your family is likely to be influenced by personal feelings and your particular culture. It's best to do what makes sense to you without making a fuss about it one way or the other. Here are some additional suggestions and guidelines:

- If your family has wine with dinner or for special occasions and rituals, you may wish to include your children in that experience. If so, a few drops of wine in a cordial glass filled with water will do nicely.
- If for any reason one parent has strong feelings against drinking, it's better for both parents to respect those feelings. It's best that parents agree on the approach to alcohol they are going to take, and not argue about it in front of the child.
- Even if you choose to allow your child to take an occasional sip, it's important to store alcoholic beverages out of your child's reach. A very big drink in a very small person could cause great harm, even death.
- Don't leave the remnants of last night's party where your child can finish off the left-over drinks before you surface and realize what is happening.

Keep in mind that alcohol is a drug, and no child needs it. An occasional swallow, however, is unlikely to do your child any physical harm. Some care providers even recommend taking a bit of brandy or whisky and rubbing it on the gums to relieve teething pain. Use your own judgment and do what makes sense to you.

# ALLERGIES

Tendency toward allergic reactions may run in families, although a child's allergies may take an entirely different form from the parent's. What are allergies, and why do some people have them? The environment contains many substances that typically cause little or no bother to most people, although some of those substances have the potential to cause harm. The body of an allergic person has an abnormally sensitive reaction to one or more substances that for most people would cause no problem.

The four main categories of substances that can trigger allergic reactions are divided according to the way a person comes in contact with them:

- things that are swallowed (foods, drinks, medications)
- things that are breathed (dust, pollen, feathers, smoke, animal dander, etc.)
- things that are touched (dyes, plants, wool, plastic, detergents, etc.)
- things that are injected (medications, venom from bites)

## THINGS THAT ARE SWALLOWED

A high percentage of allergic reactions in babies and toddlers seems to involve food. A child's sensitivity to food substances may result in digestive problems, breathing difficulties (asthma), or skin rashes (eczema or hives). A bottle-fed infant may develop an allergy to cow's milk. If so, a soybean-based formula is typically prescribed as a substitute. (See *Formula (for bottle-feeding)*, pages 95–96.)

If allergic reactions tend to run in your family, you should be especially careful about the introduction of new foods to your baby. Certain foods are more likely to cause a problem than others, and it's wise to be aware of such foods so you can be especially cautious and delay using them. Among the most allergy-provoking foods are products containing wheat (gluten), eggs, citrus fruits, strawberries, chocolate, peanuts, tomatoes, corn, artificial food colorings, and cow's milk.

To identify potential food problems, introduce new foods one at a time and in very small quantities. Begin with a tiny portion—a teaspoonful or less—and feed the new food as part of the diet for at least a week. If no adverse reaction occurs, then you can introduce something different. If you present more than one new food at a time, however, you won't be able to identify the culprit should an allergic reaction occur.

Many children become less sensitive to certain foods as they grow older, and it may even be possible to avoid triggering an allergic reaction by waiting a while before offering a food that might cause trouble. Some infants under six months of age, for example, tend to be sensitive to eggs. Some of those same children, however, would have no problem with eggs if they had not eaten any eggs until after their first birthday.

If you suspect that your child is experiencing any food allergies, you should work with your health-care provider to identify and manage the problem.

## THINGS THAT ARE BREATHED

There are many things around us that, if breathed, can cause an allergic reaction in a sensitive person. Among them are household dust, animal dander (the scaly stuff that flakes off an animal's skin at the base of the hair), pollen, feathers, and smoke.

Wheezing, sneezing, a runny nose, and, in severe cases, asthma can result from an allergy to something breathed. Consult your health-care provider if you suspect that your child may be allergic to something that is causing one or more of these symptoms. Even if your child is not obviously allergic to tobacco smoke, smoking in the home can result in damage to the child's respiratory system without provoking immediately obvious symptoms. (See *Smoking,* page 161.)

If dust is the problem leading to your child's allergic reaction, you'll have to be especially meticulous about cleaning the house. Keep the child's room as free of dust as possible. That process may involve getting rid of the rug, drapes, curtains, and any other surfaces which tend to hold the dust. Use a wet mop or cloth to wipe down surfaces daily. Put away dusty toys such as fluffy stuffed animals for a while until the problem is under control.

If you suspect that a household pet is the source of the difficulty, begin by keeping the animal away from direct contact with the child. Keep the pet out of rooms where your child crawls, walks, or spends any significant amount of time. Use the vacuum cleaner at least once a day to remove animal hair and dander from the rugs and furniture. Your veterinarian may prescribe a spray to use on the animal to reduce the amount of loose dander. Keep the animal well groomed, but don't do the grooming in the presence of the child. If the animal is an important part of your family, ask your health-care provider to recommend an allergist who works with children. Before you resort to giving your pet away, you should find out for sure if the animal is causing your child's problem, and whether there are remedies available. It would be very unfortunate to banish the family dog from your household and then find out that your child's problem was not the dog at all, but feathers from the sofa pillows.

## THINGS THAT ARE TOUCHED

If your child seems prone to skin irritation or rashes, you might suspect a contact allergy. Try to figure out what substance regularly comes in contact with the affected part. A rash around the waist and top of each leg, for example, would suggest that the plastic from the edge of a disposable diaper or waterproof pants might be causing the problem. A rash around the neck might be from a wool sweater. A rash in various places under the clothing might be a reaction to detergent residue remaining in clothes after laundering. Once you've identified the suspect, keep that substance away from contact with your child's skin. If detergents are the problem, run the clothes through an extra rinse cycle to remove as much of the residue as possible.

## THINGS THAT ARE INJECTED

Certain types of allergic reaction—to penicillin or bee stings, for example—can be very serious, even life-threatening. You won't know for sure if your child has such a problem until the first time he actually has an allergic reaction to an injected medicine, sting, or bite. If your child shows any signs of an allergic reaction to an injection, sting, or bite, obtain medical assistance immediately. Call your health-care provider or make a rapid visit to an emergency room. Be especially alert for the appearance of breathing difficulty, swelling, fever, or rash.

A useful organization to contact for further information on allergies is:

Asthma and Allergy Foundation of America
1233 20th St. NW, Suite 402
Washington, DC 20036
www.aafa.org
1-800-ASTHMA

# ANTIBIOTICS

Antibiotics can be very useful and, in some cases, lifesaving drugs. You should not, however, administer any such medication to your child without a doctor's prescription for the specific condition and time at issue. Antibiotics are specifically able to fight bacteria; they are not effective against viruses. It is important, therefore, to find out what is causing the child's illness and not assume that an antibiotic would be a cure-all. Unnecessary use of antibiotics may sensitize a child and result in allergic reactions. Perhaps even more serious is the fact that overuse of antibiotics may result in development of resistant strains of bacteria in the body. That could cause a problem if the child later comes down with a serious illness that requires treatment with antibiotics.

If your child becomes ill and the doctor prescribes antibiotics, follow the directions exactly. Use up all the medicine as directed, even if the symptoms have passed. Don't save a few pills or drops for the next time. Even if your child appears to be better, the complete course of medication is needed to rid her system of the infection.

# APGAR SCALE

At birth and again five minutes later, a newborn will be observed and rated on five items: heart rate, breathing, muscle tone, skin color, and reflex response. Each item is scored on a scale of zero to two.

A total score of seven or above indicates that the baby is in good condition. Most newborns score seven or more by the time of the five-minute check. A baby who scores four or less requires immediate intervention. Among the factors that may result in a low Apgar score are premature birth and certain medications taken by the mother during labor and delivery.

**APGAR SCALE**

| Item tested | 0 | 1 point | 2 points |
| --- | --- | --- | --- |
| Heart rate | absent | slow (less than 100 beats per minute) | 100 beats or more per minute |
| Breathing | absent | slow or irregular | regular |
| Muscle tone | limp | some motion of extremities | active motion |
| Skin color | blue | pink body, blue extremities | pink all over |
| Reflex response | absent | grimace | cry |

The Apgar scale is named for Dr. Virginia Apgar, the physician who developed it in the early 1950s. It is a useful device for assessing the baby's condition right after birth. It is not, however, a predictor of long-term health, but simply an indicator of how well a baby has come through the stress of delivery.

# ASTHMA

Asthma is an allergic reaction in which the bronchial tubes swell and thicken with mucus, causing a person to wheeze. The muscle spasms that accompany an asthma attack make breathing (especially exhaling) extremely difficult. That can result in panic, which only makes matters worse. Asthma cases seem to be on the increase, for a variety of environmental reasons.

If your child has what appears to be an asthma attack for the first time, you should seek immediate medical assistance. If possible, let someone else call the doctor while you help the child. Support the child in a sitting position. Be calm, reassuring, and comforting. Getting your child to relax will make it easier for him to breathe. Diversions such as a favorite story, song, or quiet game may help. Adding moisture to the air (see *Vaporizers*, page 186) may be beneficial.

Your health-care provider may prescribe medication for you to have on hand so you can deal with future asthma attacks. If you have been instructed by a health-care professional on how to treat your child during an asthma attack, it may not be necessary for you to summon medical aid each time. Your doctor will advise you on the appropriate procedures for your situation.

If your child has a tendency toward asthma attacks, you will have to work closely with your health-care professional to identify and avoid the specific factors that cause those attacks. Feathers, animal hair and dander, wool, dust, and smoke are among the most common triggers for such allergic reactions. It's best that any house, with or without children, be a no-smoking zone, but that is especially important for the place where a child with asthma lives. Tobacco smoke is not the only culprit. Using a woodstove for cooking or heating may also present a problem for a child with asthma.

Emotional factors such as anxiety or tension as well as environmental factors may contribute to the severity of a person's asthma attacks. In order to get the help you need to bring your child's asthma attacks under control, it is important for you to be open and honest in your conversation with your child's health-care provider. Don't be afraid or embarrassed to mention any tensions or problems in the home. That information could be useful in planning appropriate coping strategies.

Some children seem to outgrow asthma attacks as they get older; others do not. It is usually possible, however, to ease the problem so that it is not as upsetting or dangerous to your child's overall well-being.

If your child has asthma, it may bring you comfort to know that you are not alone. An organization known as the Allergy & Asthma Network/Mothers of Asthmatics publishes a quarterly magazine and a newsletter, *The MA Report*, which provide information, encouragement, and updates on the latest medical advances in dealing with asthma and allergies. You can join the organization and get on their mailing list by making a donation. Contact:

Allergy & Asthma Network/Mothers of Asthmatics, Inc.
2751 Prosperity Avenue, Suite 150
Fairfax, VA 22031
800-878-4403 or 703-641-9595
www.aanma.org

Another useful organization is:

Asthma and Allergy Foundation of America
1233 20th St. NW, Suite 402
Washington, DC 20036
www.aafa.org
1-800-ASTHMA

# ATTENTION DEFICIT HYPERACTIVITY DISORDER (ADHD)

Attention deficit hyperactivity disorder (ADHD) is a currently popular diagnostic label that is widely and sometimes inappropriately used. Among some parents and educators of difficult-to-deal-with children, identification of potentially afflicted children and ADHD management via medication has achieved an almost cultlike status, complete with intensely committed Internet support groups.

Also known as attention deficit disorder (ADD), ADHD was first included in the *Diagnostic and Statistical Manual of Mental Disorders* in 1980. Since that time, it has become the most commonly diagnosed childhood behavioral disorder. According to the American Academy of Pediatrics, perhaps three to five percent of children in the United States may have a type of ADHD. That statistic, however, indicates that at least ninety-five percent of children—including many with high energy and activity levels—do not have ADHD.

At this time, there is no one foolproof test that can tell definitively whether a child actually has ADHD. Diagnosis is typically performed by testing and observation of the child and interviews with his parents and teachers. Attaching the ADHD label to a child, therefore, may have a subjective basis. In this country, a diagnosis of ADHD, whether accurate or not, is typically followed by prescription of a medication such as Ritalin. Such medication may well smooth out the child's behavior and make him easier to deal with, but such an approach may not be best for the child's long-term interests.

Parents of a child under three should be extremely cautious about seeking or accepting a diagnosis of ADHD. A correct medical diagnosis of ADHD would be very difficult to make for any toddler because a high activity level is normal for the age. Toddlers are naturally energetic, distractible, impulsive, and difficult to handle. Many of the behaviors characteristic of ADHD children are normal for toddlers. So if your child's day-care center suggests labeling the child and managing her with medication, think carefully about whether or not a change of setting might be a better first choice. (See *Hyperactivity and the normal toddler,* pages 106–108.)

# AUTOMOBILE SAFETY

Automobile accidents are the leading cause of death and serious injury for young children. What makes that statistic especially shocking is that many automobile tragedies can be avoided with the use of a correctly installed safety restraint system. Many parents who genuinely believe they are properly securing their children are actually using restraints that have not been correctly installed.

Whether or not restrained, a young child should not ride in the front seat of a vehicle with a passenger-side airbag. Children have been known to be killed or seriously injured by airbags that deployed in what should have been a minor and fully survivable accident.

## WHY USE A RESTRAINT SYSTEM?

- A properly designed and correctly used restraint system can prevent serious injury and perhaps save your child's life in the event of an accident.
- Holding a child is no protection. An infant on an adult's lap could be crushed during a crash or could be sent flying around the vehicle with great force. Even without impact, a sharp stop could catapult and severely injure or kill an unrestrained child.
- A securely restrained child cannot fall out a window or a door of a moving vehicle. A restrained child cannot interfere with or distract the driver.
- Adult seat belts are not suitable for young children. They may not restrain the child and, in the event of a crash, seat belts may even cause a child internal injuries. Adult seat belts are for grown-ups.
- In all fifty American states and throughout Canada, it is illegal to transport a child in a motor vehicle without using an approved safety restraint system.

## COMMON EXCUSES

- "It takes too much time to use the restraint system." Perhaps so, but it's time well spent. Today's restraints are easier to use than earlier models.
- "A car restraint is expensive." Your child's life is precious and priceless. If the cost of a child-restraint system is a problem for your family, it may be possible to rent or borrow one. Ask your health-care provider or local social service agency for suggestions. In many communities, organizations and civics groups such as the chamber of commerce have programs to help families of limited means obtain the safety seats they need for their children.
- "My child doesn't like to be confined." A child who is always fastened in correctly before the vehicle is allowed to move will not object to the restraint. Such a child knows no other way to travel. Once a parent makes an exception or two to that rule, however, trouble may loom ahead. Even so, that is not a time when the child's wishes should govern your actions. If your child manages to undo the restraint, pull over as soon as you can do so safely. Refasten the device and make it clear that you are going nowhere unless your child is properly buckled up.
- "We're only going to the corner store." A high percentage of accidents occur within a few miles of home. And what might be just an insignificant fender bender for an adult could cause serious injury or death to a small child.
- "I'm a good driver." Maybe so, but many people on the road are not. An animal crossing your path, a patch of ice, a sudden glare of sun in your eyes, or many other unpredictable things could cause you to have an accident, no matter how skilled a driver you might be.

## CHOOSING A CAR SEAT

When you decide which safety restraint to use for your child, you must take into account the correct type of car seat for your child's age and size, as well as whether the particular model you select will work in your vehicle. It's important to choose a car seat that is safe and easy to use; if it isn't, you may be tempted to skip it from time to time.

To make sure that the seat model you purchase meets appropriate safety standards, look for the label indicating that it meets Federal Motor Vehicle Safety Standard (FMVSS) 213. It's not a good idea to purchase or borrow a used car seat of unknown origin. If you do obtain a used seat, you should make sure that it is no older than five years and that it has never been in a crash. Even if the device appears to be in good condition, a seat that has been in a crash may have hidden damage that would make it less likely to protect your child in the event of an emergency.

## TYPES OF CAR SEATS

There are three basic types of car seats available: infant seats, convertible car seats, and booster seats. Which you choose at a given time depends on your child's age and size.

### INFANT SEATS

An infant seat, which supports an infant in a semiupright position, is always used facing the rear of the car. It should be installed in the rear seat and used until the child weighs twenty pounds and is one year old. If your child weighs less than twenty pounds on her first birthday, continue to use the rear-facing infant seat until she reaches twenty pounds. If your child reaches twenty pounds before her first birthday, you will need to switch to a convertible-type car seat that can carry her in a rear-facing position for a while longer.

There is an important reason an infant or child weighing less than twenty pounds or who is less than a year old must ride in a semireclined, rear-facing position. The neck muscles of a baby are simply not strong enough to support the head, should an impact occur. A rear-facing seat that is not completely upright is designed to protect the baby's head. It also distributes the force of impact along the baby's back in a way that helps prevent neck and spinal injuries that could be caused by whiplash, should the head not be properly supported.

### CONVERTIBLE CAR SEATS

A convertible car seat can be used in the semireclining position for an infant facing the rear of the vehicle. For an infant, the seat's shoulder harness straps are threaded through the lower slots of a convertible seat. When your child is at least twenty pounds and one year old, the convertible seat can then be used in an upright position facing forward in the vehicle. For upright use with a child who weighs more than twenty pounds, the seat's shoulder straps are threaded through the highest openings in the seat. When you purchase a convertible seat, be sure to check out the maximum weight for which it is designed. Most can accommodate children up to forty pounds.

### BOOSTER SEATS

When your child outgrows a convertible car seat but is not yet large enough for safe and comfortable use of an adult seat belt, it's time for a booster seat. A booster seat raises your child sufficiently to allow proper placement of the seat belt, so it does not put pressure on his neck.

A booster seat is suggested for children from about forty pounds (approximately age four) to eighty pounds, and until the child is at least four feet nine inches tall. Although a booster seat may not be required by law in your state, your child's safety is at risk if you fail to use one until the child is large enough for the adult seat belt to do its job properly. In fact, small children using an adult seat belt without a booster seat may actually suffer injuries from the seat belt itself, or may slip out of the belt during a crash and thus not have protection. (For additional details, see *Booster seats,* page 33.)

## INSTALLING THE CAR SEAT

Correct installation of the child car seat in your vehicle is essential. No matter how good the device may be, it won't protect your child unless it is correctly installed. Here are the steps for correct installation:

- *Read the directions.* You will need to read the directions for the seat you are using and the directions in the owner's manual for your vehicle to help you locate and install the seat correctly. No matter how obvious it all may seem, it's best to read the directions to be on the safe side.
- *Choose the safest location.* A child should travel in the backseat of the vehicle in the correct car seat for his age and weight. The center of the backseat is generally the safest place to be, unless there is a fold down armrest, in which case a rear-facing infant seat should be located on one side or the other. Of course, if you have more than one small child, only one can be in the center.

- *Use the seat belt to fasten the child seat.* The seat's directions will indicate how and where to thread the seat belt correctly. Tighten the belt as much as you can while you push the child seat as far as you can into the vehicle seat. It may take two people to do the job well—one to push the seat and one to tighten the belt. If you can move the child car seat more than an inch in any direction, it is not tight enough. Try again, read the directions one more time, and get expert help if you are still having trouble.

### ASK FOR EXPERT HELP

Many parents, no matter how smart or well educated, may find it difficult to install a child safety restraint correctly. Manufacturers have not typically made it easy, although that seems to be changing. Don't be embarrassed to ask an expert for help. Call the manufacturer of the safety seat and/or your vehicle. The service department of your car dealer may be able to assist you in installing the child safety seat correctly. In some communities, the local fire department or rescue squad has one or more trained persons who can help. You might try a local police department, sheriff's office, health department, or your health-care provider. The organization known as the National Safe Kids Campaign can provide useful information and a local referral via its Web site: www.safekids.org.

---

# WARNING

Make sure that the seat belts in your vehicle are able to hold the child car seat safely. If the lap and shoulder belts are attached to the vehicle door or the seat bench in a way that places them too far from the vehicle seat, you will need help to find a safe alternative. Consult your local safety expert for possible alternatives. This is something you should take care of before you bring a newborn home from the hospital. Don't wait until the last minute to find out that your car may present a problem for transporting an infant or small child.

If the lap portion of the seat belt in your vehicle does not remain tight, you may need a locking clip to hold the child restraint tightly in place. Consult the owner's manual for your vehicle.

*Use the harness to keep the child in the seat.* Each and every time you allow your child to ride in a vehicle, he should be placed in an appropriate car seat and fastened in using the seat's harness. Consult the car seat directions to make sure you are using it correctly. There are too many models and they change too frequently to include accurate information here.

---

It's important never to make an exception to the rule of proper car restraint use. If your child has figured out how to unbuckle the harness, you must outsmart her. A little duct tape (on the buckle, not her hands) that you remove at the end of the trip is one way to get the job done.

# BABY FOOD (COMMERCIALLY PREPARED) _____

For some parents, the convenience of commercially prepared baby food justifies the cost. If you prefer to purchase little jars instead of making your own baby food and are able to do so, go ahead and don't feel guilty about it. To a baby or toddler, home cooking need not be an essential ingredient of good parenting. You can use commercially prepared baby food to meet your baby's nutritional needs if you pay attention to the labels and choose items carefully.

• Read the list of ingredients and the nutritional information on the jar's label. Pay attention to the order in which the ingredients are listed; they are listed in order of quantity, the largest amount first. A jar with "carrots, potatoes, water, and beef," for example, contains less meat than the same size container with "beef, carrots, potatoes, and water."

- Avoid products with modified starches or added sugar if you can. Mixed dinners, which often contain fillers, are not as good a buy as plain meat or vegetables. If your child doesn't like the texture of the plain strained meats, try mixing a spoonful or two of meat with a vegetable or mashed potatoes.
- Unless you expect to feed the complete contents of the container at one meal, don't feed directly from the jar. Saliva and bacteria from the baby's mouth can speed up spoilage, and raise the risk of making the child sick from a later meal out of the same jar.
- Room temperature is fine; there isn't any need to heat the food. But if you do heat the food, be cautious. It should be warm, not hot. If you use a microwave, be especially careful not to overdo it. Stir to prevent hot spots, and test it before you put it in the baby's mouth. Heat only what you plan to use at that time. Do not store and reheat previously heated food.
- Store open jars in the refrigerator for a day or two, but discard any that remain at the end of the third day, or at least put the food to some use other than feeding the baby.
- Even if you find the food bland and boring, don't add salt to make it appealing to your adult taste. Your baby doesn't need the extra sodium.

By the time your baby is able to handle the coarser texture of junior foods, he will be able to eat many items from the family table if you mash them up. It may still be convenient, however, to use commercially prepared items from time to time.

# BABY FOOD (HOMEMADE)

Homemade baby food is an economical and nutritious way to bridge the gap between the all-milk diet of an infant and the family table meals of a toddler. Baby food is easy to prepare, and you don't need elaborate equipment.

A pot with a tight-fitting lid and a steamer basket are all you need to cook the food. (Steaming vegetables, rather than boiling them in a lot of water, helps to preserve the vitamins and other nutrients.) A blender or food processor can puree whatever you wish to serve in a few seconds. If you don't have one of those appliances, however, don't go out and buy one. The mushy-food stage doesn't last very long. An inexpensive, hand-operated food grinder will do the job, or simply use a fork to mash the food, as parents did for centuries before modern kitchen equipment was available.

To make one meal at a time for a baby, simply steam and then mash or puree a small portion. Remove the baby's food from the pot before adding salt or highly spiced seasoning to what the rest of you are eating. When adding liquid to the food to achieve a smooth consistency, something nutritious is a better choice than plain water, although water will do. The water in which you steamed the vegetables is a good choice because it may still contain some of the lost nutrients. Depending on what you are preparing, you might also consider milk, juice, or soup stock. Beware of items such as stocks made from soup cubes, however, because they are likely to contain a heavy dose of sodium.

If making one meal at a time doesn't suit your lifestyle, prepare a larger quantity and then freeze it in single-serving portions. Prepare the food as if you were going to serve it at the next meal, then divide it into serving-size portions for future use. Servings can be quick-frozen in globs on a cookie sheet or a piece of heavy-duty aluminum foil. Ice-cube trays with individual pop-out containers also work well. Place each frozen serving in plastic wrap or a little plastic bag and store in the freezer for up to a month. Thaw in the refrigerator (or for a few seconds in the microwave to get the job done quickly), as room-temperature thawing encourages bacteria growth.

When you first feed your child solid foods, puree or mash the concoctions to a very smooth consistency. By the time your child is eight months old or so, such preparation is no longer needed or even desirable. Gradually introduce little lumps to your child's food to help ease the transition to the family table. Let the child begin to use the gums and whatever teeth she has for chewing. If you give your child only smooth substances for too long, you may have trouble introducing lumps and rough textures later on. (See *Chewing,* pages 54–55.)

# BABY TALK

A baby's babbling sounds gradually become words, phrases, and sentences as time goes on. At every stage of your child's language development, you should talk to and converse with your child. Do not, however, mimic the way he speaks. Use conversational language that is natural and comfortable for you, not baby talk, when you speak with your child. That will provide the best model and social stimulation to encourage his language development.

Although baby talk should not be your way of speaking, it's fine for your child. Try very hard to understand and respond appropriately to the words a baby or toddler invents in an effort to tell you something. Don't correct the words or syntax to make the child say things the "right" way. Let your child's language development move at its own speed.

Reward your child's early efforts to use language, even if that language is a bit difficult to figure out. Go right ahead and give a bottle to a child who says "Me bah pease." You know perfectly well what the child means. Trying to make the child say *Give me my bottle, please* will be wasted energy as far as language development is concerned. Such pressure might, however, give you a frustrated child who can't understand why you aren't delighted with her efforts to communicate.

# BABYPROOFING (FOR A NEWBORN)

Babyproofing your home for a newborn is easy. The real challenge comes later when your baby begins to creep, crawl, walk, and grab for everything in sight. (See *Childproofing,* pages 57–58.)

For a new baby, just make certain that nothing harmful can fall on the baby or make its way into the bassinet or crib where the baby might get at it. Anything that should not go in the baby's mouth must be kept out of reach. That is simple to accomplish for a baby who is not yet mobile.

Never leave plastic bags anywhere near the baby. Never use plastic bags or wrap as a mattress cover or pillowcase. When you bring items back from the dry cleaner, promptly and safely discard the plastic covers. Make sure that baby-sitters and other caregivers avoid putting plastic anywhere near the baby.

Keep strings or anything else that could choke a child away from your baby. Make sure that cords from window shades or blinds are not within reach of the baby's bed. Never offer the baby a pull toy in the crib or anywhere else. Check to see that toys do not have any glued-on or removable parts that could come off and be swallowed. Watch out for eyes on stuffed animals; even a newborn might attempt to remove them.

If you have an older child, babyproofing requires that the older child not have unsupervised access to objects that could be a danger to the baby. An older child should not have unsupervised access to the baby, with or without potentially hazardous objects.

If you have pets in your home, never leave your newborn baby in a location where an animal could harm him. A pet and a newborn should never be alone together in the same room. Even if you believe that an animal is totally reliable, don't take a chance. (See *Pets,* pages 142–143.)

# BABY-SITTERS

In selecting a good baby-sitter, there aren't any absolute rules. You have to do what makes sense for you, given the options available. Here are some guidelines to keep in mind.

- If you are fortunate enough to have an extended family close by, relatives might be a good choice, if they are willing and able. Don't take advantage of the good nature of family members. Taking care of a mobile baby or toddler can be extremely taxing.
- Don't leave a newborn, mobile baby, or toddler with a very young or inexperienced teenager. A baby-sitter should have the maturity and judgment to handle a crisis, should one arise.
- Sources of baby-sitters include recommendations from friends, local church or community groups, your doctor, or other professionals. Interview before you hire. The person who worked perfectly for your best friend's child might not do well in your home.
- Make clear what the job entails. The primary responsibility is to keep your child comfortable and safe when you are not there. Don't expect a child-care expert, housecleaner, laundry worker, and maintenance engineer all rolled into one.
- Be clear about your house rules so there won't be any misunderstandings. If you do not want your sitter to have visitors, use the telephone for personal calls, use your computer or home entertainment system, or consume the contents of the refrigerator, say so. (Your child should receive the sitter's full attention. Entertaining in your home while you are out is rarely a good idea.)
- Try having a potential sitter care for your child when you are home for a short time. If things go well, you'll feel better about leaving a baby or toddler with that person when you need to go out. That will also give you a chance to point out things in your home that the sitter should know about.
- Establish and make clear the child-care procedures you expect. That may be especially important for a toddler, who would be able to manipulate a caregiver in your absence.

19

Review the rules, including bedtimes, with the sitter and your child together if she is old enough to understand. Head off the potential conflict between a child who is used to staying up until fatigue takes over and a sitter who thinks toddlers should be in bed and sound asleep at seven.

- If feeding your child will be part of the sitter's job, make clear what you want the child to be fed and how it should be prepared. If snacks are permitted, have them available. If there are things you don't want your child to eat, the sitter should be informed. If there is any special information about your family's eating practices that the sitter should know, be sure to pass that on.
- Keep things simple. It's probably a good safety precaution to have a part-time baby-sitter use as few appliances as possible. The food processor, electric mixer, and similarly hazardous items should not be used near your toddler. A curious child might try things with a sitter that he would not dare try with a parent.
- Be sure to provide whatever information might be needed in an emergency. Make sure the sitter knows what to do and whom to call if something should go wrong. Leave a number where you can be reached. The sitter should also know how to reach a reliable neighbor, relative, or friend.

If you are not happy with a child-care arrangement, change it. Your responsibility is first to your child, not to the hired caregiver.

# "BACK TO SLEEP"

For generations, perhaps even for centuries or millennia, a baby was typically placed on her tummy to sleep. That is now known to be the wrong thing to do. Infant sleep position is a significant contributing factor to sudden infant death syndrome (SIDS, or crib death). *Babies should never be put on their stomachs to sleep.*

Research has found and confirmed that a baby is much safer sleeping on his back or side. In 1992, the American Academy of Pediatrics began recommending that parents or caregivers place an infant to sleep on the back or on the side, and not on the stomach. In 1994, the U.S. Public Health Service began a campaign called "Back to Sleep" to educate parents to place infants on their backs.

No matter what well-intentioned others whose information is from an earlier era might tell you, the evidence is overwhelming that an infant does best sleeping on the back. Just remember: *back to sleep.* Make sure that all the people who care for your infant—grandparents, day-care providers, baby-sitters, and others—are well informed. *Back to sleep.*

For additional information about sleep position and related issues, see *Beds and bedding,* pages 25–26; *Sleep problems,* pages 159–160; and *Sudden infant death syndrome (SIDS),* page 165.

# BATHS (FOR A NEWBORN)

Bathing your new baby can be fun. Don't be put off by long lists of rules or the formal bath demonstration at the hospital or birth center. Just relax and remember that your baby is very small and the bath can be brief. You'll manage to hold on even if he protests.

If you can't cope with giving your baby a tub bath when you first get home after your baby is born, don't worry. You will feel more secure as time goes on. Until then, just be sure to keep the diaper area clean, and wash any milk out of the folds of your baby's neck.

## SPONGE BATHS

A sponge bath is probably easier until your baby's navel has healed. (See *Navel care,* page 127.) A sponge bath will do nicely any time you don't feel like bothering with a tub bath. Here are some things to remember.

- Use warm water. Test it with your elbow; it should feel barely warm, not hot. Use a mild, neutral soap, such as Ivory, or a special baby soap. Save the expensive soaps for yourself, because the perfume may irritate the baby's skin.
- Use a washcloth or a little bath sponge. If you prefer, you can lather the baby with your hands. Be sure to do all the creases. Rinse thoroughly and then dry.
- Plain water will do on the face. To clean the eyes, wipe quickly with a clean, wet cloth from the outside in toward the nose. Use a fresh corner of the cloth for the other eye. Cotton balls may leave lint in or near the eyes, so a washcloth is safer. To clean the baby's ears and nose, wash gently whatever you can see and leave it at that. Do not poke cotton-tipped swabs into the nostrils or ears.
- Some parents prefer to sponge-bathe the baby one part at a time, dry and re-clothe that part, and then go on to the next part. That is a good strategy if the room is very cool.

## TUB BATHS

A plastic dishpan is an excellent container for a small baby, but any clean, small container or the bathroom or kitchen basin will do. Use warm, *not hot,* water.

- Never put your baby under the faucet or allow water to run into the tub while the baby is in it. An unexpected temperature change could cause harm.
- Get everything you need before you put your baby into the water. Never leave a baby alone in the water, even for a few seconds. A baby can drown in as little as two inches of water.
- Hold the baby firmly in whatever way is comfortable for both of you. Wash and rinse the different parts as you did for a sponge bath.
- Take the baby out of the water and dry carefully. Don't miss the creases.

## SHAMPOOS

When washing your baby's head, either as part of a tub bath or a sponge bath, wet the baby's scalp with a washcloth. Use a mild baby shampoo or soap, and apply it to the wet scalp with the washcloth. Don't be afraid to touch your baby's scalp. Washing and gentle rubbing will not hurt. Rinse carefully, applying clear water with a clean washcloth. Never let water from the faucet run over your baby. You might try gently pouring from a plastic cup or other container; some newborns don't mind. It tends to be the older babies and toddlers who sometimes develop a fear of pouring water. When you are done, dry the baby's head gently with a soft towel.

# BATHS (FOR AN OLDER BABY OR TODDLER)

Baths can be a pleasant experience for parents and child. It's best to keep bathtime relatively simple. It need not and should not become a major production, source of conflict, or the highlight of the day's entertainment. The purpose of a bath is to get your child clean, although that does not preclude having fun while bathing. A daily bath is not essential as long as the child's diaper area and her hands and face are clean. Whether or not your child needs a bath on any given day depends on what the day's activities have been.

## SUGGESTIONS FOR THE BATH

* If you are using the regular family bathtub, five or six inches of water at most is all you will need. The water should feel comfortably warm (not hot) to your elbow or wrist. Your hands are not a good test, because your hands can probably stand much hotter water than your child's tender skin.
* To keep your child from slipping in the large tub, try a towel or rubber mat on the tub's bottom. A large plastic laundry basket inside the tub works well to create a confined and somewhat slip-proof space for an active child. Just put the basket in and fill the tub as usual; the water goes right through the holes. Then put your child in the

basket. The basket does not replace adult supervision and hands on your child. It might, however, make it easier for you to keep a good hold on him.

- Kneel on something comfortable and get right down to your child's level in the tub. It is difficult and risky to hold or bathe your child while bending over. Until your child is very stable and able to sit securely, always support him with at least one hand, preferably two. One accidental slip in the water can cause weeks of bathtime fears along with potential injury.
- Give your child a washcloth and let him help with the cleaning process. A small piece of soap tied into a child's sock makes an excellent cleaning tool for small hands to hold and use.
- Use a mild soap. Ivory, a family favorite for many years, works well and it still floats. Special baby lotion soaps are fine, although perhaps a bit costly. Expensive perfumed adult soaps are wasted on a young child, and may even cause skin irritation.
- Toys in the bath are fine, but don't overdo it. Something that floats and something to pour with are all your child needs. You don't need to spend money on bath toys. A plastic cup or two from the kitchen and an empty plastic shampoo bottle will keep a child busy.
- The bathroom should be warm enough so your child does not get chilled. If the room is cool, make the bath quick and get your child warm and dry as soon as possible.
- If the room is comfortable, time to play in the tub is fine, as long as you are willing to be right there to participate. Stop the bath while it is still fun for both of you. There will be a next time very soon. For a child who wants to continue to play and soak when you think the bath is ended, try a timer. Tell your child that the bath is over when the bell rings; then stick to your word. Remove your child from the tub and then let the water out.

## SOME WARNINGS FOR THE BATH

- Never leave a baby or toddler unattended in the bath even for a moment. A young child can drown in as little as two inches of water. Accidents can happen very quickly.
- Do not run water into the tub or sink while the child is in it. An unexpected temperature change could cause harm. Keep your child away from the hot-water tap. If the tap remains hot while turned off, wrap it in a cool washcloth.
- An occasional bubble bath can be a special treat, but don't build in an expected bubble-bath routine to your child's day. Avoid bath preparations intended for adults, because they may cause skin irritation. It is difficult to keep soap bubbles out of an active child's eyes and mouth. If you start using the bubbles as an enticement to get a child into the tub, you may be creating additional bathtime problems.
- Do not let the water run out of the tub before you remove your child; many children are frightened by the sight and sound of water going down the drain. But do remember to empty the tub immediately after the bath is over and you have taken your child out. Never leave a tub of water as a hazard for your mobile baby or toddler.
- Do not bathe siblings together unless you can count on good behavior. A toddler just learning to like the bath can be severely set back by one push from an older brother or sister. Keep in mind that group bathing may not save time or effort in the long run.

## BATH SEATS

If you decide to use an infant bath seat to make it easier to hold and bathe your baby, be extremely careful. Do not let a bath seat give you a false sense of security. The Consumer Products Safety Commission (CPSC) has long had concerns about the safety of bath seats, although the seats have not been banned. Dozens of children have died or been injured when bath seats broke, tipped over, or children managed to get out of them. Most such incidents, however, occurred when the child was unsupervised. *Never leave or turn your back on a child in a bath seat, even for a few seconds.* That's all the time it would take for a disaster to occur. Before you consider using a bath seat, check the latest CPSC safety records and recommendations involving their use.

## BATHTIME FEARS

Fear of the bath may suddenly become a problem for a child who previously seemed to love getting into the tub. You may be able to identify a direct cause of the problem: soap in the eyes, for example, an unfortunate slip under the water even though you were right there, or perhaps a newly discovered awareness of the water going down the drain. In some cases, however, a fear will simply show up one day for no apparent reason, and you will have to deal with it.

Force will not solve a child's fear of the bath. Putting a terrified child into the tub will not get him used to the water. Keep the child clean with sponge baths while you work on the problem gradually. Here are some strategies for getting a frightened child to trust the water again.

Don't try to bathe your child in the large tub for a while; go back to using a small container. Put the child on a plastic tablecloth on the floor next to a small basin or dishpan with an inch or two of water. Let the child play with a floating toy. If she wants to put her hands into the water, so much the better. Using a cloth or a small sponge, wash your child gently and be careful not to get soap in the eyes. If your child wants to climb into the pan of water, let it happen. Provide support so there will be no slipping or falling.

After you have succeeded with water play on the floor, try moving the basin into the large tub. Let the child sit in the empty tub next to the pan of water and play as before. Letting the pan of water spill out into the big tub can be fun—and the start of real baths again. Make the move only when you are certain your child is ready.

If fear of going down the drain is a problem, be careful not to start emptying the tub while your child is in the room. Silly as that fear may seem to you, some children genuinely believe that they will go down with the water. No amount of reasoning will get a toddler who thinks so to believe otherwise.

If you have a handheld shower, let your child sit in an empty tub and spray off the soap you have applied with a wet cloth. Keep an arm in the spray to be ready to move quickly should the water temperature change. Be careful to regulate water temperature and pressure carefully, and don't try this at all if you know your plumbing tends toward bursts of hot water. Some children will be delighted with the notion of a shower; others will hate it. It may be worth a try, but don't force it.

# BEDS AND BEDDING

Some families use a bassinet as their baby's first bed. Others go straight to a crib. A bassinet is a hooded, basket-type container for a newborn or very young baby. Many bassinets have wheels, so they can conveniently be moved from one room to another. Most are lined and beautifully decorated.

If you use a bassinet for your newborn, make sure that the decorations and lining are safe. There should be no loose ribbons or ties that your baby could grab, put in his mouth, or choke on. The mattress should be firm and fit snugly in the basket. A nicely designed bassinet is a lovely extravagance, and its mobility will add to its usefulness for a newborn. Use of a bassinet is fairly short-term, however. When your baby begins to try to pull himself up, it's time for a crib.

All full-size cribs now sold in the United States must meet safety standards established by the Consumer Product Safety Commission. Those standards are discussed in detail in *Cribs,* pages 69–70. Knowing the safety standards is especially important if you purchase or borrow a used crib. It's important to keep your baby safe.

## BEDDING

Fitted sheets are convenient because they stay put. Patterned sheets give your child something interesting to look at. Do not use any pillows or soft bedding, such as featherbed liners or down comforters, because of the potential for smothering. Young children do not need pillows to be comfortable. Do not let your child have fluffy or soft stuffed animals in the crib, because of the danger of smothering.

Crib bumpers, which soften the crib sides and keep out drafts, are fine for young babies. Make sure they are fastened safely and that the child cannot reach the fasteners. Once a child can pull herself up and stand, the crib bumpers may be used by the child as a step to climb out. Anticipate such a move and take the bumpers away before that becomes a problem.

## AFTER THE CRIB

If your child has taken to climbing and falling out of the crib, it may be time to give up the crib altogether. At least leave the side of the crib down and the mattress in the lowest position so your climber will not have as far to fall. Pillows on the landing side might be a wise precaution. Unless your house is especially drafty, the mattress on the floor is a good transition from crib to regular bed for a child who climbs and falls out.

Remember that once your child can get out of the crib or bed freely, night wandering could occur without your knowledge. Make sure that your child has access to only childproofed places if he should stray without waking you. Make sure that the child does not have the ability to get to stairs in the night without your knowing about it. Safety gates are a must.

Easy-to-install temporary sides can be purchased for regular beds to help keep a young child from rolling out while sleeping. These will not, however, keep an awake child in bed, and they should not be used for a child under two because of the danger of getting caught and strangling between the mattress and the temporary sides. It is unlikely that the side would fit tightly enough to prevent a very young child from exploring between the rails and the mattress. One side of the bed against a wall and two straight-backed chairs on the other side will do as a temporary arrangement.

If you are expecting another baby, do not force your older child to give up the crib for the new arrival. Expecting your toddler to accept and adjust to a newborn sibling graciously is demanding enough without requiring the older child to give up her sleeping place at the same time. Either make the transition out of the crib far enough in advance so there is no relationship between giving up the crib and the new baby's arrival, or buy a second crib. (See *Sibling rivalry*, pages 157–158.)

# BEDTIME (EARLY OR LATE?)

A newborn sleeps most of the time, wakes up when hungry or uncomfortable, and then returns to sleep after being fed or comforted as needed. Once your baby begins to sleep through the night and to be awake at times other than feedings, however, you'll have to work out a plan for naps and bedtime.

When should a child go to bed? There is no single right answer to that question. Decide the best time for your family based on your child's needs and your lifestyle. For some, "early to bed and early to rise" is the most satisfactory approach. Other families prefer to enjoy the company of their toddler well into the evening so that everyone can sleep later the next morning. For some, a very regular schedule works best. For others, variety seems to do no harm. You will have to figure out what is best for you and your child. Don't be intimidated or influenced by the opinions of others who disagree with your personal choices. Chances are, for at least the first two years, you can count on your child to take as much sleep as necessary. Most very young children do. If you notice that your child is overtired, however, encourage extra or longer naps.

Some people really do seem to be larks (early risers) while others tend to be owls (night birds). If you are lucky, your child's personal style will be similar to your own. If not, you may wish to try modifying your child's sleeping and waking schedule, although such efforts may not be entirely successful.

For a child who wakes too early, gradually make bedtime later. Move the bedtime rituals and bedtime back fifteen minutes each night until you are keeping the child up late enough to sleep through until a more reasonable hour of the morning. If you want your child to go to bed earlier, on the other hand, make sure that the day has been active enough so that the need for sleep works for you. But don't wear your child out to the point that overtiredness sets in and turns out to be counterproductive. Gradually begin the bedtime rituals earlier each night until you've established a time that meets your needs. Do what makes sense to you, and don't make a big deal out of it. That is the key to success.

# BEDTIME RITUALS

The routines you use to establish bedtime should be a predictable and stable aspect of your child's life. That is true no matter what type of schedule—fixed or flexible—you use for bedtime. The rituals that accompany bedtime can help your child feel secure despite the fact that bedtime involves separation. Making bedtime a comfortable experience on which your child can rely will help prevent sleep problems and enable him to take important steps toward independence.

Begin bedtime rituals at least a half hour or more before you want to have the child settled for the night. Don't rush and convey the impression that you can't wait to get it all over with. That would set the wrong tone and send signals that could create problems, especially with a naturally contrary toddler.

In the bedtime rituals, include whatever practices suit your child's personal needs and your family's lifestyle. Getting your child out of daytime clothing and into pajamas may include a bath in the process if necessary. A bedtime story, or perhaps two, and prayers in keeping with your family's personal religious preference can complete the ritual. The bedtime ritual should signal inevitable and nonnegotiable bedtime. That will give your child a secure sense that life contains some things that she can count on.

If you do not have a copy of the classic children's book *Goodnight Moon* by Margaret Wise Brown (Harper & Row Publishers, New York: 1947), be sure to get one. More than fifty years after its initial publication, this wonderful little picture book is still available in paperback, and for good reason. Many children enjoy saying good night to the people, good night to the animals, and good night to the familiar objects. You can read *Goodnight Moon* as part of a bedtime ritual, and also use it as a model to help you and your child personalize your own routine for saying good night. (For further book suggestions, see *Books for your child,* pages 31–32.)

When you have finished with whatever routine you have established for bedtime, tuck your child in, give him a good-night kiss, and leave the room. Don't stay around until your child has fallen asleep, because once you start that practice you will find it difficult to change. Make frequent but very brief appearances at the bedside to reassure a child who protests being left alone. That is a reasonable middle ground between letting a child "cry it out" and letting a child manipulate you into becoming a sleepy-time companion. It also seems to be the most effective way to encourage peaceful separation at bedtime.

(For additional suggestions on handling bedtime, see *Family beds,* pages 86–88, and *Sleep problems,* pages 159–160.)

# BED-WETTING

Wetting the bed should not be considered a problem behavior for a toddler. It is a completely normal and typical behavior. Many children—even those who are perfectly toilet trained during the day—do not remain dry at night until they are three or even four years old. For some children, dry nights take even longer than that.

Don't be concerned about using diapers at night, even for a child who successfully wears training pants all day. Your child is likely to outgrow bed-wetting earlier if you avoid making an issue of it. Creating tension at bedtime is a sure way to make bed-wetting persist. Keep in mind that a child does not deliberately wet the bed. She is asleep when it happens. Punishment, therefore, is not appropriate. Praise for staying dry is not needed, either. The less you make of the matter, the sooner normal development will take over and your child will stay dry through the night.

If your child continues to wet the bed long after you think she should have stopped, consult your child's health-care provider. Chances are you will be reassured that time will take care of it. If there is some reason to be concerned in your particular situation, however, a medical professional can make suggestions to help deal with the problem.

# BIBS

When feeding a baby or young toddler, using a bib is preferable to creating an inevitable need to launder the entire set of clothes. For a baby who is not yet taking solid foods, an absorbent terry-cloth bib with plastic backing works well. A bib that snaps in back is safer than a bib that ties. If you use a bib that ties, make sure to remove it immediately after the feeding. Never leave an infant with anything tied around the neck.

For an older baby or toddler who is self-feeding (more or less), a bib of heavy plastic with a deep pocket at the bottom is a good choice. It will protect the clothes and catch the spills—liquid and solid—in the pocket. Wash out the pocket after each use to avoid a mess that will look and smell bad. Another reason to keep the bib clean is to avoid having your toddler add the spoiling remains of last night's dinner to today's lunch.

Disposable bibs that are absorbent and handy are now available. While disposables may seem somewhat extravagant, you may find them a useful and even potentially cost-effective alternative to laundry. Do not, however, leave a disposable bib on an unattended baby or toddler. He could tear it and put pieces in his mouth. Remove the bib immediately after the feeding or meal. When bottle-feeding a young baby, you might skip a real bib entirely and drape a cloth diaper over her front to keep her clothes clean underneath.

# BITES (TREATMENT)

## ANIMAL OR HUMAN BITES

Wash the bite area well with soap and room-temperature water. If the bitten spot is not bleeding badly, let the water run gently over it for a few minutes. Control severe bleeding by putting direct pressure on the wound. When the bleeding has stopped, cleanse the area with an antiseptic and cover the wound with a sterile dressing. Call your health-care provider for advice that same day. Make sure your child's tetanus immunization is up to date. It's important to seek medical advice for a human bite. The bacteria in a person's mouth can cause the bite wound to become infected.

If the bite is from an animal, capture the animal if possible so it can be checked for rabies. If someone else's pet has bitten your child, you should notify the owner. Your local animal shelter will help if you can't find the owner. It's important that the animal's health be checked. If the animal can't be found, your child may need to have a series of rabies prevention shots. Consult your medical provider or local health department immediately. There is a small window of timely opportunity for the injections to be successful. When rabies develops, however, it is almost always fatal.

For a week or so after your child has been bitten, watch the bite very carefully to make sure it does not become infected. If you see swelling and redness, feel heat at the wound site, or your child develops a fever, report that to your health-care provider.

## INSECT BITES AND STINGS

If there is a stinger, it's probably best to leave it alone and let a medical professional remove it. Touching it may release more venom and increase the reaction. If you must remove the stinger on your own, scrape it out with a fingernail. Apply cold compresses and watch the child carefully for any reaction to the bite. If you suspect that your child may have been bitten by a poisonous spider (a brown recluse spider or a black widow, for example) get medical help immediately because such bites could be life threatening. No matter what the cause of the bite or sting, call your health-care provider right away if the child becomes pale or weak, or develops a rash or hives, fever, trouble breathing, nausea, or vomiting.

## SNAKE BITES

If you live in an area where there are poisonous snakes, be especially alert to the ongoing possibility that your child might be bitten. If you think a poisonous snake has bitten your child (you will usually be able to see one or more fang marks in the skin), call your health-care provider immediately or take your child directly to the nearest emergency room. The bite of a poisonous snake requires prompt medical treatment. If your child has been bitten, ask a medical professional to tell you what home treatment, if any, should be followed before you get to the hospital. If your child stops breathing, begin artificial respiration at once. (See *Breathing emergency,* pages 42–43.)

# BITING ────────────────────────────

If your child shows signs of becoming a biter, deal with it promptly, calmly, and firmly.

If your child bites other children, try to avoid situations where such behavior may occur. Don't permit young children to play together without close supervision. If fighting over toys or other objects seems to provoke biting behavior, make sure that there are enough playthings to go around. At the first move toward a bite, physically remove your child from the temptation. Say, "No. Don't bite."

Some toddlers bite themselves. It may actually be harder to stop a self-biter than a child who tries to bite a playmate, because the target is readily available and the act can happen quickly. The best way to stop a child who thinks chomping on his own body is a good thing is not to make a big deal of it. The parent who becomes excited and upset sends the message to the child that biting herself is a way to get parental attention.

If your child bites himself, stay calm. Ignore it if at all possible. If the bite is severe enough to break the skin, calmly deal with the wound. Wash it with soap and water, put antiseptic on it, and perhaps cover it with a Band-Aid for a little while. If the child cannot get a rise out of you, he will be less likely to repeat the biting.

If your child bites you, a sharp *No!* while firmly restraining the child will communicate that you are displeased. A baby who bites the mother's breast while nursing should be told no and removed from the breast for a moment.

Resist the impulse to strike the child who bites. Do not bite back, although some experts have suggested that as an effective cure. Such retaliation may work in the short term, but it is more likely to set a bad example than to act as a deterrent. Although biting back may show the child that biting hurts, she may also get the message that biting is acceptable behavior.

Toddlers are not always nice. They have not yet learned civilized social graces, but hopefully they will. However, if biting or other symptoms of aggressive behavior seem to be a problem with your child beyond what you feel is typical, consult your health-care provider. You may need help dealing with the underlying causes. (See also *Aggressive behavior,* pages 5–6.)

# BLEEDING

To stop heavy bleeding from cuts or bites, use direct pressure with sterile gauze pads or a clean cloth. Your hands should be clean, and sterile gloves are a good idea if you have them available. You might try an ice cube wrapped in the gauze or cloth. Apply the pressure for up to fifteen minutes. If that is not long enough to stop the bleeding, you should get immediate medical assistance. If the bleeding stops in less than fifteen minutes but then starts again, reapply the pressure.

For a very deep wound from which blood is spurting rapidly (severed artery), apply direct pressure using your fist if necessary to press the severed blood vessel hard against the underlying bone. Bleeding from an artery can be a serious, even life-threatening condition. While you are trying to stop the bleeding, have someone call for medical help.

Use common sense in deciding to use direct pressure to stop bleeding. If there is an obvious object or loose debris protruding from the wound, try to remove it before applying pressure. Don't press on an embedded object in a wound. If the child is bleeding from an eye, get help. Don't push on the eyeball. If your child is bleeding from a head wound and there is a possibility that she has a fractured skull, get help.

In a case of severe bleeding, try to prevent the child from going into shock while you are waiting for medical assistance. Cover the child to keep him warm. Elevate the child's feet a few inches unless there is a head, neck, or back injury.

For mild bleeding, wash with soap and water and then apply pressure with a gauze pad or clean cloth. When the bleeding has stopped, apply an antiseptic such as Bactine. (See also *Nosebleeds,* pages 129–130.)

# BOOKS FOR YOUR CHILD _____

Books are an important part of a child's learning experiences, as well as one of life's pleasures, and it's never too soon to begin sharing books with your child. Even a newborn will enjoy the sounds of a parent's voice reading, and many children can begin to understand words and follow a story long before you think that would be possible.

Begin by reading your favorites to your child so that your enthusiasm shows. The following list contains a number of classic children's books that have stood the test of time—some for many decades. No matter how much time passes, some of these books will remain very special and should not be missed.

For current suggestions of ever-changing contemporary titles, visit your local bookstore or library. You may wish to go online for lists of recently published books. As you look for new titles, keep in mind the criteria that have contributed to making certain books classics; clarity, simplicity, meaningful but uncomplicated story lines, and attractiveness of illustrations are ingredients to look for. But don't overthink the selection process—pick a book and read it. You and your child will know if it works. The important thing is to keep reading.

### *The Poky Little Puppy*
by Janette Sebring Lowrey
Western Publishing Company, Racine, WI: 1942, 1970, hardcover reissued 2001

### *Bread and Jam for Frances*
by Russell Hoban, illustrated by Lillian Hoban
Harper & Row Publishers, New York: 1964, 1993

### *Millions of Cats*
by Wanda Gag
Coward, McCann and Geoghegan, New York: 1928

### *The Story of Ferdinand*
by Munro Leaf
The Viking Press, New York: 1936

### *Goodnight Moon*
by Margaret Wise Brown
Harper & Row Publishers, New York: 1947

### *The Cat in the Hat*
by Dr. Seuss
Random House, New York: 1957

### *The Lorax*
by Dr. Seuss
Random House, New York: 1971

***The Tale of Peter Rabbit***
by Beatrix Potter
Frederick Warner and Company, New York: 1903

***Winnie-the-Pooh***
by A. A. Milne, illustrated by E. H. Shepard
E. P. Dutton & Company, New York: 1926

***The Complete Adventures of Curious George***
by Margret and H. A. Rey
Houghton Mifflin, Boston: Sixtieth anniversary edition, 2001

***The Little Fur Family***
by Margaret Wise Brown
Harper & Row Publishers, New York: 1946, reissued edition 1991

***Alexander and the Terrible, Horrible, No Good, Very Bad Day***
by Judith Viorst
Atheneum, New York: 1972, reissued 1987

***Where the Wild Things Are***
by Maurice Sendak
Harper & Row Publishers, New York: 1963

***A Tree Is Nice***
by Janice May Udry, illustrated by Marc Simont
Harper & Row Publishers, New York: 1956, reprint edition, 1987

***Katy No-Pocket***
by Emmy Payne, illustrated by H. A. Rey
Houghton Mifflin, Boston: 1944, 1973

***Flip***
by Wesley Dennis
The Viking Press, New York: 1941

***The Snowy Day***
by Ezra Jack Keats
The Viking Press, New York: 1962, board edition, 1996

## READING READINESS

Interest in books is an important ingredient of reading readiness, and sharing books with your child will pay off later when he goes to school. As you read, let your child look at the page with you. Encourage your child to talk about the pictures and, if you wish, point out a word or two. Remember that fun is the major purpose of reading with your child at this point. It's too soon to teach reading in a formal way. Just enjoy.

# BOOSTER SEATS _____

When your child outgrows a convertible car seat, it is not yet time for her to do without a specially designed child restraint. Before they are large enough for safe and comfortable use of an adult seat belt, children should use a booster seat (around ages four to eight). A booster seat raises the child sufficiently to allow proper placement of the vehicle's seat belt so it does not cross and create pressure on the child's neck. A booster seat helps ensure that the child does not slip out of the adult seat belt in the event of a crash.

A booster seat should be used for children from about forty pounds (approximately age four) to eighty pounds, and until the child is at least four feet nine inches tall. Even if not required by law in your state, your child's safety is at risk if you fail to use one until the child is large enough for the adult seat belt to work as it should. Unfortunately, many parents tend to push their children to use an adult restraint before they are ready. One recent study, for example, indicated that 80 percent of children ages four to eight did not use a booster seat, although such a seat has the potential to save lives. That same study found that parents had often moved children from a rear-facing infant seat to a forward-facing seat before they were ready, and had also allowed children to sit in the front seat of the vehicle, even though they would be safer in the rear. (See also *Automobile safety,* pages 12–16.)

Small children using an adult seat belt without a booster seat may actually suffer injuries from the seat belt itself, or may slip out of the belt during a crash and thus not have protection. A child who is too small for proper seat-belt use can suffer internal or spinal cord injuries in a crash. A booster seat is a very cost-effective device to protect your child's safety. It has the added advantage of raising your child high enough so she can look out and see what is going on. There are some seats on the market designed specifically for infants (rear-facing), toddlers, and small children up to eighty pounds.

When flying, check with the airline to see if a car booster seat is permitted for use in an airplane seat. It might make the adult seat belt fit better and enable the child to see out the window. Even if the seat cannot be used in the passenger compartment, take it with you as baggage if you will need it in a vehicle at your destination.

## OTHER TYPES OF BOOSTER SEATS

Booster seats for use at home—to raise the child up to an adult table, for example—are also available. Those seats are not typically designed or approved for use in a vehicle. If you need a booster seat for nonvehicle use, choose it carefully. Make sure that it can be fastened securely so it won't make a hasty exit to the floor, complete with your child. Use a safety harness to keep the child in, if necessary.

Check the safety record of whatever model you are considering. Particularly risky may be multiple-use products in which a booster seat is part of a carrier or feeding-chair package. The Consumer Product Safety Commission has recalled such products in the past. If you are thinking about a secondhand product, the recall list is a good place to check first.

# BOTTLE-FEEDING

If you decide to bottle-feed your newborn, or if you must stop breast-feeding before the baby is ready for formula or milk out of a cup, you will have to decide which kind of bottles you want to use and which method of preparation will best suit your needs and your baby. Consult with your baby's health-care provider to decide which formula to use. (See *Formula,* pages 95–96.) A child less than a year old should not be fed cow's milk, which is the perfect food for baby cows, but not for baby humans.

## EQUIPMENT, PREPARATION, AND STORAGE

If you decide to use permanent-type, reusable bottles, you will need at least a dozen of them. Dishwasher-safe plastic bottles are better than glass. They can be washed, boiled, and won't break if you drop them. Get the nipples, collars, and caps that go with the bottles you have chosen. Most brands are interchangeable, but a few are not. A few extra nipple sets will be handy when you can't find enough pieces to go around, or if you drop one on the floor just before feeding time.

If you purchase reusable bottles, start sterile. Before the first time you use them, boil them in a large pot of water. Boil the nipples, collars, and caps for ten minutes. In addition to making sure they are clean, if you boil the nipples once, you may remove the rubbery plastic taste of new nipples that some babies don't like. Most doctors say that a dishwasher set to 182°F or higher will sterilize these items as well. Microwave sterilizers are also available.

After using a bottle, rinse out any remaining milk and use a bottle brush to make sure that no formula deposits remain. Dishwasher cleaning will do, unless there is some special reason your baby's health-care provider suggests sterilization as a regular routine. Be sure everything you use to prepare the bottles is clean. Keep one can opener just for formula, and rinse off the top of the can with hot water before opening it.

Even easier than keeping reusable bottles dishwasher-clean is the use of disposable, sterile bottle liners or presterilized disposable bottles. They are reasonably priced and readily available in supermarkets and pharmacy chains. Read and follow the directions carefully. Never put disposable bottles or liners in the microwave or fill them with very hot liquid.

When you fill the bottles with formula, store them in the refrigerator. You can safely make a two-day supply in advance. If you use condensed formula, add water according to the directions. Diluting the formula more than you should will deprive the baby of essential nutrients. If your water supply is questionable, consider using bottled water or at least boil the tap water for two minutes before you use it.

Although generations of mothers dutifully warmed the bottle before feeding it to a baby, it is now known that there is no need to do so. It is safe to feed the bottle cold from the refrigerator, at room temperature (although do not let it stand around to reach that temperature slowly), or warmed. If your baby has a preference, do what he seems to like best. If your baby does not seem to care, do what is most convenient. If you do warm the bottle, make sure it is just warm, not hot. Let the bottle stand in a pan of hot water long enough to take the chill off, but that's all. Never microwave a bottle of formula, even if the container is microwave-safe. Although the bottle and a few drops of the formula might feel right to the touch, use of a microwave could produce hot spots that could burn your baby.

If your baby does not finish the entire bottle at a feeding, discard what she does not drink. It is not safe to keep the leftovers for the next time, even in the refrigerator. Put less formula in the bottles to begin with if your baby regularly fails to finish.

## HOW TO FEED

When you give your baby a bottle, serve comfort, security, and emotional nourishment along with the contents of the bottle. Cradle the baby in your arm, with your bent elbow supporting the head and neck. He should not lie flat on his back for feeding; the head should be slightly higher than the tummy. An alternate position that both of you might like is to prop the baby in your lap, facing you. Feeding times are the highlights of a young baby's day. Holding your baby for feeding is an important ingredient of developing a close relationship.

- Never prop up the bottle and leave the baby. A baby could choke, and the practice of propping a bottle deprives the child of the essential human contact that she needs for emotional security.
- Check the nipple of the bottle before feeding. When you hold the bottle upside down, the formula should drip out in little drops, about one per second. A steady stream means the hole is too large, and you should use a different nipple. If you have to squeeze the bottle to get anything out, the hole is too small. You may be able to enlarge it with a hot needle.
- Keep the bottle tilted so that the neck of the bottle is always filled with liquid. If you don't, the baby will swallow too much air.
- Burp the baby often during a feeding. To be on the safe side at first, try it after each ounce of formula. As you get to know your baby better, you will know when he needs to be burped. Hold the baby up against your chest so he is looking out over your shoulder. Put a diaper or towel over your shoulder in case formula comes up with the bubble. Rub or pat the baby's back gently. For an older baby you can hold the baby in a sitting position in your lap. Support the chin with one hand. Gently rub the back with the other.

Resume feeding after the bubble. If no bubbles come up in two or three minutes and your baby seems comfortable, go on with the feeding.

# BOWEL MOVEMENTS (NEWBORN) _____

A baby's first bowel movement is made up of a sticky, smooth material called meconium. The color of a meconium movement is generally a dark greenish-black. If a newborn baby does not have this first bowel movement within thirty-six hours of birth, the child's health-care provider should be consulted. Chances are the meconium will have passed while you and your child are still in the hospital or birth center. If you delivered at home, your birth attendant will advise you.

The frequency of normal bowel movements can vary greatly from one baby to another. For breast-fed babies, an average of three to six stools a day is usual, although some babies may comfortably go several days between bowel movements. The stools of breast-fed babies are generally yellowish in color. These stools are typically like loose cottage cheese in texture, with a sweet-sour odor.

The stools of bottle-fed babies are generally pastier and firmer than those of breast-fed babies. Their color ranges from pale yellow to dark tan, and the odor might be quite strong. Bottle-fed babies tend to have fewer movements than breast-fed babies do—one to four per day at first.

During the first few weeks, you will have changed enough diapers to become quite familiar with what a normal stool is for your baby. Some variation from one movement to the next is, of course, quite normal. A very marked change in color or consistency without a change in diet, however, could be a cause for concern. Call your baby's health-care provider if the problem persists.

# BOWEL MOVEMENTS (OLDER BABY OR TODDLER)

By the time you read this, you probably will have changed enough diapers to know what a normal bowel movement is for your child. The frequency of bowel movements varies greatly from one child to another. A baby still on breast milk and no solid foods may have several movements a day. Others, however, might have a movement as infrequently as every second or third day. A daily movement is not necessary. Most young children move their bowels when they need to. If your child is eating well, behaving normally, and passing a stool without difficulty, then it does not matter whether she is having several bowel movements a day or one bowel movement every two or three days.

## CONSTIPATION

Constipation is rarely a problem in a young baby, especially one who is breast-fed. Make sure that an older baby or toddler who is on solid food in addition to breast milk has enough fruit or juice in the diet. Never tamper with a child's normal pattern of bowel movements by administering a laxative unless your child's health-care provider specifically prescribes one at a particular time. Children, as a rule, do not need laxatives. Upsetting a child's natural rhythm will do no good, and it may cause harm by starting a dependence on the laxative. Infrequent bowel movements are not a sign of constipation or cause for concern in a young child as long as the stools are reasonably soft when they are passed.

If your child does pass small, pellet-type stools, that is an indication of constipation. In most cases, that situation can be corrected by giving dark Karo syrup (one teaspoon to four ounces of water) once or twice a day. Consult your child's health-care provider first before administering the Karo treatment.

You may also cut down on milk and increase the juice for a day or two. If your child is eating solid food, make sure that his diet contains enough fruit, vegetables, and whole-grain breads for fiber. Lots of fluids are in order. Make sure that your child drinks enough water. (See *Nutrition,* pages 130–137.)

If your child seems very uncomfortable or appears to be straining too much with a bowel movement, stimulation with a rectal thermometer may help. Before taking such a step, consult your child's health-care provider, who might have additional suggestions to address the problem.

## DIARRHEA

How can you tell if your child has diarrhea or simply the frequent, loose bowel movements typical of many young children? A child with diarrhea passes stools that have little or no formed material in them. These stools usually differ in color from normal stools. The stools are more frequent than usual, noisy, and passed with considerable force. They may contain mucus or blood.

The most serious danger from diarrhea is *dehydration,* which in severe cases can be fatal for a young child. Call your child's health-care provider immediately if your child seems to have diarrhea with one or more of these other symptoms: mucus or blood in the stools, vomiting, temperature below 97.6 or above 99.6 degrees F, lack of appetite, decreased quantity of urine, dry mouth (little or no saliva), no tears when crying, or decreased energy and activity level. It is important to catch dehydration before it gets out of hand with disastrous results.

# BREAST-FEEDING

A human mother's milk is the perfect natural food for a human baby. It contains the nutrients a baby needs, in the right proportions. Human breast milk strengthens a baby's immune system to withstand illnesses. Certain proteins in breast milk promote a baby's brain development. No matter how scientifically a commercial formula is concocted to mimic human milk, the product is never quite the same.

Colostrum, the premilk breast fluid nature intended to be baby's first food, contains antibodies to protect against a wide variety of diseases. Colostrum helps clear the meconium (material of the first bowel movement) from the baby's intestines soon after birth. Substances in a mother's milk seem to protect the baby from certain respiratory and intestinal infections. Breast milk is easier for a baby to digest fully, and breast-fed babies are less likely to suffer from diarrhea or vomiting. While as many as one in ten babies may show some signs of allergic reaction to certain formulas based on cow's milk, allergic reactions to breast milk are extremely rare.

The exercise of sucking at the breast promotes healthy tooth and jaw development. Bottle-feeding, in contrast, may increase tooth decay and has the potential to lead to improper alignment of the upper and lower jaws. Babies who are bottle-fed with commercial formula—in contrast to expressed human milk—have a greater chance of being overfed and becoming obese, both as babies and later on in life.

Breast-fed babies tend to swallow less air than babies who are bottle-fed. They may need to be burped less often during a feeding, and they are less likely to have discomfort from bubbles. The soiled diapers of a breast-fed baby do not have as strong an odor as the diapers of a bottle-fed baby. In addition to being convenient, breast milk is economical.

Commercially prepared formulas are costly. Other than the cost of a nutritious diet for the mother, breast milk is free.

It is important for a nursing mother to have a nutritious diet. A mother who is breast-feeding should not try to lose the extra weight gained during pregnancy. The food guide pyramid—the family version, not the adapted version for toddlers—can provide guidance for a nutritious diet for the entire family, including a nursing mother. (The food guide pyramid is described on pages 130–137.) Add at least eight eight-ounce glasses of water a day to its recommendations. A nursing mother should continue to take a vitamin supplement—either prenatal vitamins or whatever her health-care provider suggests.

## GETTING STARTED

Some babies breast-feed successfully from the first feeding. Others may have a difficult time getting started. Even if a mother has nursed a previous child, a new baby might react differently. Do not be afraid to ask for help right away if you need it. The birth setting where you delivered or your health-care provider might have a lactation consultant—ask. Try the local chapter of La Leche League, which may have volunteers available in your area. Your health-care provider can help you locate local assistance, or you can contact La Leche League at their toll free number: (800) La Leche. The number is staffed part-time, and a recording will direct you to emergency assistance at any other time.

While you and your baby are learning to breast-feed, it is best that no artificial nipples be offered. Inform caretakers who have contact with your newborn that you are breast-feeding. Tell them you do not want your baby to have a pacifier, bottles of sugar water, or supplementary formula. If there is a compelling medical reason to supplement your breast milk, your baby's health-care provider should discuss that with you and you should be involved in the decision making. If your baby is in a nursery, ask that she be brought to you if fussy, hungry, or in need of sucking. A sign on the baby's crib might be helpful to ensure that your wishes are known as the staff changes each shift.

38

## POSITIONS FOR NURSING

Position is key to successful breast-feeding. Find a position that is comfortable and that works for you. Your back should be straight and supported. Don't lean back in a way that pulls your breast away from the baby. Hold and support the baby in a tummy-to-tummy position, which enables him to face the breast and latch on without turning his head. Your baby should be close to your body and within reach of the nipple without straining. The use of a pillow on your lap—either a pillow specifically designed for this purpose or a regular bed pillow or couch cushion—is also helpful. Here are two possible positions:

- You can hold your baby in your arms in front of you as you feed. This is sometimes called the cradle or cuddle hold. What you call it doesn't matter, as long as you hold your baby close, with her back, legs, and head in a straight line with her face facing your breast.
- Another position is called the football hold. Try holding the baby under your arm the way a running back carries a football. If you are not a football fan, just look at the picture and think baby instead. For the left breast, hold the baby with your left arm. Support the head and neck with your left hand. Use your right arm and hand for the right breast.

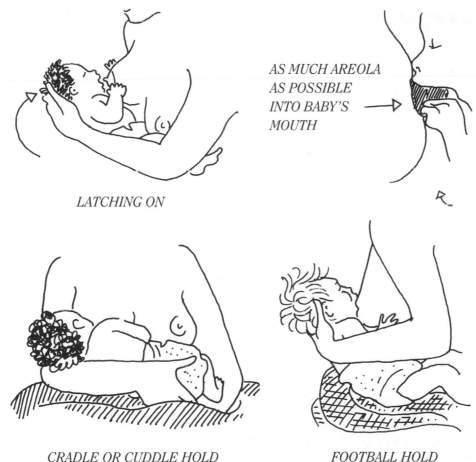

LATCHING ON

*AS MUCH AREOLA AS POSSIBLE INTO BABY'S MOUTH* →

CRADLE OR CUDDLE HOLD

FOOTBALL HOLD

Try to get as much of the areola (the dark area around the nipple) as you can into the baby's mouth. If the baby isn't getting enough of the areola, remove him from the breast and start over again. Put your little finger into the baby's mouth to break the suction so you can move the baby easily. Use both breasts at each feeding. At the next feeding, begin with the breast you used last the time before. To help you remember, tie a ribbon or put a safety pin on the bra strap to mark the side on which you just finished. Shifting a bracelet from one wrist to the other is also a good way to keep track.

## ADDITIONAL INFORMATION ABOUT BREAST-FEEDING

The above suggestions are intended to help you get started breast-feeding with a positive attitude that will help you breast-feed successfully. You probably would find it helpful, however, to consult additional, more comprehensive resources on breast-feeding to fill in the many details that have not been included here. There are excellent books available to help you. It would be useful to consult one or more of these resources before your baby is born so that you know what to expect and have a support system in place before the need arises.

*The Nursing Mother's Companion* by Kathleen Huggins, R.N., M.S. (revised edition published by Harvard Common Press, Boston, 1990) is an excellent resource for a new mother. The presentation is clear, and the text and illustrations are comprehensive and reassuring. Another excellent volume is *Bestfeeding: Getting Breastfeeding Right for You* by Mary Renfrew, Chloe Fisher, and Suzanne Arms (published by Celestial Arts, Berkeley, California, 1990). The step-by-step suggestions and excellent photographs and drawings in this book are helpful and supportive.

La Leche League is an international organization that provides information and encouragement to any woman who wishes to breast-feed. Volunteers are available throughout the country to help with problems that arise as a woman is breast-feeding. La Leche League publishes an excellent book, *The Womanly Art of Breastfeeding,* as well as a number of pamphlets. Also available is an audio guide based on the book, with information about how to prevent and overcome breast-feeding problems. The material also includes breast-feeding tips for the working mother.

## EXPRESSING AND STORING YOUR OWN MILK

Expressing your own milk is a useful technique to learn. You may find it helpful to express some milk to ease engorgement or to help your baby get started at the beginning of a feeding. If your baby is in an intensive-care nursery, you may be able to express your own milk to provide a supply for your baby's feedings. That will maintain your milk supply so you can breast-feed later. It may be convenient for you to express and store your own milk so that someone else can give a feeding to your breast-fed baby. If you plan to resume work outside the home while your baby is still nursing, you will need to express your milk and save it for your baby on a regular basis.

To express your milk manually, follow these simple steps. Use a clean container to collect the milk, and lean over the container so that the milk you express will drop into it. Hold the outer edge of the areola between your thumb and fingers to get started. Squeeze the thumb and fingers together, pulling back toward your chest wall. This may take some practice before you are able to express your milk successfully. When your milk supply is well established, you probably will be able to express several ounces at a time.

If you plan to express and store your milk on a regular basis, you might find that using a breast pump is more satisfactory than manual expression. Some women successfully use a small handheld pump that directs the milk right into a nursing bottle. These relatively inexpensive devices can be purchased at many pharmacies and baby-supply stores. Electric pumps, which are quite costly, often can be rented or borrowed. Ask your care provider or contact your local La Leche League for further information.

If you plan to feed the milk you have expressed within forty-eight hours, simply refrigerate it in its clean container. Containers washed in the dishwasher will do. If you do not have a dishwasher, wash the container and boil it for five minutes.

Milk kept longer than forty-eight hours should be frozen. Freezer containers—at least dishwasher-clean—or tightly tied plastic freezer bags are satisfactory storage containers for freezing breast milk. On the day that you plan to use the milk, move it from the freezer to the refrigerator for a few hours so it can thaw gradually. You can warm the bottle under the faucet if you wish, but don't use water that is too hot or the milk might curdle. Your own milk is not homogenized, so you should shake the bottle before feeding the baby to make sure the cream mixes back in.

How long you breast-feed is a personal choice, but it is generally considered good for the baby to breast-feed for at least six months. A full year would be even better. (See *Weaning (from the breast),* pages 193–194.)

Breast-feeding on demand is the best approach to maintaining an adequate milk supply for your baby. If you have concerns that you may not be supplying enough milk, consult your baby's health-care provider or ask La Leche League for help. Your baby's weight gain and the wetness of your baby's diapers will be a clue to the adequacy of your milk supply. Once you get started successfully, chances are all will go well. Be sure to allow enough time, and relax. Your nutrition is an important ingredient to success.

Don't panic if your child has an occasional feeding that does not go well. Relax, and try again. If problems seem to be the rule rather than the exception, however, get help soon.

# BREATH-HOLDING

Some children use holding their breath as a manipulative device during a temper tantrum. The sight of a toddler who has stopped breathing long enough to turn blue and perhaps even lose consciousness momentarily is alarming. These episodes, however, generally leave no ill effects on the child, although they may create considerable anxiety in the parents.

If breath-holding spells are part of your child's temper-tantrum stratagems, be careful not to overreact. Be reassured that a child can't and won't stop breathing long enough to cause serious physical harm. If you permit yourself, however, to be manipulated and controlled by such tantrum behavior, your child's developing personality as well as your relationship with your child may be adversely affected. If a child finds that breath-holding works to get what he wants, you are likely to find it occurring more often. Deal with the temper tantrum as you would have if it had taken any other form. (See *Tantrums,* pages 170–171.)

Consult your child's health-care provider if the breath-holding spell seems to be part of a convulsion, or if it is very severe or prolonged.

# BREATHING (NEWBORN)

The breathing of newborn babies is often noisy. They cough and sneeze frequently. Many babies snore. This is usually no cause for concern. The nasal passages of a newborn baby are very narrow; even a tiny speck of dust or dried mucus may be enough to set off a sneeze. Noisy breathing is often caused by excessive vibration of immature vocal cords as the baby inhales. Although the gasping that results may sound alarming, it is usually not a problem.

New parents often worry about the shallow, seemingly irregular breathing that is common and normal for many new babies. You may find yourself checking frequently to see if your sleeping baby is still breathing. Lots of parents do this, and are reassured when they find that all is well. Check with your baby's health-care provider, however, if you are at all concerned about the way your baby breathes. Don't be afraid to ask questions. If, for example, you feel that the pauses are too long or the pattern is too irregular, you should check it out. If your baby should stop breathing, see the following section for instructions on what to do until medical help arrives. If you have not already done so, take a course in first aid and CPR. Then you will be ready should a real problem arise.

If anyone in your household smokes, do not permit them to do so where your baby is located. Be strict, and make sure your rules apply to friends, relatives, workers, and anyone who enters your home when the baby is there.

# BREATHING EMERGENCY

When a person stops breathing for any reason—drowning, blocked air passage, electric shock, poisonous bite, or any other cause—this should be considered a life-threatening emergency that requires immediate help.

Never give artificial respiration (rescue breathing) to a person who is breathing. Here are some steps to follow if your child has stopped breathing for more than ten seconds. Do not waste any time getting started. Continue until the child is breathing well on her own or until expert help has arrived.

If drowning caused the problem, begin with Step 1. If not, begin with Step 2.

1. First, get the water out of the child's lungs. To do that, hold the child facedown with his head lower than the rest of his body.
2. Use a hooked finger to clear the child's mouth of mucus, food, or anything else that should not be there.
3. Place the child on his back on a flat surface.
4. Tilt the child's head back (neck stretched, chin up, jaw forward) to keep the air passages open.

5. With your mouth, cover the child's mouth and nose tightly. Breathe a small puff of air gently into the child's nose and mouth, just enough to make the chest wall move up a little. Remember that a baby or toddler is very small. He could not handle the entire contents of your adults lungs at once.
6. Move away so the air can come out. Put your mouth back and breathe another puff of air into the child, then move away. Do this every three seconds (twenty times per minute) until the child begins to breathe well or help comes.

These steps, in which you cover both the mouth and nose of the victim with your mouth, are designed for a baby, toddler, or young child up to about the age of eight. For older children or adults, place your mouth only over the victim's mouth and pinch his nostrils together between your index finger and thumb.

Rescue-breathing procedures are best learned from experts. Take a first-aid course, or at least a course in cardiopulmonary resuscitation (CPR), if you can.

(1)  (3)  (5)

(2)  (4)  (6)

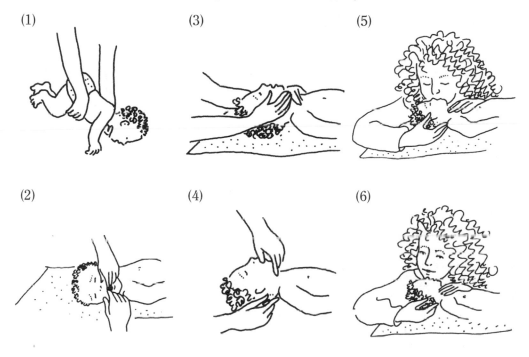

# BURNS AND SCALDS

To prevent burns or scalds, make sure that your mobile baby or toddler does not have access to hot things. Do not place objects such as coffeepots on surfaces where a child could pull them down. Turn the pot handles away from the edge of the stove when you are cooking. Never leave an unattended mobile baby or toddler in a room where there is an open fire or space heater, a stove in use, or a hot iron. Keep matches out of reach and out of sight. If your tap water is hot enough to scald (above 125 degrees F), adjust it. If you can't adjust the water temperature, make sure that your child does not have access to the taps at any time.

If your child does suffer a burn or scald, cool the injured area as fast as possible by dunking the burned body part in cold water or applying cold compresses. Continue to apply cold for several minutes until the pain stops. Then pat the skin dry with the cleanest cloth or towel you can find. Large sterile gauze pads are ideal, but if you don't have any, do the best you can. Keep the burned area loosely covered. Don't use adhesive, don't break blisters, and don't apply creams, ointments, greases, butter, jellies, or antiseptics. Call your child's health-care provider for advice on what to do next.

In the case of a chemical burn, wash the area thoroughly with cold water—lots and lots of water. The sooner you get the chemical off the child's skin, the sooner the damage will stop and healing can begin. Hold the child under a cold-water faucet or hose, if necessary. Then remove the clothes and continue to wash with cold water. After you have washed all the chemical off, call for medical help right away.

# CANDY AND SWEETS

Sweets are not good for the teeth, and too much in the way of simple carbohydrates in today's diets may also be contributing to the large number of children who become obese and are at risk for diabetes. Many parents try to minimize any contact their children have with candy or similar treats, but you may not be willing or able to enforce that.

How should you handle the issue of sweets with your child? Here are some suggestions.

- If you do allow sweets, keep in mind that those remaining in the mouth the least amount of time will cause the least harm. A piece of chocolate that melts quickly, for example, is better than a long-lasting lollipop. Chewy gumdrops, which leave particles in the teeth, are more harmful than candies that dissolve rapidly.
- Never offer your baby a pacifier dipped in sugar, honey, or jelly.
- Avoid chewing gum made with sugar. (See *Chewing gum,* page 55.)
- A handful of candy eaten quickly is better than that same handful would be if consumed a bit at a time over several hours.
- A drink of water should follow sweets. Have the child brush her teeth as soon as possible.
- Dried fruits are not a suitable substitute for candy. The unrefined sugar in chewy fruits can cause harm to the teeth if the particles remain in the mouth for any period of time.
- It's not just candy that can cause problems. Desserts such as cake, ice cream, sweet puddings, or tarts should be followed by a drink of water and a toothbrushing.
- Do not serve presweetened cereal. It adds lots of decay-causing sugar and very little nutrition to a child's diet.

The best approach to candy and other sweets is probably not to make a big deal about them. Don't encourage them, but don't make them so special that they become more enticing than they ordinarily would be. Forbidden sweets are likely to be the sweetest of all. Do not use candy or sweet treats as props in your child management strategies. Using sweets as rewards for good behavior, soothers for minor childhood crises, or bribes to get your child to behave better will increase their appeal in the long run. (See *Sugar,* pages 165–166, and *Cereals,* pages 48–49.)

# CARRIAGES

A baby carriage—especially the elegant type that looks a bit like Cinderella's coach—is probably not a cost effective investment for most families. Large carriages are expensive. They also require storage room and places to use them. They do not do well in crowded supermarkets, small elevators, or places with lots of stairs. An umbrella stroller might be a better choice. (See *Strollers,* pages 163–164.)

Nevertheless, if you can afford one, and live somewhere where it would be useful and not a burden, a traditional baby carriage or pram is a lovely way to wheel a newborn or older baby around the neighborhood. You may be able to inherit such a carriage from a previous generation, when life was less frantic and people didn't rush off to the mall with the baby in one arm and the umbrella stroller over the other.

If you purchase, borrow, or inherit a traditional baby carriage or pram, here are some things to consider. Is the carriage sturdy enough to be strong, but well designed and light enough to manage? Is it deep enough to be safe? Is the inside well lined? Is the lining well secured? Avoid linings attached with brads or other decorative bits of hardware that might come loose and become a choking hazard. Does the hood protect well from the sun or rain? Does it lock securely in place so that it will not collapse with small fingers in the way?

Can you push the carriage easily? Is the handle at a convenient height for you? Do the brakes work easily? Are they able to hold the carriage in place adequately? (Even so, never park the carriage unattended on a slope.) Is there a place to attach a harness? Your baby will be sitting and standing soon, and a safety harness is a must for all but the tiniest sleeping newborn.

Beware of carriages in which the top part is designed to be removed for use as a portable crib. Check out the safety record for the model you are considering. Does it work easily? Does it fasten back on securely? Have there been problems with the parts becoming disassembled when they are not supposed to? Although such a carriage may be transportable in your vehicle, remember that the bed portion is not safe for your child to ride in. Always use an approved car restraint.

# CARRIERS

## BACKPACK

Different carriers work for different people. Try before you buy, and bring your baby along to test the fit. Check the store's return policy in case you can't try the carrier out and you find you have made a mistake.

Your baby is likely to outgrow a front carrier, an infant carrying basket, or a sling several months before she will be able to walk fast enough and far enough to keep up with you. Some parents find a backpack carrier to be very useful; others skip it entirely and prefer to use a stroller. A backpack is not for newborns. It is suitable for babies who can sit and toddlers up to fifty or sixty pounds.

If you want to be able to see your child while carrying him, a backpack may not be a good choice. If you are unable to pick up your child in the pack from the floor without straining your back, you will do better with a stroller when your child outgrows a front carrier. If you and your partner want to take turns carrying your toddler, make sure that the backpack you choose is adjustable to fit you both. If you are considering a backpack, here are some points to keep in mind.

- Before you buy a backpack, try it on with your child in it. Do you think it will be convenient? Does it suit your lifestyle?
- Make sure there is a safety strap—preferably a five-point harness—to keep your child in the seat, even against her will.
- Is the carrier comfortable for your back and roomy enough for your child?
- Are the shoulder straps strong, wide, and well padded?
- Is the frame strong, but lightweight enough to be comfortable?
- Can you manage the pack on your own? Will you be able to load and unload your child without help? Try before you buy.

If a backpack does not suit your personal style, don't feel that you need one to be a good parent. There are other options for transporting your child. (See *Carriers [front],* page 47.)

## BASKET

A basket carrier with a bright padded lining is a lovely luxury for carrying a newborn baby from one room to another. In this type of basket, a tiny baby is as easy to carry as a briefcase. When you get to where you are going, the basket serves as an attractive little bed as well as a great conversation piece.

A basket carrier is an extravagance that is not for everyone. Whether or not one would be useful for you depends on your lifestyle and personal preference. A basket carrier can be handy for taking a newborn to restaurants, church, an office, or to visit friends. It fits easily in the trunk or on the floor of a vehicle. When you get where you are going, you can take your baby out of the vehicle's safety restraint and put her into the little basket for carrying and putting down where you are visiting. Many car seats now double as infant carriers; the basket pops out of the seat base, and you don't have to move the sleeping baby.

# FRONT

A front carrier is designed to hold your baby resting upright on your chest, with his arms and legs unrestrained, and is designed to be used with babies from about eight pounds up to toddlers weighing thirty to thirty-five pounds. Some users find, however, that carrying a child who is near the maximum weight is difficult. Using a front carrier with a toddler on long walks may tire you out.

A front carrier does have many advantages. You can keep the baby near you where she can snuggle close and hear your heartbeat. Using a front carrier, which fastens securely around the baby, keeps both of your arms free. A front carrier is excellent in close quarters; if your body can fit the width of a space such as a narrow aisle, your baby in the front carrier will fit, too. It is difficult to breast-feed while wearing your baby in a front carrier. If you want to breast-feed as you walk and carry your baby, a sling carrier is a better choice.

If you choose a front carrier, be sure to use it safely. Make certain that your newborn is big enough to use the carrier. Follow the directions for the carrier and also use common sense. If you plan to use the carrier with a very small baby, make sure that the leg holes are adjustable to keep your baby safely with one leg in each hole and no way to slip down and out. Check the product's safety record with the Consumer Products Safety Commission.

If you delivered your baby by cesarean section, ask your health-care provider how soon it would be safe to wear your infant in a front carrier. Don't wear your baby for any activity that might be hazardous for him. Never wear the baby in a front carrier while riding in the car or driving. Your baby must always be properly secured in an approved restraint system. Don't wear your baby while riding a bike, horse, or motorcycle. Although it is safe and convenient to wear your baby around the house, don't cook or eat or drink hot things that could burn or scald while the baby is attached. Use common sense.

Things to consider when choosing a front carrier:

- Make sure it is easy to adjust, with padded shoulder straps that are comfortable and do not slip.
- Fasteners—snaps or buckles—that you can manage with one hand are best.
- The carrier must not only adjust to fit you, it must adjust to fit your baby. Look for an adjustable strap or seat that allows you to raise or lower your baby on your chest. For a very young baby, the carrier should have an adjustable headrest that offers support to the newborn's neck.
- The front of your baby will be comfortable leaning on your chest. Her little back and seat will be comfortable if the carrier has a padded back rest and seat that will keep the child in place.

# SLING

A sling carrier is a simple and inexpensive way to carry a young baby. Sling carriers are designed for newborns to toddlers weighing up to thirty pounds, but chances are most parents would find the upper limit to be a bit heavy. A sling is a piece of strong fabric that wraps around you to form a pouch for your baby.

One major advantage of a sling carrier is that—unlike a front carrier—you can discreetly nurse your baby in it. A sling carrier is intended to facilitate convenient breast-feeding. You and your baby can look at each other while you carry him in the sling. A sling folds up to next to nothing and can be quickly stowed in a diaper bag or other portable tote bag.

Some parents find the sling somewhat uncomfortable and anxiety provoking; many others simply love it. Chances are you would try to keep one arm around the baby for safekeeping rather than fully trusting the sling to do the holding and carrying. That means you would not have both hands free as with a front carrier.

If you decide to try a sling, make sure it has padding at the shoulder and an adjustable strap that holds securely.

# CEREALS

## FIRST SOLID FOOD

Infant cereal made from a single grain such as rice or barley is often the first solid food offered to a baby. Mix warm water, expressed breast milk, or formula with the dry flakes to prepare the cereal. The cereal provides essential nutrients, especially iron, which may be necessary in the diet of a baby whose main source of food is mother's milk, formula that is not iron-fortified, or cow's milk.

There is no particular advantage to cooking your own cereal for a baby. The cooking takes time and effort, and adult cereals may not provide enough iron. Beware of precooked "instant" adult cereals to which you add boiling water. These usually contain added salt. The best cereal for a baby is a packaged, iron-fortified infant cereal to which you add formula or water. (See *Solid foods,* pages 161–163, for guidance on when to introduce cereal or other solid foods to your baby.)

Before you buy a particular cereal, read the list of ingredients and the nutritional information. Stick to the plain infant cereals such as rice, barley, or oatmeal. The mixtures that already contain fruit and dried formula cost more, and may include ingredients to which some children are sensitive. If your baby does react badly to a cereal mixture, it would be difficult to know which ingredient is causing the problem.

Do not add sugar or other sweeteners to your baby's cereal, even if you think it tastes awful the way it is. Serve it instead with a bit of pureed fruit, commercially prepared or homemade. Applesauce is a good first choice. It is relatively easy to digest, and many babies seem to like it.

## CEREALS FOR TODDLERS

If chosen wisely and served with milk and fruit, cereals can provide excellent nutrition for your toddler. Chosen by a young child from television commercials or supermarket displays, however, cereals could be the start of a toddler's junk-food habit rather than a source of healthful meals. Before you buy a cereal, read the list of ingredients and nutritional information. Remember that ingredients are listed in the order of their importance in a particular product. A cereal that lists sugar first contains more sugar than any other ingredient.

Avoid "instant" hot cereals, which have salt already added. Your toddler does not need the sodium, and it's a simple matter to cook the regular cereal without salt. Some instant hot cereals have added sweetener or artificial flavorings.

Labels like "all natural," "fortified," and "high fiber" are intended to convince you that the contents of a container are more nutritious than similar products which are not so labeled. Don't be fooled. Many of the granola cereals, for example, convey the impression of high nutritional standards. They tend, however, to be sweeter than your child needs, and relatively high in calories for the nutrition provided.

If you serve a dry cereal, opt for a whole-grain cereal. Always serve a dry cereal with milk or calcium-fortified soy milk, which provides calcium and additional protein.

Avoid presweetened cereals and any which contain artificial colorings and flavorings. No matter how appealing the advertising, do not let your child manipulate you into purchasing a product that is, in effect, junk food. Some cereals contain more than forty percent sugar by weight. Avoid them. Before you buy any cereal, check the nutritional label for sucrose carbohydrates (sugar content). If you feel that your child must have some sweetness with his cereal, purchase one that is nutritionally sound and sprinkle on a tiny bit (less than a teaspoon) of sugar.

# CHALLENGED CHILDREN

If any aspect of your child's development causes you concern, do not hesitate to discuss the matter with your child's health-care provider. If you suspect that there might be a developmental disability of some sort, pretending that there is nothing wrong will not make the problem go away. If you are being too sensitive and there is no real cause for concern, it is important that you be reassured.

Support and encourage a child with a specific disability to develop normally in whatever areas that development is possible. Make every effort to limit the effects of any disability to the function that is impaired, and help the child to develop as fully as possible in other ways. Actively seek whatever assistance might be available from state or private agencies and support groups of parents with similarly disabled children. Your health-care provider may be able to advise you of specific facilities and useful contacts in your area.

Here is a list of resources from which further information about various specific disabilities and problems can be obtained:

Alexander Graham Bell Association for the Deaf and Hard of Hearing
3417 Volta Place NW
Washington, DC 20007-2778
www.agbell.org
202-337-5220
Information center on hearing loss focused specifically on children. Provides support and advocacy services for parents and professionals.

American Academy of Child and Adolescent Psychiatry
3615 Wisconsin Ave. NW
Washington, DC 20016-3007
www.aacap.org
202-966-7300
Information on developmental, behavioral, and mental disorders that affect children and adolescents.

American Academy of Pediatrics
141 Northwest Point Blvd.
Elk Grove, IL 60007-1098
www.aap.org
847-434-4000
General information on common childhood problems.

American Council of the Blind
818 18th Street NW, Suite 700
Washington, DC 20006
www.acb.org

American Foundation for the Blind
11 Penn Plaza, Suite 300
New York, NY 10001
www.afb.org
1-800-AFB-LINE
212-502-7600
Information on blindness and low vision, directory of services, agencies, and organizations.

American Speech & Hearing Association
10801 Rockville Pike
Rockville, MD 20852
www.asha.org
800-638-8255 (voice and TTY)
Information on speech, language, and hearing. Online directory of speech-language pathologists and audiologists.

Association for Children with Learning Disabilities
4900 Girad Rd.
Pittsburgh, PA 15227
www.acldonline.org
412-881-ACLD
Information and services for individuals and families coping with learning disabilities.

Autism Society of America
7910 Woodman Ave., Suite 300

Bethesda, MD 20814-3067
www.autism-society.org
800-3AUTISM
301-657-0881
General information, local support contacts, and additional resources.

Birth Defects Research for Children, Inc.
930 Woodcock Rd., Suite 225
Orlando, FL 32803
www.birthdefects.org
407-895-0802
Provides fact sheets on various defects, support, and resources for parents.

Centers for Disease Control and Prevention
1600 Clifton Rd.
Atlanta, GA 30333
www.cdc.gov
404-639-3311
800-311-3435
Provides general information on health topics from A to Z.

Cleft Palate Foundation
104 South Estes Drive, Suite 204
Chapel Hill, NC 27514
www.cleftline.org
919-033-9044
Provides information to parents of children with clefts and other craniofacial birth defects.

Council for Exceptional Children
1110 North Glebe Rd., Suite 300
Arlington, VA 22201-5704
www.cec.sped.org
1-888-CEC-Sped
703-620-3660
(TTY) 703-264-9446
Information for parents of handicapped and gifted children.

Easter Seals
230 West Monroe St., Suite 1800
Chicago, IL 60606
www.easter-seals.org
312-726-6200
(TTY) 312-726-4258
800-221-6827
Information and services to help children and adults with disabilities gain greater independence.

Epilepsy Foundation
4351 Garden City Drive
Landover, MD 20185-7223
www.epilepsyfoundation.org
800-323-1000
301-459-3700
General information on epilepsy and ongoing research. Programs and services for parents of children with epilepsy.

Health Resources and Services Administration
U.S. Department of Health and Human Services
Parklawn Building
5600 Fishers Lane
Rockville, MD 20857
www.hrsa.gov (Maternal and Child Health Bureau, www.mchb.hrsa.gov)
301-443-6652
Helps provide health resources for medically underserved populations.

March of Dimes Birth Defects Foundation
1275 Mamaroneck Ave.
White Plains, NY 10605
www.modimes.com
888-MODIMES
Information on birth defects and referral services for the public.

National Hemophilia Foundation
116 West 32nd Street, 11th Floor
New York, NY 10001
www.hemophilia.org
212-328-3700
Essential information on symptoms and treatment of bleeding disorders for patients and families.

National Mental Health Association
1021 Prince St.
Alexandria, VA 22313-2971
www.nmha.org
Mental Health Information Center: 800-969-NMHA
703-684-7722
Resource for information on mental illness and treatment; referrals to local agencies.

Sickle Cell Disease Association of America, Inc.
National Headquarters
200 Corporate Pointe, Suite 495
Culver City, CA 90230-8727
310-216-6363 Office

800-421-8453 General Public
www.sicklecelldisease.org
General information, various programs and services, and educational materials.

Spina Bifida Association of America
4590 MacArthur Blvd., Suite 250
Washington, DC 20007-7226
www.sbaa.org
800-621-3141
202-944-3285
Information and referral services.

United Cerebral Palsy Associations
1600 L Street NW, Suite 700
Washington, DC 20036
www.ucp.org
202-776-0406
800-USA-5UCP
Information on local services and ongoing research developments.

# CHANGING DIAPERS

Changing a newborn's diaper is relatively easy. The how-to diagrams on a disposable diaper package are an excellent guide. Lift the baby by the feet with one hand, remove the dirty diaper with the other hand, clean the baby's bottom, and put on the new diaper.

Make sure everything you need is within reach before you begin to change the baby's diaper. You will find out how important this is the first time you open a badly soiled diaper and have nothing handy to clean the baby's bottom. If you have disregarded step one and do need something, don't leave the baby unattended—*even for a moment*—on a surface from which he could fall. Reapply the soiled diaper and take the baby with you to get what you need.

Many babies wet again right in the middle of the changing process. They almost seem to plan it that way, so be prepared. Shield a little boy's penis with the diaper you have just removed until you are ready to fasten the new one. That will keep you from being sprayed in the face as you bend over your baby. If you have a little girl, put a cloth diaper or a waterproof pad under her to catch the puddle.

Be sure to clean the baby's bottom thoroughly at every change. Even if the baby was just wet rather than soiled, it's important to remove traces of urine that could irritate. A spray bottle of water and paper towels are handy. Disposable diaper wipes are costly and unnecessary. If you do use them, make sure that the perfumes or detergents they contain do not irritate your baby. If you buy a jumbo-size container of wipes, you can make your own little travel packs by putting a few wipes in a plastic pantyhose container.

If you use cloth diapers, sticking the pins in a bar of soap will make them easier to use. The soap won't flake away if you leave it in its paper wrapper to serve as a pin cushion. When you push a pin into the baby's diaper, put your other hand behind the spot where the pin is going to protect your baby from a stab. Many cloth diapers now use Velcro closures, eliminating pins altogether.

## CHANGING A MOBILE BABY OR TODDLER

Changing a newborn is easy. As soon as your baby becomes mobile, however, the once-simple procedure can become a conflict. Many children add variety to the diaper-changing process by rolling, wriggling, or scooting along on the changing surface. An interesting (but safe) object thrust into little hands might divert attention long enough to finish the change. That strategy works better than force. Talk to your child as you change the diaper. Describe each step as you do it, but do it quickly.

Few toddlers lie still for a diaper change. You will quickly become skilled at removing and changing diapers while the child is standing or even trying to move somewhere else. As with rolling babies, an interesting object might help. Involving your toddler step-by-step in the process works for some children. Talk her through each step and try to get some help. The corner of a room is a good place to change a standing toddler, because there is no place to go until you are done.

# CHEWING (LEARNING HOW) ⎯⎯⎯⎯⎯⎯⎯⎯⎯⎯⎯⎯⎯

A baby's first chewing experience is with the gums, even before the chewing teeth come in. As soon as your baby can put his hands (and whatever they contain) in his mouth, he is beginning to learn the motions of chewing.

The first teeth a baby gets are front ones, for biting. (See *Teething*, pages 172–173.) These are not chewing teeth, but the baby is already gumming things in a chewing motion. As soon as your child begins a regular practice of putting things into her mouth, you should provide some safe, hard food objects for chewing practice. Teething biscuits or zwieback are excellent. Give your baby the chewing experience on a hard real food such as a biscuit when the impulse to explore with the mouth is strong. That will help him make the connection between chewing and eating. If you serve nothing but pureed foods until the chewing teeth (molars) are well established, your child might resist having to chew to eat.

Be careful what you offer your child to eat. Teething biscuits are designed to be useful and safe. Do not offer bits of apple or raw carrot until you are certain that your child can and will make the proper chewing motions. A baby with only front teeth could bite off and inhale a bit of apple and choke on it. Do not let your baby chew on any food while lying down.

# CHEWING GUM

It is probably best for everyone concerned if your toddler does not chew gum. Gums flavored with sugar should definitely be avoided because they are harmful to the teeth. A wad of sugarless gum won't cause tooth decay, but it will, like any other kind of gum, tend to seek out the most unwanted locations—a chair seat, the dog's ear, your child's hair, or the place you are about to put your foot.

No matter how careful you are, however, you probably won't have the good fortune in today's world to keep your child and chewing gum apart forever. Even if your child does not chew, chances are a playmate will.

Here are some hints to remove chewing gum from hair. Try cold cream, baby lotion, baby oil, or hair conditioner. Massage it well into the area that contains the wad of gum Wait at least five minutes. After the cream has had a chance to penetrate, try to separate the hairs (which by that time should be somewhat slippery) a few at a time from the gum. Shampoo to remove the remaining mess. If that does not work, probably nothing will. Resort to scissors.

# CHILD ABUSE

Child abuse is a major problem in our society. Many parents who abuse their children were themselves abused as youngsters, and they are following that example. When child abuse starts, it is often difficult to stop it without help. Many abusive parents love their children and simply lose control. Some are not even aware of how damaging their actions are. Not all abusers are parents; friends, relatives, baby-sitters, and other caregivers have also been known to hurt other people's children.

Many cases of child abuse involve physical harm—beating, battering, bruising, burning, shaking, or otherwise causing pain or physical injury. Physical neglect—failing to nourish, clothe, clean, or otherwise care for a child—is also a form of abuse. Some children are abused sexually. Verbal abuse—screaming, ridicule, constant fault finding—can cause emotional damage and may escalate into physical abuse. More subtle examples of abuse are failing to protect a child from preventable risks—not using a child restraint in a vehicle, for example—or doing something that causes harm to the child's health, such as smoking in the home or vehicle in the presence of the child.

Abuse of a young baby often starts as a desperate reaction to constant crying and the frustration of being unable to quiet the child. (See *Colic,* pages 62–63, *Crying,* pages 71–72, and *Shaken baby syndrome,* pages 155–156.) Abuse of a toddler or older child may involve discipline and punishment that has gotten out of hand. Toddlers are especially vulnerable to abuse because what is normal behavior for a toddler—curiosity, never-ending questions, exploration, abundant energy, contrariness, and dawdling—has the potential to provoke even the most easygoing adult to lose his or her temper.

Be alert to signs that your child might be having difficulty with a caregiver or family member. If your child seems fearful or unwilling to spend time with a person, quietly try to figure out why. If your child becomes uncharacteristically withdrawn or undergoes other unexpected personality changes, it's important to get to the bottom of what is happening.

If your child seems to bring out the worst in you, remember that no parent is perfect. No matter how hard you try, there will be days when things will go wrong. Here are some warning signs to watch for if you seem to be having more bad days than good days.

- Are your days full of conflict and combat with your child? Do you feel out of control or unable to cope a lot of the time?
- Do you scream at your child a lot? Do you find yourself thinking that she can't do anything right? Do you use ridicule and verbal put-downs?
- Do you frequently lose your temper with your child? Do you dish out discipline or punishment while in a fit of rage?
- When you lose your temper, do you hit, push, shake, or otherwise touch your child in a way that might hurt him?
- Do you find yourself using punishment far more than praise? Do you use or are you tempted to use punishment tactics such as beating, tying the child up, or locking the child in a room or a closet?
- Do you find yourself resenting your child? Do you often wish that you did not have any children?

If a *yes* answer to any or all of the above questions would be the rule rather than the exception for you, do yourself and your child a favor and get some additional support to make life easier. Find someone you can trust—a friend, relative, or volunteer recommended by your church, temple, or community agency. When things become unbearable, let that person stay with your child for an hour or two or more while you get out of the house. It is better to leave for a while than to stay and do something you will regret.

If you can't get help to come to you at a moment of need and you feel you are about to hurt your child, put the child in a safe place such as a playpen. Sit down in your own adult version of a time-out chair. Take some deep breaths. Count to ten. Try to put yourself in your child's place. Count to ten again. Call the local parent help hotline. Talk to someone. Write the number here, and on page 4, so you have it handy.

## PARENTS ANONYMOUS, INC.

Parents Anonymous, Inc., was founded in 1970 to help strengthen families and provide coping strategies to prevent child abuse and neglect. Parents Anonymous has a national network of hundreds of local groups that meet regularly. For a continuing source of support and communication, find your local chapter of PA and go to a meeting. Find out the local toll-free hotline number and write it on page 4 so you will have it if you need it.

Don't be embarrassed or afraid to call. You will receive understanding and supportive help from people who know what you are going through. Parents Anonymous meetings and services are available to all community members—married, single, divorced, separated, teen parents, grandparents, or stepparents. If you have not abused your child yet but feel your ability to cope gradually slipping away, call PA to get suggestions and strategies before you lose control and hurt your child. If you and your child are already caught up in a cycle of abuse, PA can help. Parents Anonymous is not a reporting agency, and no one will judge you or report you because you call and ask for help. You can call the hotline anytime—twenty-four hours a day.

To locate the closest PA group, look in your local phone book or ask your health-care provider. If you can't find the number and would prefer not to involve anyone else, you can reach Parents Anonymous, Inc., by telephone at 909-621-6184 to obtain a local contact. You can also find your accredited state PA organization on the Parents Anonymous Network map on the Internet at www.parentsanonymous.org.

# CHILDPROOFING _____

This book contains numerous, perhaps even repetitious references to techniques of keeping your baby or toddler safe. The world is full of interesting things that could cause harm to a child whose need to explore is not yet matched by good judgment.

Childproofing your surroundings—especially for an energetic mobile baby or toddler—seems to be a never-ending process. No matter how carefully you have gone over everything and taken every precaution, chances are your child is busy creating another way to get into trouble. That is an almost inevitable characteristic of the age.

To childproof your home effectively, you must look at everything from your child's vantage point. Just before your baby becomes mobile, you must concentrate on making safe everything within a crawler's reach. Chances are it has been a long time since you have had to focus so intently on the environment between your knees and the floor. Then, as your child becomes bigger, stronger, and able to stand and climb, you must extend your childproofing efforts to everything she can reach—or climb to reach.

There are devices you can purchase to help you make your home a safer place for your child. You may find it helpful to use safety latches for cupboards and drawers, cover plugs for unused electric outlets, foam tape for padding sharp edges, child-resistant lids for medications and household products, and safety gates to close off high-risk areas such as stairways and forbidden rooms. Windows above the ground floor should have window guards.

Do not, however, depend on safety gimmicks to do the entire childproofing job for you, no matter how effective such devices may seem. Be as careful in childproofing the environment as you can be, but remember that nothing is an adequate substitute for adult supervision of your child's activities. Thorough childproofing simply makes your job a bit easier.

No matter how careful you have been about childproofing your own home environment, you can't be sure that friends, relatives, neighbors, or parents of other children have done the same. When you visit other places with your child, take nothing for granted. Always take the position that an unsupervised child is a child at risk. *Keep an eye on your mobile baby or toddler at all times.*

# CHOKING _____

Choking is a common cause of accidental death among children between the ages of one and five. The best way to deal with choking is to prevent it in the first place, because when it happens it may be too late. A baby or toddler is going to put anything within reach into the mouth.

Young children have been known to swallow an odd assortment of small objects which, in most cases, pass right on through the digestive system. If an object gets into the windpipe instead of the esophagus and digestive system, however, breathing can be blocked, with immediately disastrous results. The best way to keep a child from choking is to keep any objects that could cause choking away from the child.

- All small objects (one half-inch in diameter or less) should be completely out of reach at all times. Do not let your child play with coins, buttons, tacks, erasers, screws, or any other objects of similar size.
- Examine your child's toys to make sure there are no small parts that could be removed. Be especially careful of things like the eyes of stuffed animals or the wheels of model cars. Even if an item looks appealing and is sold in a reliable toy store, it may not be safe. Use your own judgment. The Consumer Product Safety Commission does test toys, and recalls particularly hazardous models. Those procedures, however, happen too late for some children. You must monitor carefully whatever objects your child plays with.
- Don't offer your toddler food items such as popcorn, peanuts, grapes, or raisins. Those items do not break apart easily, are small and light, and can easily be inhaled into the windpipe instead of swallowed. Many care providers suggest that such snacks be avoided until a child is five or six years old.
- A child who has no molars to enable complete and adequate chewing could choke on some foods that would seem to be harmless and healthful. Celery stalks, raw carrot sticks, or apple wedges, for example, could easily be bitten off by a toddler's front teeth into tiny pieces, which could then be inhaled. Save those snacks until you are sure that your toddler has the teeth, the know-how, and the discipline to chew them properly.

## FIRST AID FOR CHOKING

If your child begins to choke, do not waste time finding someone else to help. Seconds can be precious. If she is able to cry or speak and is breathing or coughing, do nothing. Chances are the child will cough up the obstruction and all will be well.

If the child can't breathe, you must do something immediately. First, if you can see what is causing the obstruction, try to remove it with a hooked index finger. If you cannot, do not probe. You would risk pushing the object further in. If you are unable to remove the object, hold your child upside down and hit him sharply between the shoulder blades. That should remove the obstruction.

If the above measures have not worked, you will need to try the Heimlich maneuver. Holding the child in front of you, wrap your arms around her. Place one fist over the child's stomach, the other hand over the fist, and make a sudden sharp motion upward toward the chest and under the breastbone. This procedure, the most effective for adult choking victims, is best done by someone who knows how. Done wrong, it can harm a child. Nevertheless, at this point you would have little choice. If you succeed in removing the obstruction but the child does not begin to breathe, begin mouth-to-mouth rescue breathing immediately. (See *Breathing emergency,* pages 42–43.)

You should ask your health-care provider about first-aid procedures for choking so that you are fully informed and prepared in case you ever need them. It is advisable to take a first-aid course if you can.

# CIRCUMCISION

Circumcision is the surgical removal of the foreskin that covers the tip of the penis. If your baby is a boy, one of the earliest decisions you will have to make is whether or not to have him circumcised. You should consider the issues carefully before your baby is born so that your decision will be an informed one.

Because circumcision has been such a widespread practice, many parents assume that the procedure must be done. That is simply not so. Circumcision is unnecessary surgery. If you do not wish to have your baby boy circumcised, do not allow yourself to be pressured by practitioners who still suggest the procedure.

The American Academy of Pediatrics no longer recommends routine circumcision. The potential medical benefits are not as significant as once believed, and a program of good personal hygiene, including regular bathing, can prevent the problems that circumcision prevents. There is some evidence that men who have been circumcised may have less penile sensitivity.

Circumcision is a painful surgical procedure routinely done without anesthesia. Newborns do feel pain. Some practitioners are now willing to use a local anesthetic for circumcision, but that may involve risks that could outweigh the benefits. There are risks involved in the procedure, although the rate of complication is small—about one in five hundred babies. Most complications are relatively minor, such as local infection or bleeding, and can easily be treated. Damage to the penis is very rare, but it can occur.

In the early 1970s, more than 90 percent of baby boys in the United States were routinely circumcised. Now that percentage has dropped to about 65 percent. The United States is the only industrialized nation in which routine circumcision is still practiced. One reason for continuation of the practice is a circumcised father wanting the boy to look more like him. Religious ritual circumcision, required in Judaism and Islam, accounts for many circumcisions.

Most nonritual circumcisions are done before the baby leaves the birth setting. Some physicians routinely perform circumcisions in the delivery room. Although that may be convenient for practitioners, it is not what is best for the baby. It does not make sense to follow procedures for a gentle birth, promote a positive bonding experience, and then immediately inflict the painful surgical procedure of circumcision on the child. Insist that the doctor wait at least twenty-four hours before circumcising your newborn.

## CIRCUMCISION CARE

If you have had your baby boy circumcised, it will take at least a week, perhaps longer, before the sensitive area is completely healed. It can be kept clean with plain warm water applied with a sterile gauze pad. To protect the unhealed circumcision, some care providers recommend placing generous amounts of petroleum jelly on a sterile gauze pad and wrapping it loosely around the tip of the baby's penis. Change the pad at each diaper change. A tube of petroleum jelly is easier to use for this than a jar, because you will be able to use the right amount without getting any on your hands. If the baby's penis bleeds or becomes swollen, consult your health-care provider.

## INFORMATION OPPOSING CIRCUMCISION

If you are uncomfortable about making a decision regarding whether or not to circumcise your child, and are interested in obtaining additional information and research findings about circumcision, the National Organization of Circumcision Information Resource Centers (NOCIRC) is a nonprofit educational organization committed to "securing the birthright of male and female children and babies to keep their sexual organs intact." Founded in 1986, the organization now has more than one hundred centers worldwide. It maintains offices open to the public and responds to mail and telephone requests for information. You can reach NOCIRC by mail at P.O. Box 2512, San Anselmo, CA 94979-2512. Telephone: 415-488-9883; fax: 415-488-9660. Their Web site is NOCIRC@concentric.net.

# CLOTHING

The clothing your baby or toddler wears will depend on where you live and the time of year, as well as your personal preferences and resources. There is no one "right" list of things you should have. Here are a few things to keep in mind as you plan what to buy.

- Until your child is toilet trained, dress her in clothing that provides easy access to the diaper area.
- Remember that the things your child eats and plays with will inevitably leave their marks on the clothes. Ease of laundering is a must. If an indoor garment requires dry cleaning, it's not a wise choice for a young child.
- During and after toilet training, dress your child in clothes he can easily remove or pull down without help. Pants should be fairly loose with a wide elastic waistband. Avoid items with complicated fasteners or garments that require complete disrobing before your child can use the toilet or potty.
- Pajamas should be flame retardant and meet appropriate safety standards. Wash them according to the directions so they won't lose that quality.
- Clothes that your toddler can learn to put on or off by herself are a plus for developing independence.

# COLDS

A cold is a contagious viral infection of the membranes of the nose and throat. Contrary to popular belief, people do not catch colds from being in drafts, going out on cold or wet days, forgetting to wear a sweater or hat, or keeping the house too cool. In fact, overheated, dry, indoor air dries out the mucous membranes and may make a person more susceptible to colds. Colds are caused by viruses. The best way to keep your child from getting a cold is to keep him away from anyone who has one.

Preschool children get more colds than any other age group. They have not yet built up much immunity to cold viruses. Many young children get as many as six or more colds a year.

A toddler's cold often begins with a high fever that usually lasts a day or two. Common cold symptoms include stuffy or runny nose, mild sore throat, hoarseness or dry cough, watery eyes, and a general achy feeling. Most colds can be treated at home and will go away without problems in about a week.

- If your child is too young to blow her nose, you can use a suction bulb (available in any pharmacy) to help clear the nasal passages. Your child's health-care provider may suggest nose drops and tell you how to use them. Saline nose drops (one cup of warm water and one quarter teaspoon of salt) are easy to prepare, inexpensive, and effective.
- More moisture in the air may make the child with a cold more comfortable. Use a cold-mist humidifier. (See *Vaporizers,* page 186.)
- Fluids are important. Offer your child water or juice at least once an hour—more often if he will take it.

- Don't dose your child with an over-the-counter cold remedy. Never give aspirin to a young child with a virus cold. In extremely rare cases, the use of aspirin has been linked to Reye's syndrome, a disease which can be fatal. (See *Reye's syndrome,* page 150.) If your child has aches, fever, or a sore throat, and you feel you must give something, ask your health-care provider. Acetaminophen (Tylenol, for example) is a wiser choice.
- Antibiotics do not cure colds, so don't administer any on your own. If the cold develops complications, your child's health-care provider may prescribe an antibiotic to deal with the secondary infection. If so, use it as directed for the full time you are supposed to. Do not save a little for the next time.

Don't be discouraged if your child seems to get one cold after another. As immunity to the cold viruses builds up, the frequency of colds will decrease. Preschool children seem to pass colds from friend to friend and back again. In a few years, however, your child will probably have far fewer colds. There is not much you can do about it in the meantime.

# COLIC

Colic is a severe bellyache and irritable crying spell for a baby. It can also lead to a severe headache and crying spell for parents. Some babies go through infancy without a sign of colic; others are afflicted on a daily basis for as long as several weeks.

The causes of colic are somewhat mysterious. It is not known for sure why some babies develop colic and others do not. Colic is not, however, caused by bad parenting or nervous mothers, so you should not add guilt to your feelings of despair when trying to soothe a colicky infant. A tendency for colic just seems to be built into the temperament of certain babies. One child in a family may have it while another may not.

If a baby is going to be colicky, the onset of the problem is likely to occur between two and eight weeks of age. Although it can occur at any time of day, colic is more common in the late afternoon and early evening. Colic is not the same as formula intolerance, so switching formula for a bottle-fed baby is unlikely to help. (See *Formula,* pages 95–96.)

A baby with colic cries inconsolably, sometimes for hours at a time. The crying may escalate to a rhythmic bout of screaming. She may pull the legs up toward her abdomen, clench her fists, or flail her little arms. Her belly may feel tight as if full of gas, and the baby may release gas explosively or have a bowel movement.

Parents through the ages have tried many techniques to cope with a colicky baby. If nothing works, try to keep calm and be reassured that colic does not last forever, even though it may seem so at the time. By the fourth month, as the baby's digestive system becomes more mature, the worst of colic is likely to be over. Here are some hints to help get you through.

- Hold the baby upright for feeding, in a position that is more vertical than horizontal. Be sure to burp the baby frequently—after each ounce of formula or four to five minutes of breast-feeding—to help the bubbles come up.
- Hold the baby securely in your arms in a vertical position and pace the floor. Being walked may help the baby feel better, and it will give you something to do besides worry.

62

- Check to make sure that the crying is not a result of some discomfort other than colic. Check for a wet or dirty diaper. Changing the baby's diaper will provide a few moments of diversion for you both. Make sure that the baby is not too hot or too cold.
- Offer the baby a bit of warm water in a bottle, or try a few sips of a mild herbal tea such as chamomile. Dilute the tea to about half-strength, and make sure that it is just warm, not hot. A tiny sprinkling of sugar in the warm liquid might help.
- Difficult as it might seem, try to create a relaxed and calm atmosphere. Play soft, soothing music. The gentle ticking of a metronome or a nondigital clock adds soothing rhythm.
- Try swaddling your baby. (See *Swaddling,* page 168.) The security of being tightly wrapped helps some colicky babies, although it may upset others even more.
- If you have a front carrier or a sling carrier, put your baby in it and walk. If you have a rocking chair, hold the baby in your arms while you rock. It may make you both feel better. If you have an infant swing, that might help.
- Take a warm (not hot) hot-water bottle, or heating pad turned on low, and place it on the baby's abdomen. A warm bath may work, too.
- Some colicky babies respond positively to rhythmic noises and vibrations. Turn on the vacuum cleaner or a dryer. Put the child in the car restraint and take him out for a ride. The sounds and motion of a moving vehicle may help, and it will give you a diversion as well.
- For some babies, the various techniques involving movement, sounds, or other efforts to soothe simply do not work. Some babies become overstimulated rather than soothed. If your child does not respond to efforts to soothe, you may have to resort to letting him cry for a while to see if that works.

If you are having serious trouble coping with a colicky baby, don't let your exasperation get the better of you. You may be able to find a local support group that will help you. Parents who have survived colic can be an excellent and empathetic resource. A well-chosen online chat room on the computer will give you an opportunity to know that you are not alone. If you can find an experienced baby-sitter who can handle the child for an hour or two, get out of the house if you feel you are at the breaking point.

No matter how tempted you might be, *do not shake your baby* in an effort to stop the crying or to let out some of your own rage. It is better to let the baby cry than to hurt him. If you are exasperated and irritated beyond your ability to cope, shaking could quickly get out of hand and cause serious harm. (See *Shaken baby syndrome,* pages 155–156, and *Crying,* pages 71–72.)

# COMFORT HABITS

Many babies develop personal little habits that they use to comfort themselves and provide a sense of security at bedtime, naptime, or times of stress. These habits usually persist through toddlerhood and, for many children, last even longer. These personal comfort habits are typically no cause for concern. They diminish and disappear when the need is no longer there. Do not make a fuss over them.

For many children, sucking—fingers, thumb, or an object such as a pacifier—becomes a comfort habit. Some children adopt a rhythmic motion of some sort. Rocking back and forth, twirling the hair, pulling at an ear, or banging the head are different forms of rhythmic comfort habits. Severe head banging that causes pain, however, should not be assumed to be a harmless habit without further investigation. (See *Head banging,* pages 98–99.)

The popular *Peanuts* character Linus, complete with blanket, has many counterparts in real life. Many children adopt a special object such as a blanket, an article of clothing, a stuffed animal, a rag doll, or a tiny pillow.

- Use of a cuddly object for comfort is normal and healthy behavior for a baby or toddler. A child who uses such an object for solace at bedtime is beginning to develop a sense of security that is under her control.
- Protect the precious object from loss or destruction if you can. A duplicate held for safekeeping might be a good idea, although it will never feel or smell quite the same.
- If you travel, be sure to take the object along. A child in unfamiliar surroundings will need it more than ever.

Continuous use of an object as a comfort habit at times other than bedtime or naptime may signal a potential problem. If you are with your child and there are other things to be done during the daytime, and your child persistently refuses to put down the object to do those other things, explore the situation further. Your child may need additional support and comfort from you to make giving up the object easier. If you think your child avoids other activities and relies too much on the comfort object, consult your health-care provider for advice.

# CONJUNCTIVITIS (PINKEYE) ——————————

Conjunctivitis, commonly called "pinkeye," is an irritation of the lining of the eyelids and the outside covering of the eyeballs. The eyelids may be swollen, and the eyes may be weepy and red. The discharge from the eyes may form a crust that sticks the lids closed while the child sleeps. Pinkeye can be extremely uncomfortable.

Conjunctivitis that is caused by a bacterial infection can be highly contagious. Keep the affected child's washcloth and anything else that comes in contact with his eyes away from other members of the family. Wash your hands immediately after touching the child. Try to keep the child from rubbing his eyes, although with a baby or toddler that may be close to impossible.

If your child develops the symptoms of pinkeye, consult your health-care provider promptly. Treatment will vary according to the exact cause of the problem. Bacterial conjunctivitis will probably be treated with antibiotic drops or ointment. Because of the highly contagious nature of the disease, do not use the same dropper or ointment on more than one member of the family. There are several possible causes of conjunctivitis, which is why medical advice to ensure the correct treatment is essential. Don't use medicine from a previous outbreak unless your health-care provider tells you to do so. Occasionally, an allergic reaction causes symptoms of pinkeye. It's important to find out what you are dealing with to get the correct treatment.

# CONSUMER PRODUCT SAFETY COMMISSION

The U.S. Consumer Product Safety Commission (CPSC) is a federal government agency that considers the safety (or lack thereof) of various products, sets standards for certain products, and recalls products that are found to be unduly hazardous.

No matter how well the CPSC performs its watchdog functions, parents still must be attentive to the products they buy and use with their children. By the time a product is found to be dangerous and subject to recall by the CPSC, it is likely that children have already been injured or killed. You must be careful about what you use with your child, whether or not the product has government approval.

The CPSC is a useful source of information to check on the safety status of products. Its records can be particularly helpful if you are considering purchasing a secondhand item, such as a used crib or stroller. Check the safety record and recall status of intended purchases.

U.S. Consumer Product Safety Commission (CPSC)
Washington, DC 20207
800-638-2772
www.cpsc.gov

# CONTRARINESS

Contrariness is an ingredient of a child's effort to develop independence, and an inevitable characteristic of being a toddler. At some point during your child's second year, *no* is likely to become a highly favored word and cause you considerable frustration. Coping with your child at this stage will probably be easier if you approach the contrariness with cleverness. Do not use it as an invitation to combat. Here are some specific suggestions.

- Make cooperation fun whenever possible. Instead of issuing an order to pick up the toys, for example, make a game of it. "Let's see who can put the things away faster—you or Daddy." Having the child pick up two items while you pick up five or six is preferable to a situation in which no one picks up any—or you pick them all up in anger.
- Keep in mind that a toddler who says no doesn't always mean it but may just be saying it on general principles. Allow for your child to change her mind without losing face.
- Warn your child when you are going to make a demand that is likely to provoke contrariness. Say, for example, "In five minutes you will have to wash your hands and get ready for lunch." Or, "When this program is over we are going to turn off the television and go outside." That builds in time for the child to get the defiance out of his system before doing what you want.
- Avoid elaborate explanations. Keep your requests and your reasons simple and to the point. There are times when all the reason you need to offer a toddler is, "Because I want you to do it." It is possible, however, to maintain control without being mean or confronting. Try to be calm and kind.
- Give your child choices between desirable alternatives whenever possible. That leaves you in control, but gives the child a chance to express independence. For example, "Which sweater do you want to put on—your blue one or your green one?" is less likely to start a battle than simply, "Put on your sweater."
- A family is not a democracy. Let your child be independent in ways that make sense, but do not relinquish control in ways that would compromise the child's safety or the well-being of the rest of the family. Encourage your child, for example, to feed and dress herself as much as possible; do not, however, permit her to play with dangerous objects or ride unrestrained in the car to find out what it's like without a car seat.
- Do not argue. There will be times when you must enforce your wishes against your child's will—period. Do it calmly, kindly, and firmly. Say, "I know you would rather stay outside, but now we are going to . . ." Then pick up your child and get on with it. Such times will be less frequent and less upsetting if you act in a matter-of-fact way and avoid anger.

No matter how well you manage to cope with your child's contrariness, there still may be days when nothing seems to go right. Try not to lose your cool. The contrary stage, although very trying at times, does not last forever. Soon your child will become more competent in language and other activities. Contrariness will give way to cooperation as the desire to imitate adult behavior becomes stronger than the desire to defy you. Contrariness as a way of life will reappear when your child becomes an adolescent, but you will have a few years in between.

# CONVULSIONS (SEIZURES) _____

Convulsions in a young child are a frightening experience for the parents, but these seizures generally pass without lasting harm. A convulsion is caused by irritation to the brain, which often accompanies high fever. Some children are more susceptible than others to convulsions. If your child tends toward feverish seizures, your child's health-care provider will advise you on steps you should take to keep fever as low as possible whenever your child is ill. (See *Fever,* pages 91–92.)

If your child does have a seizure (convulsion):

- Put the child on her abdomen or side on a surface where thrashing about will not cause injury. A carpet will do nicely. A bed is acceptable as long as you make sure the child does not fall off the edge.
- If you can, loosen the child's clothing, especially anything around the neck.
- Look at your watch or a clock to note the time. Observe carefully what is happening so you will be able to describe it accurately to your child's health-care provider.
- Let the seizure carry on as it will, and don't try to hold the child still. When the seizure is over, put the child on his side with his head slightly lower than the rest of his body.
- At no time during or right after a convulsion should you give the child anything by mouth. Don't try to force the jaws apart or use any object to hold the mouth open.
- If the seizure lasts longer than fifteen to twenty minutes, get help and proceed to the nearest hospital as fast as you can. Prolonged seizures (forty-five to sixty minutes) have the potential to result in lasting damage.

If you are alone, tend to your child first and call for medical assistance as soon as the seizure has passed. If someone is with you, have that person call for help while you take care of your child.

If your child seems to have a tendency toward convulsions, your health-care provider may recommend further testing to make sure that the seizures are fever-related and not due to a more serious problem, such as epilepsy.

# CRADLE CAP

Cradle cap is a scaly crust that is often found on a baby's scalp and behind the ears. It may be yellowish or simply dirty in appearance. Cradle cap is a normal accumulation of shed dead skin and dried oil from the many oil glands in the scalp. On other parts of the body, such shed skin is typically rubbed away by routine friction or washing. Many parents, however, are overly cautious about washing a baby's scalp, particularly the soft spot.

Cradle cap is rarely a serious health problem, but it's best to deal with it before it gets out of control. When you wash your baby's head using a mild soap or baby shampoo, rub vigorously with your fingertips or a terry washcloth to loosen and remove the scales. Don't be afraid to rub the soft spot; it's tougher than you think. If the washing and rubbing doesn't take care of the cradle cap, apply baby oil or a bit of petroleum jelly to the baby's scalp. An hour or two later, when the scales have softened, gently remove as many as you can with a fine-tooth comb, and then shampoo. Frequent brushing with a soft brush may help, even if your baby doesn't have much hair.

For a severe case of cradle cap that does not respond to this treatment, consult your child's health-care provider. If your baby's scalp becomes red and/or weepy (oozing), don't self-treat but get prompt medical advice.

# CREEPING AND CRAWLING

Sometime around six months of age or a bit later, your baby is likely to figure out a way to get around without being carried. When that happens, life with your child becomes more interesting—and considerably more demanding.

Different children devise different techniques of locomotion. Watch your child carefully. You will probably be quite fascinated at the way she develops into a mobile baby. Some of the methods of moving about look quite comical. Some children push along on the stomach long before they can support themselves on hands and knees. Many children begin their creeping by moving backward, which seems to be easier. Children who can sit often learn how to move along in a sitting position, with a hand behind to push and a leg stretched out to pull.

True crawling—supporting oneself on hands and knees and moving the arms and legs in some coordinated way to cover distance—usually takes a while longer to develop. Some babies have it worked out by eight months; others take a year or longer to crawl efficiently. A few seem to skip the crawling stage almost entirely and go right to "cruising," holding onto pieces of furniture. Some babies get the crawling position right, but take days or even weeks to figure out how to move the arms and legs in a way that propels them forward.

Whatever method your child develops to move about, the most important task for you is to reevaluate your house for potential hazards. Try to view the world from your newly mobile baby's vantage point, less than a foot above floor level. Here are some precautions to take.

- Keep your baby off the stairs by installing secure gates at the top and the bottom. Use gates to keep the child out of certain rooms if you wish.
- Place safety caps in all unused electric outlets, or cover them securely with electrician's or duct tape so your child can't poke fingers or objects into the outlets.
- When your child is on the floor, make sure that lamps and small appliances are unplugged, with the cords out of reach to prevent the baby from pulling things down on his head. (Of course, as soon as you unplug a lamp, you should put a safety cap in that outlet.)
- Make sure the floor is reasonably clean and tidy, and free of all tiny objects that could present a choking hazard or be swallowed.
- Install childproof latches on all low cabinets. Even with safety latches (which are not truly childproof), it is safest to store dangerous substances such as cleaning materials in cabinets that are completely out of reach.
- Keep breakable objects out of reach, both for the sake of the objects and for the sake of your child.

It will take some effort to get used to your new responsibilities when your baby becomes mobile. The child can be literally under your feet one moment and seconds later can be in another room getting into trouble. Some children are more difficult to handle than others. A good rule to follow is never to trust a mobile baby who has crawled out of your sight.

# CRIBS

Many children sleep in a crib for at least the first two years, and some continue to use a crib for a year or two after that. All new full-size cribs now sold in the United States must meet safety requirements established by the Consumer Product Safety Commission. If you purchase or inherit a secondhand crib, make sure that it meets current safety standards. Even if the crib is safe, where it is placed in the room and how it is used are important aspects of your child's safety.

- The bars in the sides of the crib should be no farther apart than two and ⅜ inches. Even if you are sure that your child's head cannot fit through the spaces, it is equally important that her slender body not be able to squeeze through sideways. Children have been known to hang themselves by trying to exit through the bars feet first.
- The mattress must be firm and fit tightly in the crib. There should be no room for a child to squeeze any portion of his body between the mattress and the sides of the crib. A good test of tightness is whether or not you can put the sheet on the mattress easily. You should have to lift the mattress to get a fitted sheet on it. If your hands can easily put the sheet on without lifting the mattress, the mattress does not fit the space tightly enough.
- The surfaces of the crib should be nontoxic and splinter-free.
- The hardware should be safe and secure. There should be no sharp parts, things that could break off, or movable features that move when they are not supposed to move.
- Decorative features, if any, must be safe. There should be nothing that could trap or injure a child. Do not use a crib with corner posts that extend upward and beyond the end panels. Children have been known to catch their clothing on such posts, and some have even strangled. Avoid cribs with decorative cutouts in the headboard or footboard. Such decorations could entrap the child in some way and cause serious harm.

## PLACEMENT AND USE OF THE CRIB

Place the crib in a safe area in the room. It is best not to locate the crib by a window if you are able to place it elsewhere. If you must put the crib by a window, the window should have a safe and secure window guard. Make sure that the crib is not within reach of any cords from drapes, window blinds, or shades. It is not just the pull cords on blinds that could be a problem; children have been known to hang themselves in the tiny little space at the connecting cords between the slats on certain kinds of blinds. Although blinds of this type have been recalled and are no longer sold, some homes may still have them. Do not locate the crib near heaters, fans, or lamps.

Do not use soft bedding in the crib, since it could smother a child. Do not use a pillow or a featherbed. The mattress should be firm and the sheet tight. Babies and toddlers are quite comfortable sleeping without a pillow. If you have a mobile over the crib, make sure it is securely fastened and well out of reach of the child. Remove mobiles as soon as your child can pull herself up and sit. Make sure that there is nothing near the crib that the child could reach and swallow or strangle on.

## CRIB BUMPERS

Crib bumpers keep your sleeping baby's hands and feet inside the crib; they provide a comfortable cushion; and, perhaps especially important for a newborn, they keep your baby out of drafts.

A crib bumper should fit well and fasten securely with safe snaps or ties that the child cannot reach. The bumper should attach to the crib in at least six places so that it will stay where it belongs and your baby won't be able to dislodge it or get caught in it. Be sure to check from time to time to make sure that the fasteners are firmly secured. Some babies manage to find them to chew on, and that could be a danger.

Crib bumpers are fine for young babies. Some children, however, once they can stand, will use the bumper as a step to climb out, so it's best to remove it at that point. (See *Beds and bedding,* pages 25–26.)

# CROUP

Croup is a type of laryngitis, a viral infection of the vocal cords, that can be an emergency requiring immediate help. Croup can be a very frightening experience for the parents as well as for the sick child, whose breathing passages are still very small and easily compromised.

An attack of croup usually occurs at night, when the child coughs, wakes, tries to cry, and has difficulty breathing. A child with croup sounds somewhat like a cross between a strangling crow and a barking puppy. If your child has an attack of croup, have someone else call your health-care provider, if possible, while you attend to the child. Here's what to do, unless advised otherwise by a medical professional.

- Turn on the hot taps in the bathroom, especially the shower, so that the room becomes steamy as fast as possible. If you don't have hot running water, boil water in a teakettle or pot to make steam for a small room. While waiting for the room to steam up, try the step that follows (even though it appears to be a contradiction to the use of steam).
- A few breaths of cold air may help reduce swelling of the larynx. If it is cold out, hold the child at the window for a few breaths of chilled night air. Otherwise open the freezer door and hold your child (warmly wrapped) where he can breathe the cold, moist air. Even being in front of an air conditioner might help.
- Spend about ten to fifteen minutes holding your child in an upright position in the steamy room you have prepared. That should relieve the breathing problems.
- Keep the moisture going with a vaporizer or cool-mist humidifier. (See *Vaporizers,* page 186.) You might find it helpful to create a croup tent with sheets around the crib to concentrate the mist and keep it close to the child.
- You might also try taking the child for a short ride in the car, which serves as a diversion as well as an exposure to the cooler air outside.
- Make sure that no one in the home smokes. Smoking can aggravate an already serious condition.
- Although it is easier said than done, try to keep the child calm. A relaxed child needs less oxygen than a child who is in a panic. Although the situation is likely to make you very anxious, try not to communicate your fears to your child.

When the worst of the attack seems to have passed, you can deal with getting medical help. If you have not been able to reach your health-care provider, don't hesitate to take your child to the nearest emergency room. If you have reached your health-care provider, you may be told to bring the child to the hospital or clinic by car or ambulance, or you may be advised to continue the moisture in the air at home for a while.

A serious, potentially life-threatening disease that resembles croup is epiglottitis, the inflammation and swelling of the little flap that goes over the windpipe. Epiglottitis can completely close over and stop the child's breathing. It is a serious medical emergency. If your child has a high fever, is leaning forward and gasping for breath, drooling, has poor color, and the crouplike symptoms progress despite your treatment, call for an ambulance or take the child immediately to the nearest emergency room. If you suspect epiglottitis, do not open the child's mouth to examine it; opening it up can make matters worse and stop the child's breathing altogether.

The first attack of croup your child has is likely to be the most upsetting because you will not have been prepared for it. If your child seems to have a tendency toward this problem, your health-care provider will tell you what to do to minimize the chances of a serious attack. It may be necessary to provide extra moisture in your home's air throughout the winter months, or at least any time your child shows signs of a cold. Prevent all smoking in your home or any vehicle in which the child rides. If your child has an attack, stay in the room with her through the night. Croup is very scary. Your child should not have to face it alone.

# CRYING

A newborn or even a settled baby cries because he needs something. You may not always know what that something is, but you should try to figure it out. Do not worry about spoiling your baby; you won't. Letting a young baby cry does not build character. What it may do, however, is communicate to the baby that you are not attending to his needs.

Attend to your crying baby promptly. That will help him to feel loved and secure. Prompt attention does not reinforce the crying. In fact, babies whose needs are met quickly tend to cry less frequently and for shorter periods of time.

Some mothers seem to be able to distinguish a "wet cry" from a "hungry cry" or a "bubble cry" with uncanny accuracy. Do not be upset if you can't. Some babies are easy to figure out right from the start, while others are not. Just do the best you can. Here is a list of questions to help you figure out why your baby is crying.

1. Is she hungry or thirsty?
2. Does his diaper need to be changed?
3. Does she need to suck?
4. Does he have a bubble and need to be burped?
5. Is she tired and in need of sleep?
6. Is he startled? To break the startle cycle, pick the baby up and hold him securely, or leave him lying down and firmly hold one of his arms or legs. That seems to work.

7. Is she uncomfortable? Is she too hot or too cold? Is something pinching or irritating? Has she been in one position for too long?

8. Could the problem be some or all of the above? Sometimes you will need to fix more than one discomfort before your baby settles down. Try different things in whatever order makes sense to you.

9. Is the problem none of the above? That is the tough one. Occasionally you won't be able to figure out why your baby is crying. Walk around, holding him close to your body. At least he will sense that you are trying. In the long run, those efforts will pay off.

If your baby is colicky and that is the reason for the crying, you may have to try a number of things to give her some relief. (See *Colic,* pages 62–63, for specific suggestions.)

# CURIOSITY

Curiosity is a vital characteristic of a young child, and will keep her very busy. That has its drawbacks, but it is an important part of learning. Keep your child safe, but try not to stamp out the curiosity and inclination to explore. A curious child is not being naughty, but is doing what comes naturally.

The strong curiosity of a newly mobile baby or toddler is not matched by manual dexterity or understanding of cause and effect. You must keep dangerous substances out of reach. (See *Accidents (prevention),* pages 1–4, *Childproofing,* pages 57–58, and *Poisoning,* pages 146–147.)

You also need to remove from reach any object that could be damaged by a curious child. Remember that it is curiosity, not badness, that causes a young child to head for the crystal vase on the coffee table. If the vase should meet the floor and smash, count yourself as the naughty one. It is unreasonable to expect a mobile baby or toddler to act contrary to nature and stay away from enticing objects or situations. As language and understanding develop, you can teach your child some self-discipline, but that will take time, patience, and longer than the toddler years. Crystal vases are not a good item on which to practice.

As your child grows, the physical capacity to follow where curiosity leads will increase. No longer confined to crawling, the child will walk, run, and climb. Good judgment does not develop at the same pace as mobility. Unless carefully supervised, therefore, a toddler's self-initiated exploring and learning activities can easily lead to trouble.

Many young children enjoy hearing the popular stories about Curious George, the little monkey who has been getting into scrapes and entertaining children for many decades. Many of the *Curious George* books are available in paperback. Do not count on your toddler, however, to make the direct connection between Curious George getting into trouble and what could happen to a curious child in his own home. There are lessons one can learn from these books, but keeping the crystal vases and dangerous substances out of reach is safer for all until you are absolutely certain that these lessons have been well learned.

# DAWDLING

Dawdling is a typical toddler behavior that can exasperate caregivers. Try not to allow your annoyance at dawdling to escalate into combat with a child who is simply doing what toddlers normally do. Try to come up with coping strategies to minimize conflict.

- Allow additional time for what once seemed like simple daily routines. Leave enough time for bathing, getting dressed, cleaning up the clutter, getting out of the house, shopping, and other activities. Such events are likely to happen slowly when a two-year-old is "helping" you. If you build in extra time for things to take longer, you won't be as irritated when they actually do take longer.
- If you don't have the luxury of extra time for routine tasks, plan in advance. If, for example, you must limit the time spent shopping, skip the walking and keep your child in a stroller or shopping cart. If dawdling in the bath is a problem, set a timer and gently but firmly remove your child from the tub when the bell rings. If an activity is dragging on too long, change it before you get angry. Diversion is an excellent management device.
- Some of a toddler's slowness is an inability to cover as much ground as an adult can. Short legs must take several steps to every one of yours. If you are in a hurry, don't depend on your child to match your pace. Use a stroller or backpack.
- Understand that some dawdling may involve a bit of contrariness as a toddler is learning to be independent. Taking her own sweet time is one way a toddler can exert control. That can be a valuable learning experience. If it is inconvenient for you to permit such a learning experience at a given time, don't feel guilty about intervening. Do not, however, become angry and blame the child for being a normal toddler. Just change the scene or the activity as calmly as possible. (See *Contrariness,* pages 65–66.)

Try to take some time to enjoy dawdling along with your child. Seeing the world through a toddler's eyes can be a refreshing and wonderful experience. Remember that a toddler does not yet have a clear concept of time. He will not worry about the future or fret about the past nearly as much as an adult would. Enjoy the moment with your child when you can—you will both benefit.

# DAY CARE

If yours is a single-parent family or both parents work outside the home, you must make appropriate day-care arrangements for your preschool child. Although some child-development experts point out that nurturing care by a parent is preferable to full-time child care by others, many families simply do not have a choice. If you must work outside the home and make other arrangements to care for your child, make the best choice you can and don't feel guilty about it.

A recent long-term study of child care in the United States found that children who spent more than thirty hours a week in child-care settings were more likely to be more aggressive, demanding, and disobedient than children who spent less than ten hours per week in child care. While the results of that study are not reason to avoid placing your child in outside care should you need to do so, careful choice of the quality of care your child receives is important. That same study also found that children in day-care centers with high-quality programs did better on language tests and thinking skills than those who were not in such programs. Try to find a high-quality program that respects children and provides suitable learning activities.

How you choose to handle day care and what arrangements you make will depend on what is available in your area, as well as on what you are able to pay. The most cost-effective solution to day care may be relatives, such as grandparents who are willing and able to provide such care in their home or yours. The downside of that is potential family conflict over issues such as discipline, childproofing the environment, or other child-rearing practices.

A hired caregiver who comes to your home on a regular basis is likely to be the most flexible in terms of scheduling and procedures, as well as the most expensive. An alternative to day care in your own home is day care in someone else's home. You may be able to find a family near you that takes one or more children on a regular basis for day care. Or you might choose a professionally staffed day-care center, such as one affiliated with an agency—for example, a community center, a religious group, or an educational organization.

Find out whether or not the facility you are considering is licensed by the state or otherwise accredited in any way. Although a license is not a guarantee that the facility is suitable or well run, it does suggest at least occasional reviews or inspections and minimal basic standards. You still need to visit the facility, ask questions, and make an informed decision.

Before selecting a day-care situation for your child, visit the available choices with your child. Schedule your visit during caregiving hours so you can see what actually goes on there. Look around, and listen. Observe how the children interact with each other and with the caregiver(s). See how your child responds, but don't let your decision be strongly influenced in a negative way if your child prefers staying by your side to entering the activities. You may have to settle for the feeling that your child would participate in such a place once she got used to it.

If your child is still an infant, look at how infants are nurtured and cared for, the safety of the cribs, the attitude of the caregiver(s), the number of children per adult, attention to bodily needs such as diaper changing, cleanliness, and the general atmosphere of the place. Activities would not yet be your concern. You might also wish to consider the age range of the children. Does care of infants interfere with quality of care for older children, or vice versa? Are infants or very young children suitably supervised to keep them safe from aggressive older children? Trust your feelings as you observe.

As you consider a day-care facility, discuss with the caregiver(s) topics of importance to you. Don't be afraid to ask questions. Try to phrase your questions so they promote conversation, rather than simple yes or no answers. Among the subjects you might bring up are books for children, available toys and activities, formal instruction (if any) such as reading readiness, use of pacifiers, toilet training, discipline, safety, aggressive behavior, television, policy regarding sick children, staffing, feeding, and anything else of importance to you. While there may be no single correct or incorrect view on many of these topics, finding out how the views of the caregiver(s) mesh with your own can help you evaluate the suitability of the facility for your child.

If the person you are interviewing about the day-care facility seems nervous, uncooperative, or somewhat unwilling to address your questions and concerns, consider that a warning sign and be very careful. Ask about the visiting policy for parents. A parent should be able to drop in at any time without an appointment. A center should have nothing to hide.

Check out the safety and security of the facility. While drop-in parents should be allowed and even encouraged, make sure that the center's open-door policy is not so open that a stranger could enter unnoticed and possibly cause harm. Staff should be immediately aware of and attentive to any visitor who enters.

Once you have found out as much as you can about potential child-care facilities available to you, go with your instincts. After your child is actually attending a child-care facility, your best clues to the quality of care will be your child's daily behavior and reaction. Although any child can have a bad day from time to time and beg to stay home, if those days are frequent and your child seems fearful or anxious, there is likely to be good reason. Listen to your child and your instincts. Use common sense. If a situation is not working out, change it.

# DEATH

Death is a difficult matter for most people to discuss, and there really isn't any best way to explain the concept to a young child. Do what is consistent with your family's beliefs, and don't make up stories you will have to undo later. Answer your child's questions honestly and sincerely. By the age of two, many children will be able to grasp some notion of what death means, although the permanence of death will not be understood. And even a younger child will notice the absence of a significant person, although the reason for that absence may be beyond his comprehension.

## QUESTIONS ABOUT DEATH

A young child might hear about someone dying and ask you what it means to die. Your answer should be simple and direct. If you believe in a life beyond this world, you will probably find it easier to talk about death in a religious context. If you do not believe in an afterlife, you can tell a child that to die means to stop being alive.

Do not describe death as "going to sleep," or you may create bedtime fears and problems. Avoid talking about death as "going away," because that expression may lead a child to worry when you go away even for a short time.

If a child asks, "Am I going to die?" be truthful in a way that does not cause fears. You can say that everyone will die someday, but that most people die when they are very old, or very sick, or if they get very badly hurt. Reassure your child that you do not expect that to happen, and you expect her and yourself to be around for a long, long time.

## DEATH OF A PET

The death of a pet is often the first experience a child has with death. Allow your child to be sad and to engage in appropriate rituals to accompany the death of a pet. That can be an important learning experience. Respect for animals is an important lesson for young children.

Do not flush a goldfish down the toilet or toss a deceased cat out with the trash and hope your toddler will not notice. The child will notice, and his trust in you is likely to be shaken. A simple burial for a beloved pet will help your child deal with the reality of the loss, as well as demonstrate a reverence and respect for life. If a child wants to add a departed animal to the list of "God bless _____" at bedtime, such remembrance is appropriate and comforting.

## DEATH OF A LOVED ONE

If a person close to a young child dies—a parent, grandparent or other relative, or even a neighbor or family friend—the child must face not only the loss of the person who died, but the grief and preoccupation of those who remain. That can be a very upsetting situation for a child.

If someone has died and you are grieving, be honest with your child. Admit that you are sad because someone dear to you has died. Reassure the child that she was not in any way the cause of the death. Explain the death in religious terms if that fits in with your beliefs.

It is important that you be able to provide the child with comfort and support. Do not force a young child to go to a funeral if he does not want to go. Use common sense and follow your instincts.

# DELIVERY-ROOM PROCEDURES _____

As soon as a baby is born, she must make the transition from being totally dependent on the mother to functioning on her own. Birth attendants assist the newborn to make this transition. If the baby is in respiratory distress, helping him to breathe is a top priority. If necessary, mucus is suctioned from the baby's mouth. Because the room temperature is significantly lower than the mother's body temperature, which the baby has been used to, the baby must be kept warm. The baby may be placed on the mother's abdomen and a blanket used to cover them both.

To complete the baby's passage to life outside the mother, the umbilical cord must be cut. If you and your partner have specific preferences about who will cut the cord and how quickly after delivery that will be done, be sure to discuss the procedure in advance with your prenatal-care provider so there will be no surprises in the birth setting.

At birth and five minutes later, the baby's condition will be rated in five areas on a scale of zero to two, called the Apgar scale. (See *Apgar scale,* page 10.)

## ADDITIONAL MEDICAL PROCEDURES

In most states, babies are required by law to receive treatment to prevent eye infection. Silver-nitrate drops have traditionally been used, but more recently antibiotic ointment (erythromycin), which is less irritating, has been the treatment of choice. Ask your health-care provider in advance what will be used for your newborn, and don't be afraid to express a preference. Both silver-nitrate drops, which may irritate, and antibiotic ointment, which may temporarily blur the baby's vision, can interfere with eye contact during bonding. Many birth attendants are willing to delay that procedure until after the parents have had a chance to hold the baby for a while. That is another matter you should negotiate in advance if it matters to you.

In the nursery, babies usually receive a shot of vitamin K to aid the blood in clotting. After twenty-four hours, a drop or two of blood will be drawn from the baby's heel for a newborn metabolic screening. That screening tests for PKU disease and hypothyroidism, which can cause mental retardation, and perhaps other conditions such as sickle-cell anemia or HIV. Ask to find out which conditions are included in the metabolic screening for your baby. Some birth facilities now test newborns for hearing problems. Depending on where you live, other tests might also be done. If you have any questions or concerns about the medical procedures that will be scheduled for your new baby immediately after delivery, be sure to ask.

## IDENTIFICATION AND SECURITY

Before mother and newborn leave the delivery room, they receive matching identification bracelets to make certain that mother and baby are correctly identified and the correct baby is brought each time to the mother. Two bracelets may be placed on the baby—one on an ankle and one on a wrist—as an extra safeguard. As part of the permanent birth record, the baby's footprints may be recorded along with the mother's thumbprints.

In today's uncertain world, with heightened concern about security, some birth settings have implemented additional procedures to safeguard newborn babies. Specific details of the procedures are not typically made known, but electronic devices are sometimes used. A noninvasive device attached to the baby, for example, may trigger an alarm if removed from the child, or if the child is carried beyond certain security checkpoints.

# DENTAL CARE (PROFESSIONAL) —————————————

By the time your child is two or three, and certainly before she begins kindergarten, it is time for her first visit to the dentist. If the child has a problem, you would make that visit sooner rather than later. From then on, visits twice a year are recommended.

It is important to take good care of your child's baby teeth even though they will be replaced by permanent ones later. Even in baby teeth, cavities should be filled because tooth decay can cause painful toothaches, and the premature loss of a baby tooth can cause the position of the remaining teeth to shift. Regular visits to the dentist can help keep potential problems under control.

For most people, going to the dentist does not rate as one of life's preferred activities, and there is no point in making the experience any worse for your child than necessary. Avoid communicating your personal fears or dislikes, if any, about the process. If you are comfortable with your family dentist and feel that he would be patient with a young child, it is fine to take your young child to that office. A pedodontist is a dentist who specializes in the care and treatment of children's teeth. If you can find one near you, that might be a good choice for your child's early years.

Daily care of the teeth at home is essential. A young child will need help in doing a good job. (For detailed specifics, see *Tooth care [daily]*, pages 180–181.)

# DIAPER RASH

Diaper rash can be very painful. It occurs when a baby's tender bottom remains in contact with wet or soiled diapers too long. It can also signal a food allergy, when concentrated around the anus. Diaper rash can occur whether you use cloth diapers or disposables. To help prevent diaper rash, change the diaper frequently and wash the child's bottom at every change. Here are some suggestions for dealing with diaper rash.

- Clean the diaper area with water and mild soap after every change. Do that even if the diaper is wet rather than soiled. The ammonia left by urine can be extremely irritating to tender skin, even if the child's bottom appears to be clean.
- Avoid packaged wipes that may contain scents or other potential irritants. To cope with diaper rash, stick to plain water and mild soap. Don't use perfumed lotions or powders. If you use powder, it should be plain cornstarch.
- Change the diaper more often. This is especially important if you use disposable diapers, which can hold a lot of irritating moisture without seeming to be wet.
- If you use cloth diapers, skip the rubber pants for a while. Use two diapers at once, or a cloth diaper cover that breathes.
- If the leg bands fit tightly, cut them with scissors to open them up and let some air in until the rash is gone.
- Allow your child to go without any diapers when possible. Exposure to air helps cure the rash. Put several layers of cloth diaper and a rubber or plastic pad in the crib to protect the mattress while your child has a bare bottom. If your location and time of year permit, a little sunshine and fresh air might help. (But be careful not to trade diaper rash for a sunburned bottom!)
- To clean a baby's soiled bottom with a minimum of irritation, use a spray bottle with lukewarm water and then wipe clean and dry.
- A sitz bath may provide some relief to a child who is suffering greatly from diaper rash. Put a little warm water in a plastic dishpan or the tub (depending on the age and size of the child) and let the child sit in it for a few minutes several times a day. As when you give a child a regular bath, you must be there to hold, support, and supervise.
- An ointment such as A & D Ointment, Desitin, or a similar product may help protect your child's bottom from further diaper rash and give it a chance to heal. Zinc-oxide ointment is effective and inexpensive.
- If you use cloth diapers, make sure they are well rinsed so no soap or detergent remains. Raise the temperature of the wash water if possible. A cup of white vinegar in the rinse water will neutralize traces of ammonia from the baby's urine. Make sure the diapers are very clean. Stained or dingy cloth diapers seem to increase the risk of diaper rash.

If you have tried these suggestions for two or three days and your child still has a severe diaper rash that does not seem to respond to treatment, consult your child's healthcare provider. Your child may have a food allergy or an infection of some sort along with the diaper rash, and you will need medical advice to prescribe the correct treatment.

# DIAPERS (CHOICES) _____

Whether you use cloth diapers, disposables, or some combination of the two is a personal choice. It should be an informed choice and meet your needs. If your original choice does not work well for you, don't feel guilty about making a change.

Some people decide to avoid disposable diapers for ecological reasons. The gel they often contain may be bad for the environment. Others choose cloth diapers because they are less costly than disposables. If you have chosen cloth diapers for either ecological or economic reasons and the choice works well for you, there is no reason to change. But if you feel that you are drowning in laundry and spending time that you would rather spend enjoying your baby, you might wish to reconsider.

If your reasons for choosing cloth diapers are ecological, remember that the laundering of cloth diapers adds detergent wastes to the environment, and a washer and dryer consume energy. If you use a diaper service, the delivery truck also uses energy. If you have chosen cloth diapers for economic reasons, be sure to add in the costs of doing laundry (detergent, hot water, electricity) and reasonable compensation for your own time before you decide for sure that cloth diapers are cheaper.

## CLOTH DIAPERS

If you use cloth diapers, you will need at least four to five dozen of them. You will want more if you take your laundry out to a commercial laundromat. You may be able to make do with a dozen less if you have a washer and dryer right in your home. Even if you plan to use disposables, you should have at least a dozen cloth diapers on hand. They make excellent bibs and mops, and are a handy backup for those times you run out of disposables.

Cloth diapers come in several different types of cloth and shapes. Prefolded diapers already have the extra thickness where it is needed, but some prefolded types will require additional folding to fit the tiny bottom of a newborn. Shop around until you find the kind that makes the most sense to you. There are several ways to fold a cloth diaper. What you end up doing should be what you find easy as well as the best fit for your child. For a boy, you will want extra thickness in the front, while for a girl that thickness should be in the back.

## DISPOSABLE DIAPERS

Try different brands of disposables until you find the ones that work best for you and your baby. As your baby grows and changes shape, you might find a change of brand as well as a change in size to be helpful. The disposable diaper that fit perfectly and did the job just right two weeks ago may not be the best choice now. Shopping in bulk at warehouse clubs can save you up to $1,000 a year in diaper costs.

# DIET (NURSING MOTHER)

The balanced diet recommended during pregnancy will serve a mother well as she breast-feeds her baby. A nursing mother needs about a thousand calories of additional nutritious foods and fluids more than she would need if she were not pregnant or breast-feeding. (See *Breast-feeding,* pages 37–41.)

Any medications a nursing mother takes can be excreted in the breast milk. If you are breast-feeding, you should not take any medications—even over-the-counter items—without consulting your health-care provider. If you must take medication, you can minimize its effect on the breast milk by taking it right after you finish feeding your baby. By the time you begin the next feeding, the level of the medication will be lower.

There is no evidence that certain foods in a mother's diet are not good for a breast-feeding baby. Nevertheless, many people seem to believe that hot, spicy foods or foods that cause gas will have an adverse effect on a nursing baby. Research does not, however, support that.

Sometimes a baby will be sensitive to a particular food the mother eats. There is no point, however, in eliminating favorite foods until you know that they do cause a problem. If you suspect a relationship between a food that you eat and discomfort or fussiness in your baby, then try to avoid that food. Be sensitive to your own baby's reaction to what you eat. Do not worry in advance about what bothers your friends' children, or what you might find on a list of possible problem foods.

Let your own baby's responses be your guide, and eat any nutritious food you want until your baby indicates that you shouldn't. There is, however, one exception to these suggestions. If food allergies are prevalent in your family, it might be prudent to avoid foods to which other family members are allergic. If an older child, for example, is allergic to milk or to soy products, you should consider avoiding such products while you are nursing even if they cause you no problem. There is a possibility that your use of those items could trigger an early allergic reaction in your baby.

# DISCIPLINE

Everyone needs discipline, which is a structure or set of rules for behavior. To provide effective discipline for a mobile baby or toddler, it is best to arrange and childproof the environment so that the child does not have the opportunity to do things that are dangerous or unacceptable. It is important for a child's well-being to have predictable limits set on his behavior, and to have those limits enforced. Your child may frequently contest the limits you set, but her sense of security depends in part on those limits being there—despite protests.

A young child is usually incapable of thinking through the consequences of behavior, understanding cause-and-effect relationships, or understanding elaborate sets of verbal instructions, so the first step in providing effective discipline involves stacking the deck in your favor. Arrange things so that it is easier for your child to do what you want, and difficult to do otherwise.

When—despite your best efforts at prevention—a mobile baby or toddler gets into something you wish he hadn't, remove the child physically from the situation. This is not the time for attempts at reason, lengthy verbal requests or explanations, or lack of firmness. Keep your comments brief and to the point. There is no point in launching into a lecture that is beyond the child's ability to comprehend.

As you provide structure for your child, it is important not to confuse discipline with punishment. Punishment is the penalty for breaking the rules. Until your child is old enough to understand the rules and relate breaking them to the consequences, punishment is almost always an inappropriate way to manage the child's behavior. (See *Punishment,* page 148, *Child abuse,* pages 55–56, and *Contrariness,* pages 65–66.)

## TIME OUT

Time out is an effective method of providing discipline and structure when a child misbehaves. Time out involves removing the child from the problem situation and having her take "time out" in a predetermined and identified location, such as a chair (call it the "naughty chair," for example), a cushion on the floor in a corner, or any other place that makes sense and will cause no harm. Do not use a location such as a playpen or a crib, in which the child should have happy experiences, for a time out.

Time out typically works well, but only for children who are old enough to understand the concept. A child less than three is probably unable to use time out effectively. Putting a two-year-old in the naughty chair is likely to be followed immediately by the child's exit from the chair, thus setting up further conflict and defeating the purpose.

If you do use time out with a two-year-old, the key to success is the firm, physical placement of the child in the time-out location, not the length of time he spends there. Seconds will do, and that will be more effective than holding the child in the chair, arguing with him, or sitting there to provide supervision and entertainment—all of which defeat the purpose. Place the child in the location and promptly—before he gets up to leave—give permission to end the time out. As the child makes the connection between your displeasure and being placed in the time-out location, you can lengthen the stay a few seconds at a time. That's probably the best you can do with a two-year-old, whose natural contrariness is likely to be a strong force. But if you have placed the child in the time-out location and given him permission to leave even a few seconds later, you have kept control and have started to introduce the concept.

A three-year-old is better able to understand the use of time out, but don't make it too long. Two or three successful minutes are preferable to conflict or further disobedience. The older and more mature a child becomes, the more likely she is to make the connection between her behavior and consequences.

# DIVORCE _____

If divorce or separation becomes part of your family situation during your child's early years, try to minimize the negative impact. Make whatever adult decisions you must, and do not try to maintain or live in an impossible situation "for the sake of the children."

Reassure your child that his needs will still be met even though both parents will no longer be living together. Then make every effort to keep your word. Try not to communicate to your child any bitterness or hostility you might have for your partner. Allow the child to retain whatever feelings he might have for the other parent, no matter what your personal feelings might be.

Do not burden a toddler with specific details of adult problems. Reassure your child that he is in no way to blame for the breakup.

# EARS (CARE OF)

The ears of a baby or toddler require no special care unless you suspect a problem. If so, you should consult your child's health-care provider for advice.

Ear infections are common among children, and a very young child might not be able to communicate clearly to you just where the pain is. You might suspect an earache if your child seems unusually cranky, feverish, and is pulling at or touching the side of the face. Before the child is old enough to use language effectively, ear pain is sometimes confused with teething pain.

If the area around the ear seems tender or warm, or if you note blood or other discharge, call your health-care provider. It is best to treat an ear infection with the correct medication as soon as possible. If you have any doubts about whether or not your child has an ear infection, it is better to get medical advice than to wait and see what might happen.

One treatment often used for young children with chronic ear infections is the implanting of ear tubes to help drain fluid and prevent further infections. One recent study, however, suggested that this popular treatment may not be as necessary or effective as thought. Children who received the ear tubes after three months of fluid buildup (the standard guideline) did not differ significantly at age three in speech, language learning, or behavior from those who had waited up to nine months for the tubes to be inserted. It is not known at this time, however, if problems not noticeable at age three might show up later. Research is ongoing.

If your child seems to suffer from chronic ear infections and your health-care provider suggests the implantation of ear tubes, discuss the matter thoroughly and ask any questions you might have. Some professionals are quick to recommend the tubes, while others tend to take a wait-and-see attitude. As more is learned about the effectiveness of the procedure, it may become easier to make the most appropriate decision for a given child.

If your child puts an object into her ear, don't try to remove it on your own unless you are sure you can do so without making the problem worse. Something soft that can be grabbed easily with tweezers is worth a try. Wedged-in beads, beans, and similar objects are best left to experts, and a call to the health-care provider or a trip to the emergency room would be in order.

As far as cleanliness of the ears is concerned, wash what you can see and leave it at that. Do not poke cotton-tipped swabs into the ears or dig around to remove the wax.

# ECZEMA

Eczema is an allergic reaction in which the skin becomes dry and scaly and extremely itchy. Eczema tends to run in allergy-prone families, and it is most common in children under three.

If your child develops eczema, work with your health-care provider to identify the specific cause. Think about any recent change in the child's diet that might have triggered the attack. If the first eczema attack coincided with weaning from breast milk, for example, you might suspect an allergy to cow's milk. A switch to a soybean formula might be helpful. Think about any new substances that might have touched your child's skin and set off a problem. Did you change brands of disposable diapers, for example, or switch to a new bedcover? The answers to questions like these can help track down the cause of the problem.

Here are some suggestions to make a child with eczema somewhat more comfortable.

* Skip as many baths as possible, because soap and water may make the situation worse. Use baby oil or lotion for cleansing your child's skin. Ask your child's health-care provider to recommend a bath soap to use when you do bathe your child.
* Avoid dressing your child with clothes that irritate. Leave off, for example, the scratchy sweater, and use several smooth layers instead for warmth.
* Use a vaporizer or humidifier to add moisture to the air in your home.
* Keep the child's fingernails very clean and cut short, so that his scratching doesn't make matters worse.
* Try to keep the child busy and diverted from the discomfort as much as possible. Try not to add further stress to an already difficult situation.
* For severe cases, your health-care provider may prescribe a cortisone ointment to reduce the discomfort. Don't medicate your child without professional guidance, but be sure to ask for something to alleviate the symptoms. There is help available.

# ELECTRICAL SHOCK

A child who pokes at a live electric socket, chews a plugged-in appliance cord, or otherwise comes in contact with a live electric connection may become part of the electrical circuit. That can be a life-threatening emergency. Immediate but careful intervention is necessary.

If possible, turn off the power source at once by removing the appropriate fuse or tripping the circuit breaker. If you are unable to do that, separate the child from the circuit, but *do not use* your bare hands. If you touch the child directly, you too will be shocked. If you also become part of the circuit you will not only be injured, but you will be unable to help your child.

Touch and move the child only with dry things that will not conduct electricity—heavy rubber gloves or boots, a wooden chair, a broom handle, a dry cushion or pillow, large wooden spoons, or a rubber spatula. If the child is not breathing, begin rescue breathing (mouth-to-mouth resuscitation) or CPR immediately. Get medical help without delay.

# EYEDROPS

If your child's health-care provider prescribes eyedrops or ointment for any reason, here are some suggestions to help get the medication where it belongs.

- Place the child on her back across your lap. Put one arm (your left arm if you are right-handed) around the back of her head and reach around to her eye with this hand. Hold her eyelids open with your fingers.
- Hold the dropper with the correct dose of medication in your other hand, an inch or two above the child's eye. When she blinks, squeeze the dropper and release the medication into the inner corner of the eye. If you squeeze when the child blinks, the drop will reach the eye just as it opens again.

For a very young child, medication in ointment form may be easier to administer. Hold the child the same way, and apply the ointment to the inner corner of the eye. The child's blinking will help spread it.

# EYES (CARE OF)

Under normal circumstances, eyes need no special or elaborate care. If necessary, gently cleanse the lids with a cotton ball dipped in plain, clean water. Use a fresh piece of cotton for each eye and wash from the outside corner in.

## INJURIES TO THE EYE

- Any injury to the eyeball should receive immediate medical attention. Skip the home remedies and call your health-care provider or take your child to the emergency room. A clean, loose bandage over the eye while you are in transit may help prevent further injury and keep the child's hands away from it.
- A bit of soap or shampoo in the eye may cause discomfort and perhaps some redness, but no significant harm. A little rinse with plain water is all that is needed. Try to keep the child from rubbing the eye.
- Any household chemicals other than mild soap or shampoo—cleaners, detergents, deodorants, window sprays, aerosol cleaners, polishes, etc.—should be treated as a potentially serious problem. If your child gets one of these substances in his eyes, flush immediately with lots of plain water. That won't be easy, but it is necessary. Turn on the tap and gently pour water into his eyes again and again from a cup or a glass. If only one eye is affected, hold the child so you don't wash the harmful substance into the other eye. Don't worry about the mess you are making. Your child's sight is more important than a dry floor. Continue to pour the water until you are absolutely certain that no trace of the chemical remains. Ten minutes is probably enough.
- A foreign body such as dirt, sand, or an insect in the eye may wash itself out if the child cries. Gently pulling the top eyelid down over the lower lid may stimulate tears. If not, medical attention may be necessary.

## PROFESSIONAL EYE EXAMINATION

A child should receive a least one professional eye examination during infancy or the preschool years. An exam during infancy is especially important in cases of premature or low birth-weight babies, or children with a family history of vision disorders.

The most common visual problems include refractive problems such as nearsightedness, farsightedness, and astigmatism, and amblyopia (lazy eye) and strabismus (misaligned or wandering eye). A baby or young child with strabismus may cover her other eye or tilt her head to help see things more clearly. Your baby's health-care provider may do some vision screening during routine pediatric visits. If you suspect a problem, don't be afraid to ask questions and seek professional help.

# FALLS

Falls and the injuries that result from them are a major cause of emergency-room visits for babies and toddlers. Prevention and fallproofing your child's environment is important, although as a baby learns to walk and climb, some falls are inevitable. The key is to prevent situations in which a fall could cause serious injury.

## PREVENTING BABY'S FALLS

Right from the start, even a newborn is vulnerable to falling. You may think that your baby won't roll or slither off a surface, but it's best not to take a chance. Here are some suggestions.

- Before you change the baby's diaper, make sure you have all the supplies you need on hand and within reach. Don't leave the baby on a changing table or other surface even for the few seconds it would take to retrieve something you have forgotten. Take the baby with you rather than leaving him unsecured.
- Don't trust the strap on a changing table to hold your baby in place. It's best to keep at least one hand on the baby at all times and not to turn your back. Don't be distracted while your baby is on a high surface. The phone or doorbell can wait.
- Don't leave your baby lying unattended on a bed or sofa. Infants learn to roll far sooner than you would think, and it only takes a few seconds for a harmful fall to occur.
- Don't leave a baby in an infant carrier on a table or chair where it can be knocked down.

## PREVENTING A MOBILE BABY OR TODDLER'S FALLS

Falls, with their accompanying scrapes, bumps, and bruises, are an inevitable part of a child's first few years, especially as she learns to walk and climb. You can't always prevent the normal little falls of a child learning to become independently mobile, nor should you exhaust yourself trying. You can and must, however, eliminate situations from your child's environment in which a fall could cause serious injury. Here are some warnings and suggestions:

- Windows must be secure, and those above the ground floor should have properly installed safety guards. A screen is not sufficient protection to keep a child in. An unprotected window that is open as little as five inches can be dangerous or even lethal for a young child. Do not place chairs or other pieces of furniture in front of windows where they might be used for climbing to the window ledge.
- If your floors are uncarpeted and slippery, a toddler can move more safely in bare feet than in socks. When you purchase shoes for a toddler, avoid smooth leather soles; try to find shoes that provide good traction. Buy socks with nonslip treads on the bottoms.
- Stairs should have two gates—one at the top to prevent falling down, and one at the bottom to prevent climbing up to a position where a fall could occur.
- Mobile babies and toddlers should not be left alone—it doesn't take very long to get into trouble. No child should be left unsupervised long enough to climb to a height from which a fall could be serious.
- When a child reaches the climbing and falling out of the crib stage, it's time to make alternative sleeping arrangements—such as a mattress on the floor.
- Allowing young children to run in the house is not a good idea. Set a no-running rule, and make it apply to visitors as well as to your own children.
- Remove sharp objects that your child might fall on from your environment. If you must keep the coffee table right where it is, consider padding sharp corners until your child is better able to move about without falling.
- A protective helmet is necessary if your child is participating in an activity that might lead to a fall. For example, children who skate, use a scooter, ride a tricycle or bicycle, or ride a pony should be given the extra protection of special headgear.

## SERIOUS FALLS

If your child has fallen, be alert for signs of head injury. Loss of consciousness, onset of vomiting, bleeding from the ears, nose, or mouth, lack of eye response, or one pupil noticeably larger than the other are symptoms of a possible problem after a fall. If one or more of these conditions follows a fall by your child, you should get prompt medical attention. Unusual loss of appetite or excessive sleepiness after a fall may also signal a problem.

In addition to noticing the signs of head injury, you should be alert to any difficulty or discomfort your child may have when moving one or more limbs after a fall. When in doubt, call the doctor right away or take your child to the emergency room.

# FAMILY BEDS

The family bed—parents and young children sleeping together—is a child-rearing practice about which there is considerable difference of opinion. At one extreme are proponents who advocate co-sleeping for as many months or years as each child wishes to do so. At the other extreme are those who advise letting a child cry it out each night until he finally realizes that separation at bedtime is inevitable. Most families will choose a course somewhere in between those positions.

Family-bed enthusiasts, led by Tine Thevenin, author of *The Family Bed* (Avery Publishing Group, Wayne, NJ: 1987), claim that their children are happier, more secure, and ultimately less dependent than children who are forced to sleep alone. Others, such as psychologist, author, and columnist John Rosemond, in contrast, strongly disagree with the family-bed concept and claim it leads to anxiety, excessive dependence, and social immaturity of children, along with widespread parental dissatisfaction regarding bedtime arrangements.

Sleeping customs are social behaviors strongly influenced by the culture in which we live, but they are also a very private matter and must suit the personal preferences of the individuals involved. In other words, what other people think and do should not be of great concern to you as long as your sleeping arrangements work for your family. Nevertheless, you can learn from others' mistakes. Here are some points to ponder before you decide that sharing the same bed would be a satisfactory solution to sleeptime problems in your house.

- The family bed is not something you can try out casually. Although many nursing mothers find that a newborn's night feedings are most comfortably accomplished in the parents' bed, taking a mobile baby or toddler into your bed may start a routine that is difficult to stop until the child is willing. Unless you are prepared to continue family sleeping arrangements for a long time—months or even years—it's probably best not to start.
- Sleeping in one's own bed involves separation, which for a young child (and parents, too) includes some anxiety. Learning how to cope with such anxiety is an important aspect of development. A secure, supportive, and warm family environment can help a child take steps toward independence. Parents can provide security and support for their children in many ways that do not involve sleeping in the same bed.

- Many couples feel that the quality of their own relationship depends in part on private time together. Making bedtime and the night that follows a family affair makes less time available for parents to be alone together.
- Taking a screaming child into the parental bed every night because that child refuses to settle down in her own bed may achieve the immediate goal—peace and quiet— but such a practice may also teach a child that her parents can be controlled by screaming. Such an outcome could have long-term negative effects.

If you believe that sharing your bed with your child would be a positive step toward enhancing your family life and meeting everyone's needs, you should feel free and comfortable to take that step. If, however, you are considering the family bed in desperation because bedtime is battle time and nothing else seems to work, it's probably best to try some other techniques to make your child feel content and secure enough to go to sleep.

For suggestions on how to manage bedtime problems in a sensitive, caring way without inviting your child into bed with you, see *Bedtime rituals,* page 27, and *Sleep problems,* pages 159–160.

# FAMILY PLANNING

The number of children you decide to have, and when, shouldn't be anyone's business but your own. Nevertheless, it seems that many people—relatives, friends, and even casual acquaintances—are willing to offer opinions on such personal matters. Specific techniques of family planning are beyond the scope of this book, but you should seek professional advice as needed for your personal circumstances.

There are advantages and disadvantages to being an only child, or to being one of several siblings; to being close together in age, or to being several years apart. The one guideline you might well consider on this very personal matter is that each child you choose to have should be wanted for his own sake. There is no one right way to plan a family, so you should try to do what makes sense to you in your particular circumstances.

If you have recently given birth, it's especially important to consult your health-care provider to discuss your family-planning intentions. Keep in mind that breast-feeding is *not* a reliable method of birth control. Although some nursing women do not ovulate as long as they are breast-feeding, others do. Even if you haven't menstruated yet, you may still be fertile.

# FEARS

Many young children have fears that might seem somewhat silly to an adult. Such fears are, however, very significant to the child. Efforts to make light of a child's fears are unlikely to ease them, and may convince the child that she can't count on adults for support.

Among the common fears of toddlers are separation (see *Separation anxiety,* page 153), water (see *Baths,* pages 21–24, and *Swimming,* page 169), dogs (see *Pets,* pages 142–143), insects, loud noises, shadows, and the dark. Take care not to communicate to your child any personal fears *you* might have. Some childhood fears are learned from adult caretakers, and there is no need to let that happen.

To help you deal with your child's specific fears in a sensitive way, first try putting yourself in his place. Imagine what it must be like to be a person of such small size in an enormous world. Try to think back to your own childhood and remember things you once found frightening. Are there things that still scare you even though you know they'll probably cause no harm?

If your child is not yet able to use language to tell you what she is afraid of, you'll have to be alert to other signs of fear. Sudden tears and efforts to move away from something are, of course, obvious clues. Unusual clinging to you or other caregivers might be another indication that the child is frightened of something.

How can you help a fearful child? Be supportive and reassuring, but be careful not to say or do things that would validate the fear. Say, for example, "I know that the big dog frightens you. But don't worry, I'm here to hold your hand and the dog won't hurt you." Don't say "How awful that the horrible nasty dog is scaring my little boy. I'll have to chase the bad monster away before it hurts you."

Even if a feared thing is unlikely to cause your child harm, it's unwise to force that thing on your child in an attempt to prove that the fear is unfounded. Such an approach is likely to exacerbate the anxiety and might even push an ordinary fear into becoming a phobia.

If your child has a fear that has escalated into a phobia, you may need professional help in dealing with it. If your best efforts to handle a child's normal fears in a kind and reassuring way don't quite do the job, or if a phobia seems to be upsetting your child, ask your child's health-care provider for advice.

# FEEDING PROBLEMS

Many mealtime problems of early childhood are aided and abetted by well-intentioned caregivers who were themselves brought up as members of the "clean-plate club," or were encouraged to eat a little more for the poor starving children of East Somewhere. The child who becomes a fussy or picky eater is often one whose parents have made a big deal about cleaning the plate and/or eating neatly. Parental efforts to force food, when combined with a toddler's natural contrariness, can result in tensions that do no one any good. Here are some suggestions to prevent feeding problems.

- Let your child actively participate in self-feeding as soon as possible. Most children will do that before the first birthday, but some may take a little longer. Encourage independent eating as soon as the child shows an interest. If you continue to push the spoon long after your child could take on that task, you may find that dependence on you during mealtime has become a habit that is difficult to stop.
- Provide a balanced diet over a period of time, such as a week or two. Don't worry about balancing each meal, because it's next to impossible to do so without creating problems. (See *Nutrition,* pages 130–137, for suggestions on how to adapt the food guide pyramid for healthy choices for feeding a toddler.)
- Don't panic if your child goes through stages of seeming to eat less than usual, or even nothing at all, for a meal or two. That is not unusual. Unless there is some other reason to suspect illness or a problem, let your child's appetite determine how much she will eat, even if you think the quantity consumed should be greater.
- At any meal, when your child is no longer hungry, physically separate him from the food without comment and consider the mealtime finished. Skip the "eat another bite for Daddy" and "now one more for Aunt Andrea" routine. Don't add unnecessary emotional baggage to the act of eating.
- Remember that it's impossible for a baby or toddler to be neat. Don't allow the inevitable mess create tensions at mealtime. Newspapers or a plastic cloth can keep misplaced food off the floor. Have your child wear a suitable bib. (See *Bibs,* page 28.)

# FEEDING TABLES

A feeding table is an alternative to a high chair for a child who is ready to sit up unassisted. Here are some things to consider before you choose a feeding table in preference to a high chair.

- Feeding tables tend to be somewhat safer than high chairs. They are less likely to tip over, and a climbing toddler has a shorter distance to fall. If you use one that does not have a built-in safety harness, you should attach and use a harness to keep your child in place.
- The larger table surface means less food and drink on the floor when the meal is done. (It is on the tabletop instead.)
- A feeding table takes up considerably more space than a high chair, and it cannot be folded up and put away for storage.
- A child using a feeding table is at a lower level than much of the interesting adult activity nearby. You can't use a feeding table at the family dinner table as you could use a high chair. You could place it nearby, but it does set the child apart.
- Although the surface of a feeding table can be used for activities other than eating, many parents find that the device is not as practical as they had hoped. Chances are, your toddler will not want to sit confined in a feeding table for any significant period of time, no matter what enticing objects you place on the table in front of him.

# FEVER

The only way to tell for sure if your child has a fever is to use a thermometer to take her temperature. (See *Temperature (taking child's)*, pages 175–176.) Feeling the child's forehead with your hand is not an accurate source of information. A rectal thermometer provides the most accurate reading for babies and young children, although an ear thermometer or an infrared forehead thermometer may be easier to use. Taking the temperature by mouth with an oral thermometer is not recommended for children under five.

If you think your child is sick and decide to call the doctor, take the child's temperature before you call. A question about the child's temperature is inevitable, and it's best to have the correct information when you make the call—unless, of course, you are dealing with an emergency situation, in which case you should make the call immediately without any delay. If your child has a fever and you wonder whether or not to call the doctor, the list on page 92 contains suggestions to help you make a prudent decision.

A normal rectal temperature for a child is 99.6 degrees F (37.6 degrees C). Report the temperature and the method you used to take it. A normal temperature taken via an ear or forehead thermometer may vary slightly from a rectal reading. Call the doctor if your child's rectal temperature reading is 100.6 degrees F or above and other symptoms of illness are present.

It's important to remember that a fever is a symptom, and not the disease itself. A fever generally indicates that the body is fighting an infection, bacterial or viral. It is usually not necessary to take extraordinary measures to combat the fever directly unless it is over 102 degrees F. Try to keep the child comfortable in a room that is not overheated. Dress the child in lightweight fabrics and cover her with a light blanket, or perhaps only a sheet.

For a fever of 103 degrees F or higher, or if your health-care provider directs you to try to bring the fever down, undress the child and sponge him off with a washcloth or clean sponge saturated with lukewarm (not cold) water. As the water evaporates off the skin's surface, the child should become cooler. If he starts to shiver, however, the water is too cold.

Washing a feverish child down with rubbing alcohol used to be a popular technique to reduce the child's body temperature. That treatment is no longer recommended. The rubbing alcohol may chill the child too quickly and cause uncomfortable shivering, which may also have the counterproductive effect of raising body temperature by causing the child's body to fight back. Rubbing alcohol also produces irritating fumes, and may soak through the skin to cause a toxic reaction in sensitive individuals.

Your child's health-care provider might suggest acetaminophen ("fever drops," such as liquid Tylenol for children) to help reduce fever. If so, be sure to follow the recommended dosage for your child's age exactly. Twice the dose is not twice as good, and an overdose could cause serious harm. Do not give aspirin to a baby or young child. Aspirin is suspected to increase the risk of a serious, sometimes even fatal ailment known as Reye's syndrome (see *Reye's syndrome,* page 150). Offer a feverish child lots of fluids. Small sips on a frequent basis, especially if the stomach is upset, will work best. A breast-fed baby should be able to obtain enough fluids during regular nursing. Sips of water from a small spoon may also be helpful.

---

# CALL THE DOCTOR IF . . .

If your child has a fever, follow your instincts and common sense and call the doctor if you feel a need to do so. It's preferable to get professional advice early to prevent a situation getting out of hand, although many fevers can be successfully handled without medical advice. If your child has a fever in combination with one or more of the following symptoms or circumstances, make that call promptly.

- discomfort that results in continuous, inconsolable crying
- irritation or discomfort that does not appear to ease within an hour of taking medication, such as acetaminophen (fever drops)
- persistent vomiting, diarrhea, or signs of dehydration
- breathing difficulties
- seizure or a history of previous seizures
- unusual confusion or delirious behavior
- unusual difficulty in being awakened
- stiff neck or extremely painful sore throat

If your child's fever persists for more than three days (seventy-two hours), consult your health-care provider even if other concerning symptoms are absent.

---

# FIRE

Fires in the home are a major cause of accidental death and serious injury of young children. Here are some tips on preventing fires and protecting your family in the event that a fire does break out in your home.

## PREVENTION

- Check out your residence carefully, and eliminate any obvious fire hazards such as faulty wiring, frayed appliance cords, stored flammable liquids, or dangerously located space heaters.
- Keep your mobile baby or toddler well separated from matches, lighters, space heaters, fireplaces, stoves, and similar items that raise the risk of fire.
- Smoking in the home is a preventable cause of fire. The risk of fire in the home is just one of many reasons not to smoke. (See *Smoking,* page 161.)

## DETECTION AND ESCAPE

- Install a smoke alarm on each level of your house. It's important to have one in the bedroom area. More than 75 percent of the injuries and deaths from fires in the home are caused by smoke or toxic fumes. Because young children are especially vulnerable to such hazards, a smoke detector in or near the room where your child sleeps is an important investment in your family's safety.
- Make certain that the batteries in your smoke detectors are fresh. No matter how carefully you may have located and installed smoke alarms in your home, the devices will be useless if the batteries are dead. When you adjust your clocks from daylight savings time to standard time and back again is a good time to change the batteries in your smoke detector. That way you will be sure to check on and renew the batteries twice a year.
- A smoke alarm can wake you, but it can't lead you outside. Plan in advance what escape route you would take to get out in the event of a fire. Plan an alternate route in case a fire should block your intended exit path.
- For floors above the ground level, a fire exit ladder is something a homeowner should keep handy. Know where it is and how to use it. Have a family fire drill and rehearse getting out.
- Keep fire extinguishers in locations such as the kitchen, basement, or garage, where they might be needed. A fire extinguisher can help put out a very small fire, such as in a frying pan, while there is still time to do so. Do not, however, attempt to fight a fire yourself if doing so would delay your departure from the house and place you at greater risk. Calling the fire department promptly is usually a safer bet than trying to cope on your own.
- Identify your child's bedroom window with a symbol to let firefighters know at a glance where their assistance in rescue might be needed. Highly visible decals are available for this purpose from many local fire departments.

93

## CLOTHES ON FIRE

If a child's clothes catch on fire, act quickly to put the fire out. Save the lecture on not playing with matches for later. Use a coat or rug to smother the flames. If there's nothing handy to smother the flames, you can use your own body. Put the child down on the ground with the flames on the side facing up. Cover the child quickly and completely with your own body, which will deprive the fire of oxygen and extinguish it without causing you significant injury. Treat the child's burns as necessary. (See *Burns and scalds,* pages 43–44.)

# FIREARMS

Guns and children together are a tragedy waiting to happen. If you keep firearms in your home for protection or for sport, it's essential to ensure that your child does not have any access whatsoever. In a house with children, firearms must be stored in a secure, locked location. Hidden is not good enough. Locked up with the key absolutely unavailable to a child is the safest strategy short of simply having no firearms in the home at all.

Handguns are especially dangerous because they are small enough for a child to hold easily. If you believe that a handgun is useful for protection, consider that a gun in the home is statistically less likely to harm an intruder than it is to kill friends or family.

Here are some safety tips if you do keep firearms in the home for any reason.

- Store firearms unloaded in a securely locked location that is not routinely opened and closed for other things. Unlocking the cabinet, closet, or drawer for other things stored there increases the risk that one day it will not be properly locked.

- Store ammunition in a securely locked location separate from the guns. *Never leave a loaded gun in the house.*
- A trigger lock is an added safety device, but you should not let one lull you into a false sense of security. Firearm safety involves keeping guns and ammunition away from children, but if a child does get his hands on a gun, a trigger lock may help delay any potential disaster.
- After you have locked up firearms and ammunition in their respective safe locations, it's important to secure keys so that they are not available to the child. Keep the keys as well as guns and bullets out of sight and out of reach.

Make sure that the adults in any place your child visits are as careful about firearms as you are. It's also important to tell a child that a gun is not a toy. She should be instructed to tell an adult right away if a friend tries to show her a gun.

# FLUORIDE

It is generally agreed that fluoride is an effective aid in preventing tooth decay. Many cities or towns add fluoride in controlled amounts to the municipal water supplies. If the water in your area is fluoridated, you won't have to give this matter further thought other than making sure that your child drinks some each day. If the water supply you use is not fluoridated, your child's health-care provider or dentist may prescribe a fluoride supplement.

Fluoride supplements are available by prescription in liquid form, in combination with liquid vitamins, or as chewable tablets. If your water supply contains more than one part per million of fluoride, you should not give your child a fluoride supplement. Too much fluoride can be toxic or can cause discoloration of the tooth enamel.

Whether or not your water contains fluoride, you may have your child brush his teeth with a fluoridated toothpaste. Do not worry about any small amounts swallowed during normal brushing. It would take ingestion and swallowing of the contents of many tubes of toothpaste to be a cause of concern.

If a fluoride supplement is advisable where you live, ask your child's health-care provider to suggest when to begin and to prescribe a suitable supplement. Some practitioners endorse the use of fluoride supplements within the first few weeks, while others prefer to wait until a child is several months old before beginning treatment. If you have any questions about the need for fluoride or the timing, be sure to ask. (See *Tooth care (daily)*, pages 180–181.)

# FORMULA (FOR BOTTLE-FEEDING)

If you have decided to bottle-feed your newborn, your baby's health-care provider will advise you about which formula to use. For routine feeding of healthy, normal newborns, any of the readily available brands of prepared formula will do. They are designed to have characteristics similar to mother's milk—although, of course, there are some qualities of mother's milk that cannot be duplicated. If the brand used at the hospital or birth center where you delivered agrees with your baby, it makes sense not to change.

It doesn't matter which size containers you buy, as long as you prepare and use the formula as directed. Prefilled bottles and eight-ounce ready-to-serve cans are the most expensive. The large (thirty-two-ounce) cans of ready-to-serve formula cost less per ounce than the smaller cans. Powder or large cans of concentrate are the least expensive, but they require preparation and a safe drinking water supply.

If your baby is doing well on the formula you are using, do not switch brands. If, however, your baby is continuously fussy or irritable, with spitting up or vomiting, it is possible that the formula is causing a problem. Some babies, for example, are unable to tolerate formula with iron supplement added, and require the iron-free version. Some babies are allergic to cow's milk with or without iron, and they must be fed using a milk-free formula. Those babies are usually placed on formula made from soy protein.

If you suspect that the formula you are using is causing problems for your baby, consult your child's health-care provider. It's best not to attempt to change the baby's diet on your own.

(For more information on bottle-feeding your baby, see *Bottle-feeding,* pages 34–35.)

# FURNITURE (NEWBORN)

Baby furniture need not be expensive or brand new. At first, all you will really need is something for the baby to sleep in, a surface on which to change the baby's diapers, and somewhere to store clothes and supplies so they will be handy. It is possible for many families to meet those needs without buying anything for the first few weeks.

A newborn baby can sleep in a large dresser drawer (out of the dresser, of course) until you make more permanent sleeping arrangements. Pad the bottom with a folded blanket. A pillowcase makes a fitted sheet. Do not pad the drawer with a soft pillow because that could cause smothering. If your birth setting uses disposable cardboard sleeping containers in the nursery, bring one home for your baby. It is a useful, very portable sleeping container. Locate the container on a nondrafty part of the floor or on a secure surface such as a sturdy table, but not near the edge. You will need a proper crib soon, but you can probably make do for at least a month before you get one.

An elaborate and specially designed changing table is not necessary. You can change your baby's diaper anywhere. Spread a towel on any flat surface—a countertop, a table, a bed, or even the floor if your back can handle it. Make sure you have all your supplies with you before you put the baby down on the surface.

You can use any comfortable chair for holding and feeding your baby. A rocking chair is ideal if you have one; it can soothe both you and your baby. If you don't have a rocking chair and can't borrow one, try garage sales or secondhand shops. You can, of course, survive quite well without a rocking chair, but you will find one helpful, especially if your baby tends to be fussy.

You can store your baby's things in cut-down cardboard boxes from a local package store. Be careful about the source; avoid boxes that might contain roaches or other insects. Cover the boxes with bright contact paper to make them attractive.

# GENITALS (CARE OF)

Your baby or toddler's genitals require no special care other than the bathing you give the entire diaper area to keep it clean and free from irritation. Don't attempt to force back the foreskin of an uncircumcised boy in an attempt to clean under it. Don't push apart a girl's labia for washing. A good rule for care of your child's genitals is to leave alone what you can't see. Regular bathing is all that's necessary.

If you have your baby boy circumcised, the penis will need special care until it has completely healed. In most cases it will take at least a week, perhaps even two, until the sensitive area recovers from the procedure. (For specific suggestions on care for a newborn who has been circumcised, see *Circumcision care,* page 60.)

# GIFTED CHILDREN

In today's high-pressure society, parents tend to wonder and worry very early about the abilities and talents of their children. Is the child gifted? What does it mean to be "gifted," anyway? What special measures can or should be taken to prepare a child for the best nursery school, prep school, college, or graduate school? Is it a good idea to be worrying about all this when your child isn't yet two years old? Is your child gifted? How can you tell?

Every child is gifted in her own way. Whether those gifts ultimately add up to a high score on an IQ test, early admission to a good college, a career as a professional athlete, or stardom as a concert musician is far less important at this point than the process of learning to learn. It's helpful for you to enjoy learning with your child. Provide suitable stimulation and learning experiences. Without undue pressure, try to nurture your child's many different abilities as they emerge and develop. (See pages 116–120 for specific activities and suggestions.)

Just as children differ greatly in appearance, they differ in the combination of strengths and weakness that make up their different abilities and talents. To maximize the special gifts your child has, concentrate on his uniqueness. Encourage his curiosity, creativity, and excitement about life and learning.

# GROWTH

Your child's height and weight will be measured and recorded at routine well-baby or well-child visits to the pediatrician or other health-care provider. If you also wish to keep track of your child's growth, ask your child's health-care provider for a copy of the chart used in the child's medical file.

If your child is too young to stand tall and still, measure the length when she is lying down. Two adults are needed to accomplish the measuring accurately. If your child can and will stand, a flat stick (such as a ruler) can be held level on top of the child's head at right angles to the wall. Mark the wall where the stick touches, and then measure the distance from the mark to the floor. The child should be barefooted when you mark the height. For recording the child's weight and making meaningful comparisons from one time to the next, you should use the same scale each time.

# HANDEDNESS

Although most babies begin using both hands equally, preference for one or the other may develop early. Some children seem to favor one hand and then switch to the other, perhaps even changing back again before establishing dominance. It's best not to interfere. Allow your child to develop a preference for one hand or the other naturally.

If your child favors the right hand, it's not likely to remain an issue for long. If your child seems to favor the left hand, let it be. There is nothing wrong with left-handedness. Harm could come from forceful efforts to make him change. It's better to be supportive and avoid criticism of the child's natural choice, regardless of what that choice might be. Be positive and don't try to make him switch. Here are some additional suggestions if your child is definitely left-handed.

- Help the child use crayons or other writing tools. Assistance with placement of paper on the desk or table may be necessary.
- When the time comes for your child to cut, provide a pair of left-handed scissors to make the process easier.
- Be sure that baby-sitters, grandparents, teachers, and other caregivers know that the child is left-handed, and that you intend to let her remain so. Make them aware that they must not offer negative comments or pressure the child to change, no matter how well-intentioned they might believe such efforts to be.

# HEAD BANGING

Some babies or toddlers develop a habit of head banging, in which the head is hit rhythmically against something hard. This habit often occurs at bedtime, when the object being hit is the headboard or side of the crib. If a child engages in head banging while not in the crib, he may bang the head on a wall, the floor, or a piece of furniture.

If your child is a rocker and head banger at bedtime, don't get into a panic over it or overthink the problem. It is not uncommon or abnormal for a child to get on her hands and knees and rock to sleep. Sometimes banging the head on the crib becomes part of the rocking routine. If the child uses the rocking and head banging as a technique to go to sleep and does not seem to be hurting himself, let it be. Your intervention may cause unnecessary dependence and additional bedtime or sleep problems that will be difficult to deal with. (See *Sleep problems,* pages 159–160.) Crib bumpers or other safe padding may make you feel less anxious about your child's safety. Chances are, the rocking and banging will disappear within a matter of months, and it will have caused no harm.

Some children, however, use head banging outside the bed almost as a type of attention-getting temper tantrum. If your child engages in severe head banging against hard surfaces in a way that causes pain, bruises, or risk of more serious injury, you should not ignore it. Be careful, however, not to engage in combat with your child; that may reinforce her head banging as an attention-getting device. Remember that toddlers are contrary by nature. (See *Contrariness,* pages 65–66.) Don't react in a way that makes a toddler's anti-social behavior more enticing to the child as a way to get to you.

Some experts may advise to leave the head-banging child alone and simply ignore the behavior until it disappears. There are dangers, however, to such an approach. Your aggravation at your child's behavior is likely to show, and may intensify the head banging even if you think you are ignoring it. And, if your child really goes at it, he might get hurt.

Psychologist and syndicated columnist John Rosemond suggests a rather unusual way to deal with head banging without reinforcing it and without ignoring it. The approach may appear a bit odd, but it seems to work. Give your head-banging child her own special place on a wall to bang her head. Draw a two-foot in diameter circle as a target. Tell your child that she must go to that place and nowhere else for head banging. You may have to remind her calmly at first. Such an approach simply takes the fun out of the behavior, and removes it as a provocative attention getter. Chances are, the head banging will stop considerably sooner than it would have if you had either ignored it or punished it.

If your child's head banging is so severe that it causes pain or injury beyond what seems to fall within acceptable limits of toddler antisocial behavior, perhaps you should think about whether there is anything in your child's life or environment that is causing special anger, tension, or insecurity. A child who uses self-inflicted pain as a comfort habit may be trying to tell you something. It might be a good idea to figure out what that something is. If the strategy recommended above, extra doses of kind, positive attention throughout the day, and efforts to substitute less painful comfort habits along with careful attention to bedtime rituals bring no improvement, you may want to seek professional guidance. (See *Comfort habits,* pages 63–64.)

# HEARING (PROBLEMS) ———————————

Even before birth, a healthy baby is able to hear. Newborns show signs of responding to sounds right from the start. A loud noise will usually startle a baby. Most newborns are soothed by a parent's voice and will turn their heads, seeking the source of the sound (even though the turn might be in the wrong direction at first).

Hearing problems are the most common disability at birth, and tests are now available for detection of hearing impairment in newborns. The American Academy of Pediatrics recommends that all infants be checked at birth for hearing loss, although such testing is not yet universal. Early detection of hearing problems can help prevent serious delays in language development.

Hearing testing is noninvasive and painless. One popular test uses sensors to record brain waves when a sound is played through earphones. The test can be done while the baby sleeps. Another type of test measures the vibration of the small hair cells in the cochlea when sounds are presented. If problems are detected, follow-up testing and early intervention are important. Because not all birth facilities test newborns for hearing, you should ask if your child has been tested.

Sometimes hearing impairment develops later on. Even if your newborn has been tested and no problem was found, ongoing observation is prudent. As your child grows, be alert to any possible signs of hearing loss. Have your child professionally tested if you suspect any problems. Here are some observations you can make informally.

## BIRTH TO 6 MONTHS

A baby who can hear will typically be awakened by loud sounds and, if already awake, will react to them. A hearing baby will be soothed by a parent's voice and seem to recognize the parents' voices. He will turn toward a parent when spoken to and react facially when spoken to. If it appears that your baby does not turn toward the source of what should be familiar sounds, try making a familiar sound about three or four feet away. If the child does not turn or react, mention this to your health-care provider and request a hearing evaluation.

## ONE YEAR

Does your baby seem to be trying to talk (even if what she is doing does not sound much like real talking)? If not, request a hearing evaluation. Babies learn to talk by imitating, and they have nothing to imitate if they can't hear.

## 18 MONTHS

Is your child able to use simple words? Can he follow a simple spoken direction? If not, hearing loss may be part of the problem. Have your child's hearing checked to find out.

## TWO YEARS

If you tell your child (without using visual clues) to do something, can she follow the directions? Don't confuse a contrary child who *will not* with the hearing-impaired child who *cannot*. Is your child able to repeat a three-word sentence or simple phrase? Can he recognize an object by its sound? If these tasks seem to be a problem for your two-year-old, have her hearing tested.

If your child does have a hearing problem, the sooner treatment or corrective intervention is started, the better. Sometimes the effects of hearing loss are not recognized for what they are, and a child is incorrectly labeled retarded, emotionally disturbed, or learning disabled. If you have any suspicion that your child might have a hearing problem, consult an appropriate professional promptly.

# HEAT RASH (PRICKLY HEAT) 

In hot weather, many young children get a rash called prickly heat—very tiny pink pimples, blotches, and perhaps even blisters that are caused by plugged-up sweat gland ducts which then burst and release sweat under the skin's surface. The resulting clusters of little red bumps may look ominous, but they are not contagious and they are probably not painful.

Prickly heat usually begins around the neck, face, and shoulders, and in more severe cases may spread to other parts of the body. Places where there are folds in the skin— behind the knees, in the elbows, in the groin area—are typical sites for prickly heat. You'll probably worry about prickly heat more than the condition will trouble your child, but you should take care of it promptly even if she does not appear to be bothered.

The best treatment for prickly heat is also the key to prevention. Keep your child dressed appropriately for the weather. Remove clothes if the temperature is very hot. Choose cotton clothing in preference to synthetic fabrics that do not breathe easily. Avoid shirts or other garment tops that are tight around the neck area, a typical starting place for heat rash.

Wash the affected area with cool water and a mild soap, dry gently but well, and then leave it alone. Do not apply ointments, lotions, or skin creams, because what you want is to keep the skin dry. A light dusting with baby powder or cornstarch might help. Take care that your child does not breathe in any of the powder. Sprinkle it first on your hands and then apply it gently to the child's skin. Don't shake powder directly on the child.

Heat rash is not just a summer problem. It is also common in winter, when babies and toddlers tend to be overdressed in heated houses, vehicles, or stores. Your baby's room should not be kept at a warmer temperature than your own, and a young child does not need extra clothing beyond what makes sense for the rest of the family.

# HERNIAS

An umbilical hernia is the most common type of hernia found in an infant or very young child. An umbilical hernia is a small swelling near the baby's navel caused by weakness of the muscles in that area. The bulge may increase somewhat when the baby cries. Although tight strapping used to be the prescribed treatment for an umbilical hernia, it is now believed that the area will strengthen best on its own. Most cases of umbilical hernia put themselves right within a year or two without any treatment at all. In very rare cases, surgery may be necessary.

An inguinal hernia, which occurs most often in boys, is an opening in the abdominal wall muscles allowing a portion of the intestine to squeeze into the groin area. A "strangulated" inguinal hernia is one in which the intestine has become stuck in the passage, causing severe pain and requiring prompt emergency treatment.

If you suspect that your baby might have a hernia, consult your health-care provider. Chances are, however, if you have taken your child for regular well-baby checkups, any signs of a hernia will have been discovered.

# HICCUPS

Babies sometimes get hiccups along with their bubbles and burps. These hiccups usually stop when the next bubble comes up, and they are generally no cause for alarm. The baby is probably less bothered by them than you are. Here are some things you can do, however, if the hiccups persist for more than a minute or two.

- Put the baby back to the bottle or breast to suck. Or, if you prefer, offer some warm water in a bottle.
- Try holding the baby upright over your shoulder with the weight and pressure on her chest rather than the abdomen. A change in position often helps. Rub or pat the baby gently on the back.
- Place the baby on his stomach while you watch for a few minutes. Remember that lying on the stomach is a temporary arrangement to see if the hiccups stop. Always place your baby on his back to sleep.
- If you have chosen to allow your baby to use a pacifier, sucking on it may help. But if your baby does not use a pacifier, hiccup relief is not an excuse to start. Try the other suggestions instead.

The suggestions for an infant with hiccups should also work for a mobile baby or toddler. Here are some additional suggestions for a toddler or older child with the hiccups.

- For a child who can drink from a cup or a glass, offer water and have her take as many sips as she can without stopping. Aim for ten. That should help break the hiccup cycle.
- Have your child try to hold his breath long enough to stop the hiccups. You can hold your breath too, and time it. Make it a fun little game.
- Try a small spoonful of jelly to be swallowed in one gulp. Although some would recommend honey, jelly is a preferred and often effective alternative. Remember, you should never offer honey to a baby or child under a year because of the potential for deadly botulism. (See *Honey,* page 104.) There is no point in taking the risk of honey, even for an older toddler.

Even without intervention, a hiccup spell typically ends within a few minutes. If your child's hiccups persist for a day or longer, seek medical help. In rare instances, hiccups may signal a more serious problem.

# HIGH CHAIRS

When your baby is old enough to sit up unassisted for a meal, it is time for a high chair. Here are some suggestions to consider as you choose one.

- The chair should be sturdy with a wide base so an active child won't be able to tip it over. Shake a chair before you buy it; see how stable it is before it's too late.
- A completely removable tray is easier to clean than one that is permanently attached. A poorly designed removable tray, however, can pinch fingers (yours and/or the child's) and dislodge when it shouldn't. Check the particular model you are considering and its safety record very carefully.

- Choose a high chair with a tray you can operate with one hand. That way you will always have the other hand to keep your child secure while you put her in place.
- The chair must have a crotch strap to keep the child from sliding out under the tray. The chair should also have a safety harness or seat-belt arrangement to keep the child sitting in place.
- Avoid a high chair with multiple uses. Get the safest and most suitable chair for your child to use while eating. You don't need one that also turns into a swing, a walker, a smaller play table, or any other gadget. Multiple-use items have more potential hazards, and are likely to be less reliable than a high chair designed with one purpose in mind.
- Avoid a high chair that reclines. Your child should not use a high chair until he can sit unassisted. A reclining high chair is intended for use while bottle-feeding, which is best and most safely done with the child in your arms.
- The high-chair tray should have a wide rim to keep spilled food inside the tray and off the floor to the best extent possible. Check the bottom of the tray to make sure it is smooth and without sharp edges that could hurt your child. Don't count on a child to keep her hands on top of the tray.
- If you choose a chair that folds up for storage, make sure the locking mechanism is easy to use and strong enough to ensure that the chair will not collapse while in use. Try before you buy.
- Beware of chairs that come dismantled in cartons that say "easy assembly." Some accidents with high chairs have been known to result from incorrect assembly. It's best to purchase a chair that is assembled and ready to go.

## USING A HIGH CHAIR SAFELY

- Do not use a high chair until your baby can sit up unassisted. Even if you have the chair ready early, skip using it until it is safe to do so with a child who can remain upright on his own.
- Do not leave your child unattended in a high chair, even when the safety restraints are in use. Put your child in the chair without letting her climb or stand. Be careful that older children do not play near the chair in a way that could tip or pull it over.
- Use the restraint system every time you put your child in the high chair. If you skip it, that could be the time the locking tray fails and falls to the floor, with your child close behind. Such a scenario has the potential for serious injury.
- Put the chair in a safe, level place. Keep it away from hard surfaces, such as walls or counters, which your child could push on to move or tip over the high chair.
- Be careful when you put your child into the chair. Make sure his head and fingers are out of the way when you adjust or remove the tray.
- Check the condition of the high chair's safety features frequently. Every time you set up a foldable chair, check to make sure it is securely locked in the upright position. Every time you use the chair, check to make sure the tray is properly locked in place. If key parts such as latches or locks become worn or do not seem to function correctly, repair or replace.
- If the chair you use is padded, keep an eye on the padding to make sure that it does not wear or break away and leave pieces that a child could consume or choke on. Watch for cracks in the tray that could hold spoiled food or cut your child.

# HOLDING A NEWBORN

Many new parents are somewhat fearful about handling their newborn baby. Don't be afraid to hold, touch, and cuddle your child. Infants are not as fragile as they might seem, and they need human contact and to be held.

When you pick up your baby, use both hands. Support the baby's head and neck with one hand. Use the other hand to reach around and support the baby's bottom and back. Remember that your arms were designed to cradle an infant. Just do what seems most comfortable for you and the baby, but be sure to remember to support the head and neck. A very young baby is not yet strong enough to hold her head up without support. Hold your baby firmly enough so that a sudden startle won't send the little one flying.

It's important to touch and cuddle your baby. A baby who is held firmly and gently is likely to be more secure than one who is not. Shaking or tossing a newborn about, however, could cause serious harm, even if done in play and without any intent to injure. Handle your baby gently and with kindness. Don't play rough, even in fun. Don't bounce a newborn up and down to bring up bubbles or for any other reason. (See *Shaken baby syndrome,* pages 155–156.)

Don't pound too vigorously on a baby's back as you try to burp him. This warning is very important if your baby is tiny and new. Premature babies are especially vulnerable.

# HONEY

Never feed honey to a baby less than a year old. Contrary to what some people think, honey is not nutritionally more beneficial than plain sugar. In fact, it has potential hazards that make it an unwise choice for young children.

Honey is an unusual simple carbohydrate, made by bees from the nectar of flowers. Honey may contain dormant spores of bacteria that have the potential to produce a type of botulism in the human body. The process used to package honey involves low temperatures that do not destroy the botulism spores. The potential accumulation of toxins could make an infant seriously—even fatally—ill.

While toddlers or older children may be able to tolerate the potential risk of honey, there is no valid reason to feed raw honey to any child. Sugar, no matter what its form, is still sugar, and most children get far too much of it. No matter what you may have heard, honey is not a health food. Avoid feeding it to an infant or young child.

# HOSPITALIZATION

If your child has to go to a hospital for any reason and you have time to prepare for it, there are steps you can take to make what is likely to be a traumatic situation a little easier. Here are some suggestions.

- If the hospital permits a parent to room in with the child, by all means do so. If not, arrange to spend significant portions of the child's waking hours with her. Ask nicely, but be persistent. Don't take no, or some vague reference to hospital procedures, as the ultimate answer. If your child will be hospitalized for a long time, find out what facilities might be available for your stay. See, for example, if there is a Ronald McDonald House nearby.
- Find out as much as possible about the hospital facilities and procedures that are planned for your child. The more you know, the better you will be able to prepare him for what is in store.
- Be honest with your child about what is going to happen. Don't be unnecessarily alarming, but don't paint an unrealistic picture of what will happen. Don't, for example, promise painless procedures if that promise would be untrue. Say instead that the doctor or nurse can give something to help if it hurts. Don't promise daily pizza, ice cream, or sweets if intravenous feeding or bland hospital food is all that will be offered.
- Try to prepare your child for any specific procedure that might be especially stressful—X rays, injections, or intravenous drips, for example.

Discuss your child's case completely with the medical team so that you feel fully informed and as comfortable as possible about the procedures. Don't be afraid to ask questions, and insist on honest answers. While it is important to be truthful with your child about what is going to happen, it's also important for you not to communicate your personal fears and concerns in a way that might add to your child's tension. Be supportive and hopeful. Remember that you are the adult.

To help prepare a preschool child for a hospital stay, you might use *Curious George Goes to the Hospital,* by Margret and H. A. Rey, in collaboration with the Children's Hospital Medical Center, Boston (Houghton Mifflin Co., Boston: 1966). This humorously illustrated book, available in paperback, features the popular little monkey whose curiosity frequently gets him into trouble.

## EMERGENCY TREATMENT

If your child must be hospitalized because of an emergency—sudden illness or accident—there will be no time for elaborate preparations. Under such circumstances, it is even more important for you to remain with your child so that feelings of abandonment aren't added to the other trauma. Remember that it is your child—you have a right to be with her and to be kept informed about what is going on. While it's important that you not get in the way of a medical team providing emergency treatment, you should not be intimidated by hospital personnel who would rather have you go home and call them in the morning.

## RETURNING HOME

After a hospital stay, many children regress a bit in behavior. Don't be surprised if that happens. When your child returns home from the hospital, he may be more dependent and seem to cling to you more than usual. A hospital stay can undo toilet training, so be patient and buy disposable diapers for nighttime if necessary, even if your child previously had been able to stay dry through the night.

Make sure that your child's health-care providers have given you careful and complete instructions regarding what you should do for your child at home. Even very young children feel pain, and it's important for you to discuss pain relief with the medical team should that appear necessary. Your child may even blame you for her predicament. She may act angry for a while. Be supportive and provide extra loving positive attention.

# HOT CARS

Hot cars and children are a potentially deadly combination. The temperature of a parked vehicle can heat up to 125 degrees F within fifteen to twenty minutes, even if the outside temperature is in the seventies. With temperatures in the nineties, the inside of the vehicle can soon reach 140 or more degrees. It is never safe to leave a child in a parked vehicle, even for a minute.

In the last few years, more than a hundred children have died in hot vehicles. Sometimes the parent left the child to run what was expected to be a brief errand, and it took longer than expected. Other times a parent simply forgot that the child had been left in the vehicle. Bizarre and tragic as it may sound, children have died because the driver forgot to take the child out of the vehicle when they got home, or forgot that the child had not been dropped off at day care or the baby-sitter.

It takes only minutes in an overheated car for a child to die. Leaving the windows cracked open does not solve the problem. In a hot vehicle, the child's body temperature can increase three to five times faster than an adult's would. *It is never safe to leave a child in a parked vehicle.* Even for a minute.

To prevent a tragedy, check your vehicle every time you reach your destination, whether it be a shopping mall, a health-care provider, or back home again. Make sure to take the child with you. That may sound like obvious advice, but good people sometimes get distracted. Make a conscious effort to be certain where your child is at all times.

Even if it is not hot out, it is dangerous to leave an unattended child in a parked vehicle. The child could get out of the safety seat and put the vehicle in gear. It wouldn't take long for a carjacker or kidnapper to break in and take the child, the vehicle, or both.

It is prudent to lock your vehicle (including the trunk or cargo area) if it is parked anywhere a child could possibly get to it, including in your own driveway. Keep the keys out of reach of curious toddlers.

# HYPERACTIVITY AND THE NORMAL TODDLER

What is hyperactivity? How much activity is too much? The answer to such questions in a particular situation may depend on the tolerance level and coping mechanisms of the caregivers, rather than on an objective analysis of the child's actual characteristics. These days, some parents and educators seem quick to apply the label hyperactive to youngsters who are energetic, healthy, and normally active. Many of the behaviors characteristic of a truly hyperactive child, however, are typical of all or most normal toddlers.

What should you do if your toddler is busy driving you up the wall with energy you can't match or contain? Some children are tougher to live with than others, and no toddler is easy all the time. Here are some suggestions for coping and providing structure for an extremely active child.

- Build sensible structure into the child's day. Do it consciously and deliberately. Pay careful attention to simple routines and rituals. The environment and schedule for the child should be predictable.
- Set guidelines that your child can easily understand. (For example, spread a plastic tablecloth out on the floor and tell your child that he may dump the toys out and play there. That may not do a perfect job of keeping the occasional block from turning up under foot or in an odd corner, but it will start to introduce the notion of limits.)
- Simplify the environment. When you childproof your house, remove not only items that could cause harm, but also items that could cause chaos. Move the entire contents of your silverware or utensil drawer, for example, not just the sharp knives, to a location out of your child's reach. Offering the child two or three wooden spoons instead is an alternative that will keep you from having to pick up the tableware service for eight several times a morning.
- Be consistent. If it's not acceptable for your child to remove all the books from the bookcase today, then it should not be acceptable for her to do so tomorrow, or next weekend when you are in a better mood. Make reasonable decisions about what you will and will not tolerate, and try to stick to what you have decided. Being consistent, however, does not mean being unreasonably rigid. If you have made a silly decision that isn't working well, of course you should change it. The important thing is to avoid confusing your child with constantly shifting limits.
- Provide suitable and sufficient stimulation for your child. Many children with high activity levels are very bright and also very bored. The availability of interesting activities requiring active participation and involvement may help channel a child's energies into constructive and appropriate experiences. (See pages 116–120 for suggested activities.)
- Don't fall into the tempting trap of depending on television to keep your child occupied and under control. Television is a one-way street that bombards your child with stimulation while providing no structure or meaningful opportunity for the child to respond or interact. While television may, upon occasion, keep your child quiet and give you some brief respite from his high activity level, it will not solve the long-term problem and may even make it worse. (See *Television*, pages 173–174.)
- Some research has suggested a possible link between hyperactivity in some children and consumption of foods containing artificial colors or flavors. Excess sugar in the diet has also been blamed for hyperactivity. It would be prudent, therefore, to avoid foods with artificial colors or flavors and to reduce your child's sugar consumption. Regardless of a child's activity level, furthermore, eliminating artificial colors and flavors and excessive sweets from the diet is a step toward better nutrition.

- Caffeine is a stimulant that no child needs. Coffee, tea, and cola drinks should not be part of a toddler's menu. Such beverages not only contain caffeine, but take the place of more nutritious drinks such as milk or juice.

A very small percentage of children—for specific medical reasons, in contrast to normal toddler development—have a short attention span, extreme distractibility, and a very high activity level that exceeds normal limits. If whatever you have tried seems to fail, discuss the problems with your child's health-care provider. There are circumstances that may require professional help. (See *Attention deficit hyperactivity disorder (ADHD)*, page 12, and *Terrible twos*, pages 176–177.)

# IMMUNIZATIONS _____

A number of childhood diseases that were fairly common three or four generations ago are now quite rare because of widespread immunization programs. Immunizations are an important part of your child's health care. Today's children are given a greater number of immunizations than children in previous generations. Because of advances in preventive medicine, it is now possible to prevent many serious diseases that previously placed children at risk.

Don't let the infrequent occurrence of certain diseases lull you into a false sense of security and tempt you to skip your child's shots. In most locations, a complete series of immunizations is required before a child is allowed to enter school. And, if a significant number of parents decided not to have their own children immunized, it might not be long before some common diseases of the past reestablished themselves as serious health problems.

## RECOMMENDED IMMUNIZATIONS

The following immunizations and schedule are recommended by the American Academy of Pediatrics (AAP). Should there be any medical reason to alter the program for your child, your child's health-care provider can advise you and answer any questions you might have. The vaccines are listed below in alphabetical order. The recommended schedule follows in the chart on page 109.

- DT&P vaccine protects against diphtheria (a serious and potentially fatal infection of the throat and windpipe), tetanus (lockjaw), and pertussis (whooping cough).
- Hepatitis B vaccine protects against a virus that may cause serious liver disease. It is one of the earliest immunizations your child should be given.
- H. Influenzae type b (Hib) vaccine protects against Haemophilus influenzae type b, a bacterium that can cause spinal meningitis, pneumonia, and other serious infections.
- Inactivated polio (IPV) vaccine protects against polio, a disease which was once prevalent but now has been almost eliminated because of the success of the prevention program. Polio can cause paralysis or death. Occasionally, an oral polio vaccine may be used instead of the IPV injection. Ask your child's health-care provider if you have any questions about what is right for your child.

- Measles/mumps/rubella (MMR) vaccine protects against measles, mumps, and rubella (also referred to as German measles).
- Pneumococcal conjugate vaccine protects against the pneumococcal bacteria, which can cause pneumonia, meningitis, and infections in the brain, bloodstream, and ears.
- Varicella vaccine protects against chicken pox, which—in addition to being very uncomfortable for a child—can cause complications such as bacterial skin infections, scarring, pneumonia, and brain infections.

## RECORD OF IMMUNIZATIONS

| Recommended Age | Immunization | Date Given | Reaction |
|---|---|---|---|
| Birth to 2 months | Hepatitis B | | |
| 2 months | DT&P | | |
| 2 months | IPV (Polio) | | |
| 2 months | Pneumococcal conjugate | | |
| 1 to 4 months | Hepatitis B (second shot) | | |
| Two to three times between 2 and 6 months | Hib vaccine | | |
| 4 months | DT&P | | |
| 4 months | IPV (Polio) | | |
| 4 months | Pneumococcal conjugate | | |
| 6 months | DT&P | | |
| 6 months | Pneumococcal conjugate | | |
| 6 to 18 months | Hepatitis B | | |
| 6 to 18 months | IPV (Polio) | | |
| 12 to 15 months | Pneumococcal conjugate | | |
| 12 to 15 months | Measles/mumps/ rubella (MMR) | | |
| Booster at 12 to 15 months | Hib vaccine | | |
| 12 to 16 months single dose | Varicella vaccine (chicken pox) | | |
| 15 to 18 months | DT&P | | |

This chart contains space to record routinely recommended immunizations for your baby and toddler. Your child's health-care provider may suggest a slightly different schedule or additional precautions. Certain of these immunizations must also be repeated at a later date. For example, DT&P should be given again between four and six years. A tetanus and diphtheria shot (Td) without the pertussis component is typically administered between eleven and sixteen years, with routine boosters every ten years thereafter. The inactive polio vaccine (IPV) and the measles/mumps/rubella (MMR) vaccine should each be repeated once when your child is between four and six years old.

The proposed immunization schedule is based on the Recommended Childhood Immunization Schedule, a policy statement published by the American Academy of Pediatrics in January 2001. Should medical research lead to any changes or additions to the list in the near future, that information would be available at the AAP's Web site, www.aap.org.

## PARENTAL CONCERNS

The United States has a relatively high rate of compliance with the recommended schedule of immunizations, but concerns do exist among some parents who question whether certain of the various vaccines might pose an unacceptable risk. Such concerns, in some instances, have been escalated by Internet chat rooms and media reports. Should you worry about subjecting your child to the medically recommended schedule of immunizations? Nothing is absolutely, perfectly safe in this world. But the risk of skipping the suggested vaccinations is far greater than the risk of a serious complication.

Immunization can protect your child from various childhood diseases. Failure to provide the suggested immunizations places her health and possibly even her life at risk. And, should too many parents fail to immunize their children, there could be a serious resurgence of diseases that are now under control.

Public schools nationwide require that children be immunized in order to attend. In individual cases, exceptions may be made for medical reasons, such as immune system disorders or allergies to ingredients of a particular vaccine. All but two states (Mississippi and West Virginia) allow a parent to choose not to immunize a child based on religious convictions, and seventeen states may take into account (but not necessarily go along with) philosophical reasons to avoid immunization. Approximately 98 percent of parents immunize their children prior to sending them to school. If you decide to do otherwise, you should make a fully informed decision based on strong beliefs and an understanding of the risks to your child and others.

## REACTIONS TO VACCINES

Some children do show a reaction to certain immunizations, but the potential for such a reaction is not typically a reason to avoid the procedure. The reaction is almost never as severe as the complications from the disease might have been. You should discuss the specifics of each immunization, including any questions or concerns you might have, with your child's health-care provider. Observe your child carefully after an immunization and call your care provider if your child seems to be reacting in an unusual way or if you are concerned about his reaction.

After the DT&P immunization, there may be some localized soreness at the spot of the injection. Many children seem cranky or out of sorts for a day or even two. That is not unusual. But if your child develops a fever or seems really sick after a DT&P injection, call your health-care provider for advice. Some children react badly to the pertussis (whooping cough) component of that triple vaccine. If that is the case for your child, your health-care provider may decide to modify the dose used in future boosters.

Many children experience some fever, discomfort, and a mild rash about a week after receiving the measles immunization (typically given as MMR, in combination with vaccine for mumps and rubella). Your child's health-care provider will tell you what to do, should that occur.

# INDEPENDENCE

Striving for independence is an integral part of being a toddler. As your child tries to do things on her own, it's important to allow, encourage, and support those efforts in whatever ways you can without compromising the child's safety. There may be many times when you will be tempted to step in, take over, and do a task yourself just to get it done at a pace that exceeds toddler speed, but you should resist such an impulse whenever you can.

When your child insists on getting dressed without help, for example, compliment her efforts even if the socks don't match, the shirt is on backward, the pants are a little twisted, and the sweater is buttoned wrong—all of which took much longer than it would have taken you to dress the child to perfection. Remember that your child is learning. Tomorrow is another day and another chance to get it right. But if you do everything for your child instead of allowing independence when he tries to do things without help, you may find that you are still a personal valet when your offspring reaches school age.

Eating is another area of behavior in which you should allow your child to become independent as soon as she shows signs of doing so. (See *Feeding problems,* page 90.) While you may be the provider of nourishment, you need not personally dispense that nourishment a spoonful at a time when your child has already figured out how to get food from the plate to the mouth without your help. Self-feeding by a toddler is inevitably messy, but it's an essential ingredient of becoming independent.

There will be many opportunities during a typical day to encourage your child's independence without placing him at risk, and you should take advantage of those situations. Never forget, however, that a toddler's reach often exceeds his judgment, if not his grasp. Do not allow your child to exercise independence in ways that could be dangerous—climbing a tree, for example, or swimming in the pool, operating an appliance, walking the dog in traffic, or crossing a street. Use common sense, constant supervision, and much care as you permit your youngster to try her fledgling wings.

# INTERNET (AS A SOURCE OF INFORMATION)

In generations gone by, parents learned many aspects of child rearing in their extended family or community. In today's world, that may not always be a viable option. Some contemporary parents have turned to the Internet for information and support. If you are comfortable using a computer and have access to an online service, you may find the computer to be a useful reference tool. A number of useful professional organizations and sources of expert information are identified in this book. You will find many others as you surf the Web.

If you use the Internet for information and support as you learn to deal with your newborn, older baby, or toddler, it is important to sort out the good and useful from the irrelevant or even harmful. There are literally millions of pages out there that you might find in your quest for information. Remember that there are no professional or even practical qualifications required to open up a Web site. While some of the best expert resources are available online, there also may be material of less reliable origin. Be sure to consider the source before buying into information or advice.

Some parents find communicating with similarly situated parents via chat rooms to be supportive and helpful. Use caution, however, in such dealings. When you really need factually correct information and professional help, it is best to obtain it from a known and identifiable source. You probably would not accept advice about your child from a stranger on the street, and accepting it from a stranger behind a computer is not very different. You should also be careful about the amount of time you spend online. Your child deserves your attention and energy. Sitting in front of a computer—even if you are obtaining useful information—is appropriately a low-priority activity in the total scheme of family life, especially when your child is very young.

# JAUNDICE

Mild jaundice (a yellowish tinge to the skin) is a common condition of the newborn. Many full-term babies and an even higher percentage of those born prematurely have some degree of jaundice during the first week.

Jaundice is caused by an accumulation in the skin of a pigment called bilirubin. Bilirubin is one of the substances released when red blood cells break down. It is processed by the liver and passes out of the body in the stool.

Healthy infants are born with more red blood cells than they need. These red blood cells break down rapidly in the first few days and weeks after birth. During pregnancy, the placenta and the mother's liver process the bilirubin for the unborn child. After the child is born, however, the baby's own liver may take a few days to take over that function. The immaturity of a newborn baby's liver may allow the bilirubin level to build up faster than the liver can process it. This causes jaundice.

Mild jaundice is usually no cause for concern. In most cases, it will disappear by the time the baby is six or seven days old. Because excessive amounts of bilirubin have the potential to cause serious harm, however, a newborn should be watched carefully for jaundice during the first week, and especially for the first three days.

Many birth settings routinely test newborns' bilirubin levels. If your baby is tested, you'll probably notice a small Band-Aid on the heel where the blood was drawn. Be sure to ask any questions you might have about this.

Early treatment for a high level of bilirubin typically involves the use of light (phototherapy). In this procedure, the baby's eyes are covered and he is placed under a bright fluorescent light. A baby receiving this treatment is usually able to be brought to the mother for regular feedings.

In a small number of cases of excessive jaundice, phototherapy is not enough to solve the problem. A stronger treatment such as a blood transfusion may be needed. If your baby requires such treatment, your health-care provider will explain what needs to be done and why.

# JUICE

Juice should not be the beverage of choice for babies or toddlers. The American Academy of Pediatrics now advises that fruit juice not be given at all to infants younger than six months, and that breast milk is still the best food for the first year of a child's life. For babies who are not nursing, formula can be used. For toddlers and older children, milk should be the preferred beverage for nutrition. For thirst, offer plain water.

In the past, some health-care providers and nutritionists suggested early introduction of juice as a source of needed vitamin C. That is no longer recommended, and a liquid vitamin supplement would be preferable should additional vitamins be needed. Experts are now concerned that overconsumption of juice by young children may have contributed to the recent increase in childhood obesity and obesity-related diabetes. Here are some suggestions for using juice.

- Introduce juice to your older baby or toddler's menu when your health-care provider recommends that it's time, and not before that. Some young children find apple juice easier to digest than orange juice. Begin with a small quantity—perhaps a tablespoon or so—diluted with water. Gradually work up to a four-ounce serving of pure juice per day.
- Even unsweetened juices contain natural sugars that can add to the risk of tooth decay. Don't use juices in naptime or bedtime comfort bottles. A child who is old enough to drink juice is old enough to sip it from a cup.
- Don't use the syrup from canned fruit (even diluted with water) as a drink for your child. The syrup is very high in sugar.
- Avoid commercially packaged fruit drinks, punches, or 'ades, which are artificially colored and/or heavily sweetened, even if the product boasts "vitamin C added." When you do serve juice, it should be 100 percent pure fruit juice. Read labels carefully.
- Don't offer your child carbonated fruit-flavored beverages. These are usually heavily sweetened and contain artificial colorings. Stick to real fruit juice, and don't get your child started on the soda-pop habit.
- Juice packaged in cans is a poor choice, because the metal may leach into the contents. Small bottles or single-serving cardboard containers are preferable to large containers that may hang out in the family refrigerator beyond acceptable limits for freshness and safety.

Juice in moderation (a four-ounce serving per day, for example) can be a nutritious and appropriate addition to the diet of a child who is at least a year old. But don't allow a thirsty child to pour down the juice just because it's more nutritious than soda or fruit-flavored drinks. A thirsty child should be encouraged to quench her thirst with water. The nutritional benefits of juice for your toddler are better provided by serving snacks of fresh fruit, which supply fiber along with the nutrients.

# JUNK FOODS

Junk foods are those that contain too many calories for the nutrients they provide. Many junk foods, furthermore, contain additives such as artificial flavorings and artificial colors. Unfortunately, many junk foods are packaged and advertised to be especially attractive to young children. There may be times when you feel that you are fighting a losing battle to confine your child's food preferences to those that are nutritionally sound in contrast to those with empty calories.

Try not to get your child started on the junk-food habit. Don't stock your cupboards with junk foods such as presweetened cereals or commercially packaged beverages that are artificially colored or heavily sweetened. Don't give in to a toddler's demands to purchase junk food, even if that might result in a tantrum in the supermarket aisle. Once you begin the practice of buying food items according to your child's whim of the moment, you may find it difficult to stop doing so. Encourage nutritious snacks such as fruits and raw vegetables. A homemade milkshake is preferable to sodas and the sugar-laden shakes from fast-food outlets.

Not all junk foods are fast foods, and not all fast foods are junk foods. If your family eats a meal in a fast-food chain from time to time, it is possible to choose nutritious items from the menu. Even a sweet snack from time to time is not going to be the nutritional downfall of your child, although daily doses of candy are not a good idea. Cookies (in moderation) and milk, for example, can be not only a comfort food but a pleasant memory of childhood.

Use common sense as you plan your child's meals. Don't fall into the trap of pushing nutritious items so hard that you give junk foods the added appeal of being forbidden. And be sure to set a good example. Your child is unlikely to be content with raw carrots and celery or even a tasty piece of fruit while you consume an entire box of chocolate cookies.

# KIDNAPPING

Each year, tens of thousands of young children simply disappear. Many of these children are seized by an estranged parent in custody disputes. Others are taken by strangers, some of whom commit sexual abuse, torture, and even homicide. It is important to take special care of your child so that she does not become a victim.

Here are some precautions to keep in mind for protecting your child. Most of them are just common sense. In a simpler world, many of us would not have felt the need to give them a second thought, but now we do.

- Never leave a baby or toddler unsupervised in a public place, even for a moment. Don't leave a child in a carriage or stroller outside a store, a fast-food place, laundromat, or other such location while you run inside.
- Never leave a child alone in a parked car, even if the car is locked. A passing criminal may only want the car, but the possible danger to the child is enormous.
- Don't let your toddler "get lost" in a supermarket or department store so you can finish your shopping in peace before claiming your wandering offspring from the store

manager. Your shopping tasks might be easier without a toddler in tow, but your child's safety must come first.

- Know the persons to whom you entrust your child for baby-sitting. Make sure that any baby-sitter or other caregiver is instructed to keep your child closely in hand in places such as the park, playground, stores, streets, and sidewalks.

Don't lull yourself into a false sense of security by thinking that crimes against children only happen in big cities or in someone else's town. Children have been molested or stolen from lawns and playgrounds in the nicest of neighborhoods. Your toddler should never be out of sight or out of mind in any place (even if that place is your own yard) where someone could approach and cause harm.

A young child does not have the judgment, understanding, or physical strength to cope with a problem involving an older, unstable person. No young child should be left unsupervised in a location where such coping might become necessary.

# LAUNDRY

Infants, mobile babies, and even toddlers can create absolutely amazing amounts of laundry. This is true even if you use disposable diapers. Some babies seem to go through one complete change of clothes per feeding.

Here are some tips to help you deal with laundry.

- Rinse dirty cloth diapers in the toilet bowl right after changing the baby. Flush as you dip the diaper in the water.
- Soak diapers in a small covered pail until you are ready to do a washload of them. Add a bit of Borax or some mild liquid detergent to the water.
- Use a mild soap (if you have soft water) or liquid detergent and hot water for baby's wash. The wash cycle need not be long.
- Rinse at least twice—three or more times if the water is very hard. Don't leave traces of soap or detergent that could irritate your child's skin.
- To avoid permanent stains, attack promptly any fabric on which the baby has spit up. A solution of baking soda and water may be useful. A commercial spray such as Shout may be used. Be careful to rinse thoroughly.
- It's quickest and easiest to dry your child's clothes in a dryer, but that is also expensive. In addition to cutting costs, sunshine has other benefits. Sun can kill some of the bacteria that tend to hang around on diapers, and it bleaches without leaving an irritation residue. If you live in a climate that provides the right conditions and you are able to do so, try hanging your wash out to dry.

For a newborn baby, it's best to keep the child's laundry separate from the rest of the family wash if you are able to do so. After the first several weeks, when the baby's skin is less sensitive, that may no longer be necessary.

# LAYETTE

A layette is an outfit of clothing, bedding, and other essential items for a newborn baby. As you read books about infant care or shop for your expected baby, don't be intimidated by the long lists of items presented in a way that suggests these items are essential. If you were to combine all the lists of recommended infant clothes and then purchased an average of the various quantities suggested, you would probably end up with many unnecessary things.

Perhaps the best advice on buying a layette for your baby is not to do it. See what you get as gifts, and then buy the absolute essentials to get you through the first two or three weeks. By then you'll really know what else you need.

Here is a shopping list for getting started. Fill in the numbers you think you will need for your special circumstances.

\_\_\_\_ boxes disposable diapers (have one on hand even if you are using cloth diapers)

\_\_\_\_ dozen cloth diapers (one dozen if you are using disposables, four to five dozen if not)

\_\_\_\_ undershirts (you'll need a lot of these, so get at least six to start)

\_\_\_\_ stretch jumpsuits or other sleeping garments

\_\_\_\_ receiving blankets

\_\_\_\_ rubberized sheets to protect cribs (or your lap)

\_\_\_\_ bathing and diaper-changing items

\_\_\_\_ cold-weather garments if needed (hat, bunting, blanket, sweaters)

# LEARNING AND ENJOYING (ACTIVITIES)

Each day in a young child's world is likely to contain a great number and variety of valuable learning experiences, whether or not you plan it that way. It is not necessary or even desirable to involve a toddler in formal instruction in school-related skills such as reading readiness. The way you interact with your child, nevertheless, and the early experiences you provide can pay off in successful achievement later on. Don't push or pressure your child, but do make an effort to provide positive reinforcement for his learning efforts.

## TALKING AND LISTENING

The most useful thing you can do to help your child learn to talk is to provide lots of interesting conversation. Here are some suggestions.

- Be expressive. Use gestures and intonation to help hold your child's attention as you speak. Even be a bit theatrical if you wish.
- Use the name labels for things. Say, for example, "Here is your sweater," rather than "Here it is."
- Address your child by name, and use the name rather than a pronoun. Say, for example, "Let's find Willie's toy," instead of "Let's find your toy."
- Keep in mind that your child can understand far more than she can express at this time. Be careful not to say things in front of your child that you don't want the child to repeat someday. Don't say anything that might alarm the child unnecessarily, even if you believe he doesn't understand. Assume that he will get the message even if the words to say it back are not yet there.
- As your child puts words together to make phrases and sentences, listen carefully and try to understand. Don't worry about syntax or correct the child's grammar. It will straighten out in time. When you respond to your child, however, use your syntax, not the child's.

## LEARNING TO LISTEN

Take time to call your toddler's attention to different sounds in the environment, and then talk about what you hear. The ticking of a watch or clock, a dog barking, a cat purring, cars or trucks going by, an airplane passing overhead, the kettle boiling, the bathwater running, a person hammering, footsteps, and hands clapping are examples of sounds you could use.

Try sitting (or lying down) comfortably with your child. Have both of you close your eyes and listen. See how many sounds you can identify. At first, you'll be the one to talk about what you hear. Then when your child gets better at listening and using language, she can be the one to tell you about sounds.

Encourage your child to listen to music. Share your own favorites if you wish, but be careful not to turn the volume so high that it causes fright or damaged ears.

## THINGS TO SMELL

Help your child to notice and identify different odors in her environment. As you are cooking, take the time to let your toddler sniff the ingredients as you tell the name of each one. Omit from this experience any powdered or finely crushed dry items, which could be inhaled.

Share with your child personal products with different aromas—aftershave, cologne, hand cream, sunscreen, his own baby lotion, and similar items. This must be a well-supervised activity, both for the safety of the child and the survival of the product. Use cotton balls to make a sniffing sampler for your child. Put a few drops of an interesting substance (perfume, cooking extract, fruit juice, or vinegar, for example) on each piece of cotton and let your child smell it while you talk about what it is.

Scratch-and-sniff books are fun, and they can help you provide interesting experiences to educate your toddler's sense of smell. Ask your local bookseller to recommend current titles.

## ART ACTIVITIES

Art activities for a toddler need not be elaborate to be fun. Plan in advance for the inevitable mess, and let your child create and enjoy. Here are some suggestions.

- Supplies such as crayons, paints, and paste should be nontoxic, washable, and non-permanent. Keep items such as permanent felt-tip markers and ballpoint pens out of a toddler's hands. The marks they make will outlast a toddler's childhood.
- For painting, let your child use water-based poster paints. A large plastic tablecloth makes an excellent cover for the floor; an old adult shirt can serve as a full-length smock. Large sheets of paper make it easier for your child to put the colors where they belong, rather than on the table or walls.
- If your child is tired of painting on paper, try making painted rocks. A smooth stone painted with poster paint can become an animal, a flower, a house, or just about anything a child imagines it to be.
- Vanilla pudding tinted with fruit juice or food coloring makes an excellent fingerpaint that causes no harm when bits of the mess end up in the mouth.
- A chalkboard securely fastened on the wall at child level can be good fun. Make sure, however, that the only writing tools near the chalkboard are pieces of chalk. A typical toddler is unlikely to notice the difference between chalk and crayon, and is even less likely to care.
- When your child creates something, treat the product with respect. If she tells you something is a picture of an elephant, don't say it looks like a tree or a rock. If the random scribbles on a piece of paper are identified as a letter to Grandma, there's no harm in helping the child to find an envelope.

## THINGS TO TOUCH

As your toddler touches things, call attention to any significant features of each object's texture or shape. Introduce your child to the concepts of soft, hard, rough, scratchy, smooth, wet, damp, dry, squishy, cold, hot, and the like.

Help your child to make his own touch-me book. Use heavy construction paper for the pages, and items such as fabric samples, wallpaper, sandpaper, aluminum foil, embossed greeting cards, or other textured items to paste on the pages. Use a nontoxic glue, such as library paste.

## SHOEBOX SURPRISES

An ordinary shoebox can be transformed into a container for interesting items to be experienced by touch (see illustration that follows). Here's how to begin. With scissors or a sharp knife, cut two corners of the box so the end can be pulled out to lie flat. (This is one step in which your toddler should not take part.) When the box is in use, leave the top on with the end flap out, so the end of the box is like an open door. To store the box, push the side back to its closed position, put the cover back on, and secure it all with a heavy rubber band.

The shoebox is an excellent tool for playing learning games with your toddler. Begin by placing two familiar objects (a model car and a tiny doll, for example) in the box. Have the child reach in and, without looking, find the car. Talk about how the object feels. Ask questions, such as, "How can you tell it's a car?" or "What do the wheels do?" Then have the child pull out the object and see if he is correct.

To make the game more difficult add more objects, or use objects that are not so easy to identify. To help teach your child concepts of size, shape, and texture, use objects such as a stone, a sponge, a bit of soft cloth, etc. Give the child directions such as, "Find me something very hard." "Which thing in the box would you use to dry dishes?" "Pull out the biggest thing you can find."

There are many different shoebox games you can invent as you go along. A shoebox can also become a garage for small cars, a barn for small animals, or anything else your child might imagine.

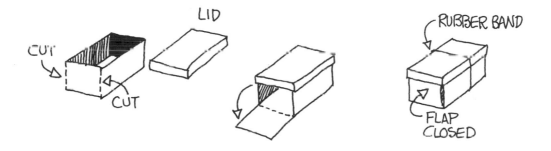

## FANTASY PLAY

Young children often engage in play that may involve imaginary props, creative use of ordinary objects, and even imaginary animals or playmates. Respect your child's imaginative endeavors and don't make fun of this fantasy world, which to a toddler may seem real and meaningful indeed. Don't think it's silliness, for example, if your child carries on a conversation using the hairbrush or similar object as a telephone receiver. Be sure to answer and supply your half of the conversation if the call is for you. But don't be surprised or disappointed if the call is not for you. Many children create imaginary playmates and involve them in complicated activities. These fantasy companions generally cause a toddler no harm and can be lots of fun; but when a clever child begins to blame naughty behavior on the "friend," it's time to introduce a bit of reality and point out that you know better.

Make toys and appropriate and safe household objects available to support your child in fantasy play. A large cardboard carton, for example, may serve as a rocket to carry a toddler to the moon one minute and a barn for imaginary horses or a hospital for sick dolls the next. An old purse, scarves, hats, and similar items can be used for dressing up. Objects that stimulate your child's creativity are better than expensive items that do it all and leave nothing to the imagination.

# LIGHTING

When you put your baby down to sleep, think of her position relative to the lighting in the room. That is especially important now that it is known that a baby should be placed on her back to sleep, to reduce the risk of sudden infant death syndrome. "Back to sleep" is something every parent and caregiver should remember.

A light right over the baby's crib would make it easy for you to see the baby; but it would be very uncomfortable for the child who is lying there looking up at it. Remember that the light should be located for the baby's comfort and well-being, not for your ease of viewing.

Be sure that your baby does not have to look directly into a light. An infant does not have the ability to change position easily if he is uncomfortable. It is up to you, therefore, to make sure that the light is not located in a way that would be bothersome or harmful to your baby's eyes. That caution applies to sunlight as well as to artificial light. Protect your child's eyes from strong direct light at all times.

# MANNERS

Teaching manners to a toddler—or any child, for that matter—is best done by example. A young child is not likely to place a high value on being courteous and considerate if the role models in her immediate environment fail to practice what they preach. It is possible, for example, or even relatively easy, to teach a two-year-old to say "please" and "thank you," but such verbal gestures will have little meaning if everyone else in the family grabs and takes.

But setting a good example is not the only consideration in helping a young child develop manners. It's important not to demand or even noticeably expect that a child will perform to a higher level than his developmental stage will allow. The typically horrendous table manners of a toddler, for example, are rarely bad manners at all, but are the result of a child's immature motor coordination not being equal to the task of eating neatly. Trying to force a toddler to hold a spoon or other utensil "properly" and to eat without spilling anything is more likely to lead to eating hassles than to good manners. Set a good example, but don't insist on or even hope for the unreasonable or the impossible.

# MASTURBATION

Exploration of their own bodies is a normal and natural activity for babies. Sooner or later, your child is going to discover the genitals and find that touching them feels pleasant. For a baby or toddler, this discovery is not any more significant than locating the fingertips, toes, or any other body part. Adults should be careful not to introduce their own sexual feelings into the way they deal with normal baby-and-toddler exploration of the genitals. Masturbation is not a moral issue for a very young child.

In most cases, the best way to deal with a young child who touches his genitals is to ignore the behavior and avoid introducing anxiety or guilt that might intensify that behavior. That does not mean, however, that you should encourage behavior that concerns or embarrasses you. Children must learn that certain behaviors should be kept private.

Tell your child that touching her private parts is one of those behaviors that should be kept private. Prevention by diversion is a useful approach to dealing with a child who masturbates in public. A child who is happily engaged in some other activity will be too busy to bother.

If you feel that your child is frequently using masturbation as a comfort habit and this concerns you or makes you uncomfortable, discuss the matter with your child's health-care provider. It may be possible to support the child in finding another comfort habit that is more acceptable. It's important to do this in a way that does not increase the child's tensions and make matters worse.

# MEDICATIONS

Keep all medications—those prescribed for your child, you, your pets, or anyone else—out of your child's reach at all times. Don't count on childproof containers to do the job, although a so-called childproof top on a bottle may slow some children down.

Be especially careful of medications intended for pets. Many veterinarians dispense medications in small paper packets or easily opened bottles, and there isn't even a child-resistant cap between your child and a potential poison.

If your child is sick enough to require medication, you should follow the advice of your professional health-care provider. Here are some additional guidelines.

- Do not use one child's medication for another family member, even if you think it will work. It is not worth the risk.
- Read the instructions carefully and follow them exactly. Follow the prescribed timing and the dosage. Don't ever give a little extra to make sure you give enough. Even something as seemingly harmless as acetaminophen has a very small margin between an effective dose and a potentially harmful overdose. Dose precisely according to the directions.
- Don't administer medicine in the dark. It's too easy to make a mistake, especially if you are tired.
- As an extra safety check, read the label and the directions one more time before putting the medication away, to make sure you did it right. If you make a mistake, it's best to catch it immediately so appropriate steps can be taken.
- Never refer to tablets or capsules of any kind—even vitamins—as candy. Do not tempt your child to view medicine as a treat. Medicine is medicine and should always be presented as such.
- Use all the medication that is prescribed, unless your health-care provider directs you to stop giving it sooner. Discard what is left over unless you are specifically instructed to save it for future use.
- To dispose of medicine you don't need, flush it down the toilet or wash it down the drain. Don't toss it in the trash where a curious toddler might find it before the trash collector takes it away.

See also *Antibiotics,* page 10, *Poisoning,* pages 146–147, and *Vitamin supplements,* page 188.

# MEDICINE CABINET (ITEMS TO HAVE)

A thoughtfully stocked medicine cabinet can help you react quickly and appropriately to many minor ills and accidents as your child is growing up. Having a particular item on hand (syrup of ipecac, for example, in the event of certain poison ingestions) may even save a life.

While it's fine to follow your instincts and use common sense in treating minor problems, you should not attempt to diagnose and treat a child's medical problems without the advice of a professional. Do not save prescription drugs from one family member's illness and apply them to a different child or problem. Certain medications—both prescription and over-the-counter—have a limited shelf life, so it's important to check the expiration date even if you are certain it's the right medicine for the job.

Here are some items you should have on hand in your home. Those marked with an asterisk (*) should be used on the advice of a professional. You may wish to ask your health-care provider whether you need to add to this list, and for recommendations of specific preparations or brand names.

- acetaminophen (such as Tylenol, in liquid form)*
- adhesive bandages (Band-Aids, for example) in assorted sizes
- adhesive tape
- antibacterial ointment (for cuts and scrapes)*
- antiseptic (iodine or Mercurochrome, for example)*
- cough syrup*
- heating pad or hot-water bottle
- nasal aspirator (suction bulb for clearing infant's nose)
- pen light (handy for examining throat or ears)
- petroleum jelly (Vaseline, for example)*
- sterile cotton balls
- sterile gauze pads (in assorted sizes)
- syrup of ipecac*
- vaporizer
- zinc oxide ointment (for diaper rash)*

# MEMORIES AND MILESTONES

Some parents enjoy keeping track of important milestones in their child's development. The chart on the following page can help you do that easily. Already listed are milestones that occur during a child's first three years or so; the blank spaces are for you to list any special events or experiences that you wish to remember.

If you decide to keep track of milestones, remember that child development is not a competitive race. Although recording milestones may be of interest, don't get carried away or use the chart to compare this particular child to her peers or siblings.

# MOBILES (FOR NEWBORNS)

A newborn baby can distinguish light from dark and can perceive several different colors. Right from the start, a newborn likes to look at faces and other objects, especially those that move slowly within his field of vision. Movement attracts a baby's attention, and every baby should have a mobile over the crib. You can, of course, go out and buy a suitable mobile, but here are two simple mobiles you can construct yourself. Because they are easy and inexpensive to make, you can vary them from time to time.

## PAPER-PLATE MOBILE

All you need for this one is a paper plate, cloth tape, and about two dozen small plastic spoons. You'll also need some strong string to hang the finished mobile where your baby can see it. Fasten the spoons around the edge of the paper plate with the tape. If you wish, you can put an interesting pattern—a face or bull's-eye target, for example—on the plate where the baby can look up at it. Then hang the mobile.

## MILESTONES AND MEMORIES

| | Date | Notes |
|---|---|---|
| Says first word | | |
| Says next words | | |
| Crawls | | |
| Sits alone | | |
| Stands, holding on | | |
| | | |
| Plays peek-a-boo | | |
| | | |
| Feeds self (more or less) | | |
| | | |
| Creeps | | |
| Waves bye-bye | | |
| | | |
| Walks, holding on | | |
| | | |
| Walks alone | | |
| | | |
| Tries to undress self | | |
| | | |
| Goes up stairs | | |
| Says "no" | | |
| | | |
| Scribbles | | |
| Has tantrum | | |
| | | |
| Knows own name | | |
| Dresses self (more or less) | | |
| | | |
| Names objects in pictures | | |
| Turns pages | | |
| Reads word or symbol | | |

## COAT-HANGER MOBILE

For another simple homemade mobile, all you need is a coat hanger (wire or very light plastic), assorted small objects to hang from it, and some strong string to hang it all up with. Clear fishing line works well for attaching the individual items and hanging up the entire device.

Make your mobile using any handy items you wish. The things you hang from it should be lightweight, varied in shape and color, and interesting. The mobile in the illustration uses well-secured decorations, small toys, miscellaneous cheerful items, and a miniature Raggedy Ann doll. Assemble your own collection of things and create a personal mobile for your baby.

## WARNING

The above suggestions are for making mobiles that your newborn can look at *but not touch.* Tie them securely—close enough to be seen clearly, but out of reach. Use lightweight objects with no sharp edges, so in case one falls it won't hurt the baby. When your baby begins to reach for the mobile and there's a chance of success, it's time to move it.

# MOTION SICKNESS

The motion of a moving vehicle soothes some young children to sleep. Some children, however, get sick from it. Motion sickness, while rarely a serious problem, can be especially inconvenient if you live in an area where you frequently must take your child in a car with you. If you used to get carsick as a child, that does not mean your offspring will be similarly afflicted. Don't anticipate travel trouble unnecessarily. It may never happen. If your child does, however, prove to be one of those who gets sick in a moving vehicle, it's best to be prepared to cope with it. Here are some suggestions.

- A light meal (never a heavy one) before you go, and easy-to-digest snacks such as dry crackers en route may help. Avoid large quantities of fluids, especially milk or sweet drinks. Give a thirsty child small sips of plain, cold water.
- Fresh air may help prevent an attack of motion sickness. Use the air conditioner or have a window partially open. Do not allow smoking in a child-occupied vehicle. (That is a good rule even if the child is not prone to motion sickness.) For a child who seems to be suffering, pull over in a safe place and let her take a few deep breaths outside the car before going on.
- Try to keep your child looking straight ahead toward the horizon rather than out the side windows.
- Diversionary tactics such as singing and little games may work with an older child. Don't let the child look at a book or pictures until the vehicle has stopped. Reading while riding can cause discomfort or sickness even for those who normally travel well.
- Be alert to the symptoms of impending motion sickness. Try to pull over and take remedial measures before your child becomes actively sick. Don't count on a toddler to tell you in time. A pale or greenish tinge to the skin, visible perspiration, drooling or watering of the mouth, and apparently unprovoked tears are signs that a child may be getting ready to throw up. A normally active and chatty toddler who becomes strangely silent may be warning you that trouble is on the way.
- Be prepared: Have a suitable container ready. The air-sickness bags found on commercial airlines are ideal. Foil-lined bags used for hot takeout food work well. You may be able to get your local store to donate a few to the cause. Avoid flimsy plastic bags. They do not work well and are not safe around young children. If your child is going to throw up, there is nothing you can do to stop it. Carry a supply of packaged wet cloths for cleaning up.
- If motion sickness seems to be a severe or continuing problem for your child, consult your health-care provider. Medication may be helpful in some cases.

If your child is one of those who does not travel well, make plans to cope with the problem and try to make the best of it. Don't blame the child; he can't help it. Clean up the mess and get on with your trip. Don't let your anger or tension make an already miserable child feel even worse.

# NAIL CARE (FOR A NEWBORN)

Keep your baby's fingernails and toenails neatly trimmed to help prevent self-inflicted scratches. Cutting a newborn baby's nails is really very easy. Just do it while the baby is sound asleep! If you prefer, you can have someone else hold the baby's fingers or feet while you do the cutting. Do not attempt to cut the nails of a wide-awake baby without help.

Use small, clean scissors—preferably the kind with rounded tips. Be sure to put them away in a safe place when you are done. Some parents prefer to use baby-size nail clippers. One advice book even suggests that you bite your infant's nails to keep them trimmed if you prefer to avoid scissors or clippers. The important thing is to keep the nails well trimmed without cutting a tiny fingertip or toe.

# NAPS

Are naps necessary? For most children they are. The naptime procedures you establish should be based on your child's personal needs, and not on a rigid routine or somebody else's chart that says a child of a certain age needs a certain amount of sleep at certain times. You know your child best. Many children take at least two naps a day—one in the morning and one in the afternoon—until they are a year old or more, but some do not seem to have a need to do so.

Many children go through a difficult stage during the second year when one nap is not quite enough and two naps are too much. Be flexible and use common sense. Encourage your child to take a nap if she seems tired, but don't force matters. Most children, if given the opportunity, will take the rest they need. Some children require and thrive on a regularly scheduled nap each afternoon until school age. Others are quite able to do without any naps at all by their second year. Insisting on a nap for a child who is not tired causes conflict, but meets no real needs (except perhaps, the caregiver's need for some time off).

Sometimes a child who does not take regular naps may just "conk out" on a given day for an hour or two. If so, let it happen. Try to be sensitive to your child's sleep needs and make provisions to meet them, even if it means temporary rearrangement of your day's plans. An exhausted child will not be good company at the supermarket or wherever else you had planned to spend the afternoon. A tired toddler is more likely to have a tantrum. Naps can be nice at such times.

# NAVEL CARE

Don't be intimidated by the stump of your newborn's umbilical cord. It will dry up and fall off of its own accord in a week or two. Be reassured that it does not cause the baby pain as the natural process progresses. Watch for signs of a problem, such as bleeding or infection, but take comfort in the fact that such difficulties are rare.

Your child's health-care provider will advise you on care of the umbilical stump when you leave the hospital or birth center. Some professionals suggest swabbing it with alcohol (on a sterile alcohol wipe or cotton-tipped swab), while others prefer that you simply leave it alone, clean around it, and let nature take its course. Ask what your health-care provider thinks is best for you and your baby.

Try to keep the cord area dry until the stump falls off. If you are already giving your newborn a bath, use a small enough amount of water so that the navel is not submerged. Many parents prefer to give sponge baths instead to make it easier to keep the umbilical stump dry.

Make sure that your newborn's diapers do not rub on the stump and irritate it with friction. If necessary, fold the diaper down to avoid the navel. If you notice more than a drop or two of blood, or the stump or surrounding area becomes hot, red, or weepy (oozing), consult your child's health-care provider. When the stump actually falls off, there may be a bit of soreness for a day or two. But it won't last. It's likely that all will go well.

# NEATNESS

Neatness is almost never a strength of a child under three. The urge to use newly developing mobility and independence to explore is just not compatible with a neatly arranged environment where things are never out of place. That does not mean, however, that you have to accept continuing chaos. It simply means that you must be clever about maintaining a balance between your child's need to be messy and your need for order. The trick is to accomplish this with minimum conflict.

Trying to make a baby or toddler eat neatly is a losing battle. Prepare for the mess, and don't make the family table a battleground. Newspapers or a plastic tablecloth under the child's high chair or feeding table will minimize floor mopping. A large bib will protect the clothes. It will be a long time until your child's manual dexterity can catch up to good intentions, so there is no point in demanding polite use of table utensils. At this stage, fingers are typically handier than forks and spoons, but many a child will attempt to imitate the grown-ups—and many a spoonful of food will end up somewhere other than the mouth. Be patient.

It does not take a toddler more than a few minutes to make a room look as if a tornado has just passed through. Putting one item away before taking out the next is not something most small children do easily. Instead of fighting with a child to put things away, try to set up a system in which some order becomes part of the fun. Cover large cartons with bright contact paper and use them to store toys. Many children will find that putting the things in and taking them out can be as entertaining as playing with them. A large plastic tablecloth or a sheet spread out on the floor makes a suitable playing surface with subtle structure and boundaries. When it's time to put things away, the cloth can be gathered up complete with toys, tied in a knot by the corners, and put away in a closet or behind a chair until the next time.

Being neat with a small child around requires ingenuity and tact. Make cleaning up a game to help overcome the natural contrariness of a toddler, but accept a certain amount of mess as part of the price of child rearing. That will eliminate a source of tension.

# NIGHTMARES

It is not uncommon for a toddler to have a nightmare vivid and terrifying enough to cause her to wake up sobbing with fear. These nightmares of a small child may contain monsters, frightening animals or persons, and terrifying or uncontrollable machines. A considerable part of the fright is that the child feels overwhelmed and helpless.

If your child is having a nightmare, provide comfort and support. Don't try to make light of it because at that point the nightmare is very real and threatening to the child, and he must be able to rely on you for protection. Help the child to wake up and become calm. Physical contact is important. Hold the child securely and provide reassurance. If the child's language is sufficiently advanced, encourage talking about what happened. If not, tell the child that you understand and that you will take care of her. Extra hugs are in order.

# NOISE (AND THE NEWBORN)

Most babies can sleep very nicely in the midst of everyday household noise. Just remember the noise level in the hospital or birth-center nursery. People there did not tiptoe about or keep their voices to a hushed whisper; nevertheless, babies slept.

Don't let your baby get used to sleeping in absolute silence. If you do, you will then find yourself with the unrealistic burden of keeping it that way. It will be easier for you if your baby can continue to sleep through whatever routine noises go on where you live.

That does not mean, however, that you should subject your infant or yourself to extreme noises that might cause upset or damage to tiny ears. Noise pollution is not good for anyone. Use common sense. Keep the stereo, television, or car radio at a moderate level. Don't scream a lot, even if you might feel like it. Don't locate your infant right next to a noisy household appliance. It is perfectly all right, however, to go on walking and talking while your baby is resting.

# NOSE (CARE OF)

Mobile babies and toddlers may try to stuff small objects into the nose. Little wads of paper fashioned from toilet tissue or napkins may also find their way into a small child's nostrils. If your child has inserted an object in his nose, be careful not to push the object farther in as you try to remove it.

Tweezers may grab a soft object such as a paper wad. Most toddlers are unable to blow out on command without sniffing in first, so asking your child to exhale to blow out an object may cause more harm than good. Because a good sneeze may dislodge the object, a bit of pepper held under the nose might do the trick. If your efforts fail, head for the hospital emergency room or call your child's health-care provider.

You may not notice right away that your child has lodged an object in the nose. It may even be days before you realize there is a problem. Suspect that possibility if you notice a foul smell or bloody discharge, or if your child seems to have pain in the nostrils. Medical attention will probably be required to deal with a foreign object that has been in the nose for any period of time.

Nasal congestion in children often accompanies colds or allergies. Your child's health-care provider may suggest nosedrops (see *Colds,* pages 61–62) or adding moisture to the air (see *Vaporizers,* page 186).

# NOSEBLEEDS

Nosebleeds are a common problem for many young children. Many nosebleeds are caused by picking, or by strenuous efforts to blow. Dry air increases the likelihood of a nosebleed.

Help a child with a nosebleed sit with the head slightly forward to minimize the swallowing of blood. Check to make sure that the bleeding is not a result of a foreign body placed in a nostril. If there is no object in the nose, get right on with the task of stopping the nosebleed. Use your fingers (with gauze or a small cloth, if you wish) to pinch the nose firmly so that the nostrils are pressed closed. Apply pressure for ten minutes to give the blood a chance to clot. If the nose is still bleeding after ten minutes, try again for a full fifteen minutes. Don't keep checking on it to see if you are making progress. Wait the full time before taking a look. If your efforts still are failing, call your child's health-care provider for advice.

For a child who seems to have frequent nosebleeds, use a cool-mist vaporizer or humidifier to put additional moisture in the air. A thin coating of petroleum jelly inside each nostril may help prevent nosebleeds as well.

# NUTRITION

The food guide pyramid is a recommended guide to balanced and quality nutrition for your family. You probably have seen the food guide pyramid on packages of food. This section explains how to use the food guide pyramid for your family. Obviously, a baby or toddler will not yet be ready for the grown-up pyramid for some time. Once you understand how to use the food guide pyramid, however, you will be able to plan your family's meals to be healthful and nutritious. This section includes special pyramids to show you graphically how to move your baby from breast milk or formula to a balanced and appropriate diet for a toddler. First, however, the food guide pyramid for parents and older children is presented.

## FOOD GUIDE PYRAMID . . . BLOCK BY BLOCK

The material that follows explains the food guide pyramid block by block and level by level to make it easy for you to use it with your family. The first thing to note is what is meant by a serving. The servings are presented for counting purposes, and are not the amount of food you would serve at a meal.

You don't need to spend time weighing or measuring the servings exactly. For mixed dishes, make your best guess. A macaroni-and-cheese casserole with tuna, for example, might count as one serving each in the bread group (macaroni), the meat group (tuna), and the milk group (cheese). If it is actually more pasta and a little less meat, don't worry about it. Things will even out over the course of a few days.

These guidelines are intended to help you provide a balanced and nutritious diet for your family. Quality of choices within each group is key to good nutrition.

## BREAD GROUP

The base of the pyramid—the foundation of a healthful diet—contains breads, cereals, rice, and pasta. The number of servings in this group is six to eleven each day. But take careful note of what constitutes a serving, and pay special attention to the quality of choices in this group.

# Food Guide Pyramid

## A Guide to Daily Food Choices

**Fats, Oils, & Sweets**
**USE SPARINGLY**

KEY
○ Fat (naturally occuring and added)    ▽ Sugars (added)
These symbols show that fat and added sugars come mostly from fats, oils, and sweets, but can be part of or added to foods from the other food groups as well.

**Milk, Yogurt, & Cheese Group**
**2-3 SERVINGS**

**Meat, Poultry, Fish, Dry Beans, Eggs, & Nuts Group**
**2-3 SERVINGS**

**Vegetable Group**
**3-5 SERVINGS**

**Fruit Group**
**2-4 SERVINGS**

**Bread, Cereal, Rice, & Pasta Group**
**0-11 SERVINGS**

SOURCE: U.S. Department of Agriculture/U.S. Department of Health and Human Services

To maximize the nutrients and natural fiber from servings in the bread group, concentrate on using whole grains as much as you can. Whole-wheat bread, for example, is more nutritious than white bread. Brown or wild rice is preferable to refined white rice. Overuse of refined flour, white bread, white rice, and similar items to make up the suggested number of servings in the bread group may have, in recent years, contributed to obesity and poorer nutrition instead of hoped-for nutritional benefits. Remember that quality of choices is important. You can increase the nutrient density of foods you prepare yourself by using whole-grain flour instead of highly processed white flour, or by adding wheat germ to items such as baked goods, cereals, meatloaf, and casseroles.

If you wonder how anyone could eat the number of servings suggested, look carefully at how a serving is defined for counting purposes. A cup of pasta with a garlic roll, hardly a lot of food, adds up to three servings. Two pieces of whole-wheat toast at breakfast would

**WHAT COUNTS AS ONE SERVING?**

1 slice bread

½ cup cooked pasta

½ cup cooked cereal

½ cup cooked rice

1 ounce ready-to-eat cereal

be two servings. The jumbo-sized muffins and bagels that have become so popular recently are large enough to count as at least two servings per item, rather than one.

## VEGETABLE GROUP

The food guide pyramid suggests a general range of three to five servings per day from the vegetable group. Vary your selections, because different types of vegetables provide different nutrients. You need leafy green vegetables (spinach, broccoli, kale, collard greens, romaine lettuce, chicory), deep yellow vegetables (carrots, yams, sweet potatoes, acorn squash), and starchy vegetables (potatoes, corn, peas, lima beans), along with miscellaneous others (tomatoes, onions, green or yellow beans, zucchini). You don't need every type of vegetable every day, but try to balance it out over the course of a few days or a week.

Legumes (chickpeas and kidney, pinto, or navy beans) can be used as a protein source as well as a source of vitamins and minerals. You can count legumes as vegetables or substitute them for meat in the meat group.

**WHAT COUNTS AS ONE SERVING?**

½ cup cooked vegetables

½ cup chopped raw vegetables

1 cup leafy raw vegetables

Fresh vegetables eaten raw or minimally cooked (steamed briefly or microwaved) are your best source of nutrients and fiber. Frozen vegetables without sauces or additives are also excellent choices, and are best if you cannot get high-quality fresh produce. Canned or dehydrated vegetables may have added sugar and salt, and are likely to have lost some nutrients in processing. Do not cancel out the benefits of vegetables by cooking them in oil or loading them up with butter or margarine. Remember to count any added cooking oils or toppings such as mayonnaise, salad dressing, butter, or margarine in your allotment at the top of the pyramid to be "used sparingly."

# FRUIT GROUP

Fruits and fruit juices are sources of key nutrients such as vitamin C, vitamin A, and potassium. The food guide pyramid suggests a range of two to four servings per day from the fruit group.

If you or your family members need more fiber, remember that whole fruits (fresh or dried) provide more fiber than fruit juices do. Avoid canned fruits packed in heavy syrup; they contain far too much sugar. Fruit punches and 'ades do not count as fruit. They are basically fruit-flavored, colored sugar water. Stick with unsweetened, natural fruit juice. For your older baby or toddler, offer water first instead of juice if the child is thirsty. (See *Juice,* page 113.)

## WHAT COUNTS AS ONE SERVING?

Fruit
Group
**2–4 Servings**

    1 medium-size apple, pear, or orange
    ½ grapefruit
    1 melon wedge
    1 banana
    ½ cup chopped, cooked, or canned fruit
    ¾ cup (6 ounces) pure fruit juice
    ¼ cup dried fruit, such as raisins or prunes

Fruit drinks, punches, or 'ades don't count as a serving of fruit because they are mostly sugar.

# MILK GROUP

The milk group in the food guide pyramid is a source of calcium, protein, vitamins, and other nutrients. In making food choices from the milk group, try to limit the fat intake for adults and older children in the family. Such limitations are not necessary or preferable for toddlers. Choose skim milk and lowfat or nonfat yogurt more often than whole milk for parents and older children. Ice cream counts in the milk group, but it also counts at the tip of the pyramid in the fats to be used sparingly. As you will see from the special pyramids presented later in this section for babies and toddlers, the milk group has special importance for very young children.

## WHAT COUNTS AS ONE SERVING?

Milk, Yogurt,
and Cheese
Group
**2–3 Servings**

    1 cup milk (whole or skim)
    1 cup yogurt
    1½ ounces natural cheese
    2 ounces processed cheese

1 cup cottage cheese counts as ½ serving of milk because it has less calcium than milk.

## MEAT GROUP

The food guide pyramid suggests two to three servings per day from this group, which includes meat, poultry, fish, dried beans, eggs, and nuts. If your family prefers not to eat meat, the group contains other options to meet your protein and other nutrient needs.

Your meat choices should be lean and prepared without additional fat. Broil, roast, poach, or boil rather than fry. Fish is an excellent lowfat choice, but it should be broiled, steamed, or poached rather than deep fried. Poultry without the skin contains less fat than poultry with the skin left on. Canned fish such as tuna packed in oil may be rinsed to reduce fat content. The same fish packed in spring water may contain less fat; read the labels.

### WHAT COUNTS AS ONE SERVING?

Meat, Poultry, Fish, Dried Beans, Eggs, and Nuts Group
**2–3 Servings**

2–3 ounces cooked lean meat
2–3 ounces cooked poultry
2–3 ounces cooked fish

Count 1 egg, ½ cup cooked dried beans, or 2 tablespoons peanut butter as 1 ounce lean meat (about ⅓ serving).

As a rule of thumb, a 4-ounce piece of meat is roughly the size of a deck of cards, so 2–3 ounces would be slightly smaller than that.

## FATS, OILS, AND SWEETS

Throughout the food guide pyramid there are little symbols for fats (naturally occurring and added) and sugars (added). These symbols appear occasionally in each of the food groups to show that fats and sugars can occur naturally or be added to each of those groups. The highest concentration, however, is at the tip of the pyramid. That is where you keep track of the fats, oils, and sugars that you add to what you prepare for you and your family to eat. That is where you can and should exercise some care and control.

It is best to limit the calories obtained from fat to 25 to 30 percent of the daily diet's total. Choosing wisely from the various groups in the food guide pyramid will help keep the daily fat intake within the recommended range. If, for example, your family's fat intake tends to be higher than it should be, use lowfat or nonfat yogurt and skim milk instead of whole milk (though babies and toddlers need whole milk). Choose fish or poultry in preference to red meat. Don't load up your whole-wheat bread with an overdose of butter, margarine, or mayonnaise. Garnish steamed or microwaved vegetables with a bit of lemon instead of butter or margarine. Use those added fats and oils at the tip of the pyramid sparingly, if at all.

What does the directive "use sparingly" mean with respect to added sugars? A person whose suggested daily caloric intake is about two thousand calories should try to limit added sugars from all sources to ten teaspoons or less. The ten teaspoons are not simply what you might put in your tea or coffee. They include sugars added to any processed, prepared, or baked food—cookies, cakes, shakes, sweetened cereals.

Fats, Oils, and Sweets
**Use Sparingly**

**Key**
□ Fat (naturally occurring and added)
☑ Sugars (added)
These symbols show that fat and added sugars come mostly from fats, oils, and sweets, but can be part of or added to foods from the other food groups as well.

As a person's caloric requirement increases, a teaspoon of sugar may be added for each hundred-calorie increase. Note that these guidelines are averages over time, not a precise prescription for any given day. If you can cut your family's sugar intake even further, so much the better. If a piece of chocolate cake or a fast-food shake should fill up the pyramid's tip with a week's worth of extras all at once, don't let that be the beginning of a trend. Try to get your family's food choices back into better balance as soon as you can.

## NUTRITION FOR A NEWBORN OR SETTLED BABY

From birth to the age of approximately six months, breast milk or formula provides the nutrition a baby needs. The infant food guide pyramid is designed to illustrate that. Feedings are typically on demand, although most babies work themselves into a fairly regular and predictable schedule.

If your baby is thriving—that is, if she is healthy and is growing and gaining weight within normal limits for a child her age—the exact number or spacing of feedings, as well as the precise quantity of formula or minutes at the breast, is not something you need to worry about. If your baby is not doing well, consult your health-care provider and discuss your concerns. If you are having difficulty breast-feeding, get support as soon as possible. Your health-care provider can refer you to a local lactation counselor or chapter of La Leche League. To find out how to reach a La Leche League volunteer in your area, you can telephone (800) La Leche. (See *Breast-feeding,* pages 37–41.)

Your baby's health-care provider might suggest beginning solid foods sooner than age six months. In the past, solids were often started fairly early. It is now known that many babies much younger than six months simply can't digest all the nutrients in solid foods. Beginning certain solids too early, furthermore, can trigger allergies that might be avoided if those foods were introduced later. Don't rush. Work with your baby's health-care provider to do what is best for your baby.

## STARTING SOLID FOODS

The first-solids food guide pyramid illustrates what your baby should be eating about four to six weeks after that first bite of cereal or fruit. Note that most of the baby's nutritional needs are still being met by breast milk or formula, so the milk group remains at the base of the pyramid, unlike its placement in the pyramid for adults and older children.

# Infant Food Guide Pyramid

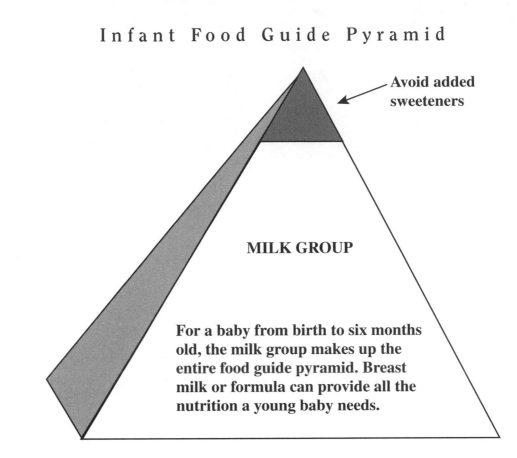

**Avoid added sweeteners**

**MILK GROUP**

**For a baby from birth to six months old, the milk group makes up the entire food guide pyramid. Breast milk or formula can provide all the nutrition a young baby needs.**

For approximately six months, your baby should be fed breast milk or formula. Avoid added sweeteners. If you offer a thirsty baby a bottle of water, it should be plain water. Do not add sugar or other sweeteners. Never give honey to a child under a year old.

If you have questions about how to introduce solid foods to your baby, see *Solid foods,* pages 161–163, for suggestions about sequence, timing, and serving size. Consult your baby's health-care provider if you have additional questions or concerns.

## TODDLER/FAMILY FOOD GUIDE PYRAMID

As you ease your toddler from her first-solids pyramid into the regular family pyramid, the key to the transition will be serving size and number of servings. Remember that quality of choices within each group is important.

Consult your child's health-care provider as needed to help you personalize suggestions for your child. At this stage, use the food guide pyramid as a rough guide for balanced nutrition, not as a rigid prescription. For a small child just adapting to solid foods,

# First-Solids Food Guide Pyramid

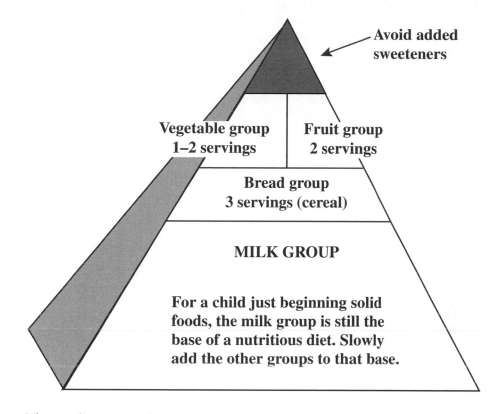

**Avoid added sweeteners**

Vegetable group
1–2 servings

Fruit group
2 servings

**Bread group**
**3 servings (cereal)**

**MILK GROUP**

**For a child just beginning solid foods, the milk group is still the base of a nutritious diet. Slowly add the other groups to that base.**

When you begin to introduce solid foods to your baby, milk is still the base of a nutritious diet. Cereals begin to develop the bread group, and in this first-solids pyramid they rest on the base of milk. Fruit and vegetables are introduced gradually. As with infants, avoid added sweeteners, the tip of the pyramid. If you offer a thirsty child a bottle of water, use plain water. Do not add sugar or other sweeteners. Never give honey to a child under a year old for any reason.

a serving size might be as small as a spoonful, a half piece of toast, or a bite or two of pizza. For an older child, serving size will increase.

We've included this material to get you thinking about varying and balancing your child's diet as he makes the transition from breast milk or formula to a grown-up diet. An older toddler might enjoy looking at the food guide pyramid in this book and comparing it to one reprinted on a bread wrapper or cereal box.

# OUTINGS FOR A NEWBORN

Fresh air is good for your baby, and you probably would enjoy getting out of the house too. Use common sense when you dress your baby for going outside. Approximately the same number of layers of clothing you need to keep yourself comfortable will work for your baby. If you need a sweater, your baby will need one too. A good rule of thumb is that since she won't be walking, she'll need an extra layer.

In summer, indoor clothing may be enough. When you take your baby out in the summertime, or even a warm spring or fall day, try to pick a shady place. Be careful that your baby does not get sunburned; an infant's skin is very sensitive. Even though your newborn might not need much clothing to keep warm, it is important to protect him from the sun. A carriage with a hood is helpful. Or, if you use an infant carrier (a soft front carrier or sling, for example), make sure that the child's skin is not exposed to direct strong sunlight.

In very cold weather, several layers might be necessary—indoor clothing, for example, plus a hooded sweater, a bunting, and a blanket. Be sure that your baby's head is well covered and kept warm. If the hands are outside the bunting, don't forget mittens. A baby who is cold will probably curl up trying to keep warm. Winter sunshine is wonderful, but make sure it does not shine directly on your baby's face.

It is fine to take even a very young baby in a carrier or a carriage out to the yard, the park, or other uncrowded places for fresh air. For the first month or so, however, it is best to stay away from crowded shopping malls, school playgrounds, public transportation, and any other places where there are lots of people. Your baby's health-care provider will advise you if there is any special reason to postpone taking your new baby out. If you have any concerns, ask.

# OVERWEIGHT CHILDREN

Although a plump baby or toddler may be charming and irresistibly cute, too rapid a weight gain even at this early age can help set the stage for a lifetime of obesity and related illness, such as cardiovascular problems and diabetes. A breast-fed baby is typically not yet at risk for being overweight. The problems start when solid food is added to the diet. Pay attention when your child is measured and weighed during regular visits to the health-care provider or well-baby clinic. Excessive weight increase relative to growth in height will be noted.

Don't place an overweight baby or toddler on a diet to lose weight. For a young growing child, it's best to slow down the weight gain so that the increase in height puts the weight and height back into balance. Follow the special version of the food guide pyramid (see pages 136–137) designed for very young children. Key to success is the quality of choices you make for your child from each of the categories. Pay careful attention to what your child is actually eating. See where you can cut calories without cutting down on essential nutrients.

Resist the impulse to tell your child to clean her plate. Servings should be modest. When she shows signs of stopping, take the food away. Cut down on fats; put half as much butter (or none at all) on bread or toast. When your child is thirsty, offer a glass of water instead of juice or soda. Try little chunks of potato (or mash them with skim milk) instead of french fries. Avoid frequent visits to fast-food restaurants, and don't supersize the Happy Meals if you do go.

As you choose from the categories in the food guide pyramid, the carbohydrates (grains, bread, pasta, etc.) will be an opportunity to allow wise choices to make a significant difference. Try to select complex carbohydrates that provide some nutrition along with a burst of energy. If sweets and junk foods have crept into your child's diet, help them creep out. Do not serve presweetened cereal as one of your choices from the grains. The best way to help your child avoid junk food is simply not to have it in the house. Provide nutritious snacks if your child seems hungry, but place a limit on the quantity. Do not let your child self-feed from bottomless bags of snack food.

If your child is overweight, cut down gradually and sensibly. Remember that your child is growing and needs a nutritious diet to support that growth. Never subject a growing child to an adult fad diet. Don't try to change your child's eating habits too quickly, or you might add other problems to the excess weight.

Try to increase the amount of exercise your child gets each day. Work with your health-care provider to bring your child's weight gain back to an appropriate rate. If you are helping your child to follow the toddler's food guide pyramid, avoid junk food, get enough exercise, and choose wisely as he eats, things should get back on the right track. If you believe that you are doing most things right and your child is still obese, discuss your concerns with your care provider. Most overweight toddlers are overweight because they eat too much of the wrong things. Occasionally, however, there may be an underlying problem that requires additional medical guidance. Don't be afraid to ask.

# PACIFIERS (FOR A NEWBORN)

If you breast-feed your new baby, it is best that no artificial nipples be offered until breast feeding is well established. In the hospital or birth center it is important to make your wishes strongly known, or you may discover a pacifier plugged into your newborn's mouth when you visit the nursery. Make sure that every caretaker who has contact with your baby is aware that you request no pacifier, no supplemental feedings or formula, and no bottles of sugar water. If your baby's sucking needs exceed the breast-feeding time, she will surely find a naturally attached pacifier—a thumb, finger, or fist.

If you decide at some point, however, to use a pacifier with your baby, here are some guidelines to help you avoid unnecessary problems.

- If your baby is content without the pacifier, don't offer it.
- Make sure you select a pacifier that is safe. It should be one piece—that is, the nipple, disk, and handle should be molded at one time of the same material. The disk must be large enough to ensure that the baby will be unable to get the entire device into the mouth.
- Some hospital nurseries use bottle nipples stuffed with cotton or gauze as pacifiers. That technique may be satisfactory for a newborn under constant supervision, but don't try that at home. Your baby could choke. Avoiding the pacifier altogether is preferable. Your baby need not be offered a pacifier simply to make life easier for the hospital staff.
- Never use a string or ribbon to tie a pacifier to your baby or to the crib. Children have been known to choke to death as a result of that practice. A lost pacifier is preferable to a dead or injured child.

- Do not substitute the pacifier for your attention when what the baby really needs is you.
- Remove the pacifier from the baby's mouth when he gets tired and starts to fall asleep. Don't allow your baby to begin to depend on the device for falling asleep.
- Don't dip the pacifier in sugar, honey, or jelly to make it taste nice. That practice can put your baby on the path to a lifetime of dental problems, along with potential for obesity and diabetes. Because of the potential for botulism poisoning, honey should never be offered—even on a pacifier—to a child under a year old.
- Do not use a pacifier beyond the first four to six months. By that time your baby will be using it to satisfy emotional needs rather than sucking needs. It is best not to let that happen.

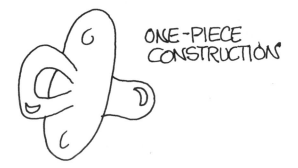

## PACIFIERS (FOR A MOBILE BABY OR TODDLER) _____

If your mobile baby or toddler is still using a pacifier, you have probably waited too long to stop the practice easily. At this point, the child has passed the stage of strong sucking needs and is probably using the pacifier as a comfort device for emotional needs. If your child still needs a transitional comfort device to smooth the way toward independence, there are probably more appropriate choices than the plug in the mouth. Unless you are comfortable with use of the device as a long-term comfort habit, it's best to take it away before your baby is six months old.

### IF YOU DO USE ONE

- The same rules for pacifier safety for a newborn apply for an older baby or toddler. (See previous section.) The pacifier should be molded in one piece, with a large-enough disk so the child cannot put the entire device in his mouth.
- Do not tie the pacifier to your child or to the crib. A dropped or lost pacifier is preferable to a choked child.
- Don't use the pacifier as a device to promote sleep. Remove it when your child becomes drowsy. If you don't, you will run the risk of having a child who will not go to sleep without the plug in her mouth. In extreme cases, a child may wake up every time the pacifier falls out. That can disturb an entire household.

- Do not stuff the pacifier in your child's mouth every time he fusses. First try to find out what he needs and take care of it. If the pacifier has become a significant tool of interaction between you and your child, try to find a better way to communicate.
- Don't dip the pacifier in sugar, honey, or jelly. That practice may please your child and keep her quiet, but it is not good for the teeth or the diet. Avoid giving honey to any child under a year.

## HOW TO STOP

- If putting the pacifier in your child's mouth has become a habit for *you,* stop. Make a conscious effort to offer the pacifier only when the demand is expressed strongly. Before you offer the pacifier, see if there is anything else you can do to make your child content.
- If your child shows any signs of rejecting the pacifier—spitting it out, for example, or not opening the mouth to take it—don't offer it until the demand is there and you see no other choice. Cut down gradually. Take a little longer to present it and remove it a little sooner each time.
- If gradual phasing out does not appeal to you, try stopping all at once, although that may not be easy if the pacifier has already become well entrenched as a comfort habit after strong sucking needs have passed. Tell your child that he can use the pacifier today, and the next day, and then no more. On the day you have chosen to stop, keep your child very busy. Plan interesting and engaging activities. Encourage other comfort devices as needed. When you make it through day one, try for the next. If you get through three days without too much misery, you will manage. If your child is still fiercely unhappy without the pacifier, you may have to put up with its use a while longer. Don't make a big deal about it or enter into continuous combat. That would only make matters worse.
- Do not try to shame or embarrass your child into quitting the pacifier. Don't push the notion that the device is only for "babies" and not for children who can walk and talk. Remember, you are the one who keeps putting it in the child's mouth.

# PANTS (WATERPROOF)

If you use disposable diapers for your baby or pre-toilet-trained toddler, they will usually keep the bedclothes or the child's outer garments dry on their own. If you use cloth diapers, there may be times when you will use waterproof pants to provide the protection that a cloth diaper lacks. No matter what you use, be sure to change the child's diapers frequently.

The better the plastic pants are at protecting the clothes or the bedding, the better they are at keeping the moisture inside near the baby's skin, where it can cause irritating diaper rash. Frequent changes and an opportunity for the child to go without any pants from time to time will help prevent irritation.

If you do use plastic pants for your child, make sure that the elastic legs are not too tight. The pants should be a bit large rather than too small, and they should not be worn around the clock. Whenever you can, substitute an extra cloth diaper instead of the waterproof outer layer. It's best for the child's bottom to get some air, even if that approach does let some dampness through.

# PETS

It is possible for pets and young children to coexist safely and comfortably in the same household, but it takes special precautions and careful planning. No matter how reliable and how much a part of your family your animals are, you must never forget that they are animals and potentially unpredictable. Some animals seem to experience jealousy toward a new baby in much the same way as an older sibling might. Be prepared.

## PETS AND A NEWBORN

Never leave your baby alone in a room with an unrestrained pet. Remember how small and helpless a newborn baby is. The cat that playfully leaps on an infant's face may mean no harm, but lasting fear as well as injury could be the result for your baby. A seemingly gentle dog could unexpectedly turn on a helpless baby with tragic results. That has been known to happen.

The fleas that irritate your dog or cat are not good companions for your baby. Do not let the baby share a pet's blanket or toys. Flea collars—on or off the animal—are toxic, and should not be within your baby's reach. If your pet takes medication, be sure to store it safely. Many veterinarians dispense medication in containers that are not child resistant.

If you have pets, make sure that your newborn's bassinet (if you use one) is sturdy enough not to be toppled by an animal. Even if you feel absolutely certain that your pets would not cause any problems for your baby, there is no point in taking the risk. When your baby is older and stronger, she will be better able to meet and enjoy your animal friends. Until then, close supervision is safer for all.

## PETS, MOBILE BABIES, AND TODDLERS

If your household does not include pets already, your child's first two or three years are not the best time to introduce a puppy or kitten to the family. If you already do have animals, however, there are several precautions you should take to keep your offspring and your pets healthy and happy.

Young children explore by touching, and as far as a young child is concerned, an animal is an object to be explored. Keep that in mind, and be prepared to protect the pet, the child, or both when needed. Here are some specific suggestions for keeping pets and children in the same house.

• Help your child learn to be kind to animals and handle them in an appropriate way. Hold the pet and show the child how to stroke it nicely. These lessons take a long time, so don't be surprised if the child tries to hold the cat by the tail with one hand while stroking it gently with the other.

- Small children and animals together need constant supervision. (Small children need supervision even if there aren't any animals.) While a reliable family pet is unlikely to turn on a toddler, it is not fair to either of them to allow a situation where that could occur. You might be sure that your faithful canine is guarding and protecting your child, but there have been examples where an animal changed its behavior abruptly. It is better to be safe than to be sorry.
- Keep your toddler away from the flea collar. If your child plays with the dog or cat, it might be best to find a different way to control fleas and ticks on your animal. A flea collar is just a toxic handle for your child to grab.
- Although your child will probably enjoy helping you feed and groom an animal, never make the care of a pet the responsibility of a young child. That would be unfair to both the child and the animal. (See *Allergies,* pages 7–9, for more information about pets and babies.)

# PICA

Pica (pronounced pī-ka) is a craving for unnatural foods such as sand, dirt, paint chips, plaster, or animal droppings. Although it is unusual for a person to desire a regular diet of such things, it occasionally does happen. In rare cases, the craving is due to a mineral deficiency in the diet. If your child seems to crave strange substances on a regular basis, discuss this with your health-care provider. Be especially careful that the child does not chew on painted surfaces or eat paint chips that might contain lead. Lead poisoning can cause brain damage and retardation.

Don't confuse pica with a child's normal curiosity about things. Don't forget that a mobile baby or toddler uses the mouth as an important tool for exploration. Most children will experiment with tasting things such as dirt or sand. A few bits in the mouth are inevitable, and will usually cause no serious harm.

Overreacting and making a fuss if your child puts a few grains of sand in his mouth may actually help create a problem where there wasn't one before. A child who wants a parent's attention can soon learn that something forbidden in the mouth will immediately bring an abundance of attention and concern. The parental reaction adds considerable fascination to a bite of sand that probably would not have held his interest without such a response. Supervise and control what your child attempts to consume. If the object about to be placed in the mouth is truly dangerous, take immediate action.

# PLAYPENS AND PLAY YARDS _____

Should you use a playpen, now often referred to as a play yard, for your child? Perhaps. Read the following pros and cons of playpen use and work out the answer that best meets the particular needs of your family.

## REASONS *NOT* TO USE A PLAYPEN

- A child can become bored during an extended stay in a playpen.
- Use of the playpen reduces opportunity for exploration of the environment, and for learning from such exploration.
- Some active children do not take well to confinement.
- Because the child appears to be safe, it is easier for caregivers to ignore or delay attention to the child's needs.

## REASONS *FOR* USING A PLAYPEN

- A playpen or play yard provides an area that is the child's own "turf." Many children find that secure and comforting.
- Use of the playpen permits parents or other caregivers to go about necessary household chores without needing to keep a mobile child under constant surveillance.
- The playpen or play yard makes it possible to keep a child safely in an area of the house that is not perfectly babyproofed or childproofed.
- An active mobile baby or toddler can wear an adult out. Both child and parents benefit if the child has periods of quiet play in structured, limited space.
- Living cannot involve total freedom at all times. It does not hurt a child to learn that fact of life early.

## HOW TO CHOOSE A PLAYPEN OR PLAY YARD

If you decide to use a playpen or play yard for your child, here are some guidelines to help make it a positive experience for all of you.

- Make a safe choice. If you intend to move the playpen from one place to another, choose one that is lightweight and easy to fold, but sturdy enough to remain firmly in the set-up position when in use. Check the safety record for the folding playpen or play yard you are about to purchase. There have been recalls of devices that folded up during use in a way that trapped a child's head, causing serious injury and, in a few cases, death. Make sure the one you buy has a locking mechanism that keeps it securely open while in use. Don't buy one at a yard sale, or accept a used one from a friend or relative, without checking the safety record of the model number.

- For a folding playpen or play yard, sides made of very fine mesh screening are the best. The larger mesh can trap tiny fingers, and anything large enough to put toes or feet into will provide a climbing ladder to the outside and defeat the entire purpose.
- Playpens or play yards with bars instead of mesh require an arm's length (and then some) safety area around them so objects don't get pulled inside. The bars, furthermore, must be close enough together so that the child cannot get her head trapped or slide a slender body partway through.

## HOW TO USE A PLAYPEN OR PLAY YARD

- Begin using the playpen or play yard before your baby is mobile. A playpen introduced after the child has started to crawl will seem like a cage for confinement, but one that has been part of the regular routine from the beginning may not.
- Make sure your child has interesting and safe toys so the time spent in the playpen or play yard will not be boring.
- Do not use the playpen as punishment. Try to keep its associations pleasant. "You've been bad, so you have to go to your pen" is a sure way to make your child dislike the playpen. If your child is old enough for you to use the time-out technique of discipline and punishment, don't use the playpen for time out.
- The older your toddler gets, the more opportunities you should provide for carefully supervised activity outside the playpen or play yard. Your child's energy level along with your tolerance level will work together to determine how rapidly you phase out using the playpen or play yard.
- Don't leave your child in the playpen or play yard for extended, uninterrupted periods of time. A few minutes of attention several times an hour will do you both good. If you can, keep the playpen or play yard where your child can watch what is going on and you can observe him. If not, check frequently to see what your child is doing.

# POISONING _____

Accidental poisoning sends hundreds of thousands of young children to the emergency room each year, and causes death to as many as three thousand or more. The only certain way to prevent poisoning is to keep poisonous things away from children.

Infants and toddlers use their mouths as primary tools for exploration. A curious child may consume something even if it tastes awful. Children have been known to drink (and be killed by) full containers of paint remover, bleach, liquid detergent, and similar substances that would hardly seem to compete with milk or juice for palatability. Research indicates that toddlers do not seem to be put off by a dreadful taste.

## MOST COMMON TYPES OF POISONS

The most common types of substances or causes of poisoning include the following:

- cleaning products
- pain-relieving drugs (analgesics) such as acetaminophen, aspirin, and narcotics
- cosmetics, including mouthwashes and nail-polish remover
- plants, including some common houseplants one would not tend to suspect
- cough and cold medicines
- creams and ointments intended for external use
- venom from bites or stings of poisonous spiders, insects, or snakes
- foreign bodies such as toy parts, other small objects, coins, or packaging materials (including Styrofoam bubbles)
- chemicals, such as antifreeze, pesticides, and the like

## PREVENTION MEASURES

- Always keep poisonous substances in their original containers. Never use soda bottles or mason jars or similar items to store household products or hazardous substances. It is dangerous to make a poisonous substance more appealing by putting it in a friendly container. If your child should ingest something harmful, furthermore, it is essential to be able to identify the exact substance immediately. You would need the label of the product in order to do that.
- Do not leave medications where your child could get to them (in your purse or on a bedside table, for example), or depend on child-resistant packaging to do the job. Keep such items out of sight and out of reach. Do not take your medications in the presence of your child, because young children like to imitate. Never refer to medication—yours or the child's—as candy.
- Be sure that all products are properly labeled, and follow the directions exactly. Read the label before opening and using a product. Store it again properly and don't leave it, even for a moment, where your child could get to it if you should be distracted.
- Store household products and food separately. They should not be in the same cabinet.
- Do not keep hazardous projects you no longer use, but don't simply toss them in the

garbage or trash bin. A hazardous substance removed from the trash can harm the child as easily as it would if taken from its shelf or cabinet. Empty (into the toilet or down the drain) and rinse the containers before discarding them. Leave them in their previously secure location until trash pickup if you can.

- Do not store household products in easy-to-reach locations, such as under the kitchen sink, unless the cabinet can be locked. Do not depend on child-resistant latches, although they may slow a curious child down.
- Obtain the telephone number of your nearest poison control center. Write it on a safe place near your telephone so you will have it readily available in time of need. Ask your health-care provider for information about which call you should make first should your child ingest something harmful. Write those numbers in the space below, so you have them in one extra place.

> *Poison control center* _____
> *Health-care provider* _____
> *Emergency room* _____
> *Local paramedics* _____

- Keep syrup of ipecac on hand in case you need it to make your child vomit. You can get it at any pharmacy. You should not use it, however, unless told to do so by the poison control center or a medical professional. Some poisonous substances can cause almost as much harm coming up as they did going down. Have a can of activated charcoal available for diluting poisons in case you are directed to do so by the poison control center or your health-care provider. You can buy activated charcoal in most pharmacies and many health-food stores.

## IF YOUR CHILD INGESTS POISON

- Call the poison control center (or your health-care provider, depending on the plan you have in place) immediately. Have the container in hand so you can describe exactly what the child has taken. You will be told what to do next. If you act promptly, some poisoning emergencies can be handled at home.
- If you can't reach the poison control center or a physician, get your child to the nearest emergency room as fast as you can. Take along the container from which your child ate or drank. If the child has vomited, take the vomitus for analysis as well.

# POWDERS AND LOTIONS _____

Powders and lotions are not necessary for care of a baby, and for a child with sensitive skin they might even create problems.

If you must use powder on your baby, use it carefully. Do not shake powder directly onto the child. He might inhale some, and that could be extremely harmful to a tiny respiratory system. It is not good for you, either. Put the powder in your hand first, and then rub it gently on your baby's skin. Cornstarch is actually a better soother for your baby's bottom and other creases where moisture accumulates. Cornstarch does the job without added perfumes.

If your baby tends toward dry skin, a bit of lotion might be helpful. Ask your healthcare provider for a recommendation of what to use, if anything. Some care providers advise against the use of any perfumed powder or lotion for a newborn or young baby. Ask what would be best for your child. Plain water and mild soap (well rinsed) are typically the safest choice for keeping the baby clean.

# PUNISHMENT

It is important for parents of young children to understand the difference between punishment and discipline. Discipline involves the structure that you set up for the child's behavior—the rules you expect to be followed. Punishment is not the structure, but the penalty for violating that structure.

Every child, no matter what her age, needs discipline. Predictable rules of family life are essential for civilized living, and are an important part of a child's security as well. Punishment, on the other hand, should not be an issue in the case of a baby or toddler, because children that young are not yet able to understand the cause-and-effect relationship between something they have done and the punishment that follows. Instead of contributing to effective discipline, frequent punishment of a very young child is likely to confuse the matter.

Aggressive behavior toward a child, such as hitting or biting the child for some transgression, brings with the punishment an example of behavior you do not want to encourage. Punishments such as withholding a treat or even confining the child to a quiet corner just don't have the intended effect with a child who is still too young to make the connection between those consequences and something he has done or failed to do.

With a baby or toddler, the best way to deal with punishment is to prevent the need for it as often as you can. Remove your child from a troublesome situation before something goes wrong. Put the china teacups away, for example, before your toddler has a chance to drop one on the floor. Don't leave your child alone with the cat long enough for her to put it in the dishwasher and then try to retrieve the animal tail first.

When a small child starts to do something he should not do (hit a playmate, for example, or crayon the wall), stop him quickly, calmly, and firmly. The word *no* and a brief comment can, in the right tone of voice, communicate all the displeasure needed.

(See also *Curiosity,* page 72, *Discipline,* pages 80–81, and *Spanking,* page 163.)

# QUARANTINE

Should you keep a child with a contagious disease away from other people? If so, for how long? It is generally a good idea to keep a contagious child isolated for a while so that others who have not had the disease do not catch it. Anyone who came in contact with the child just before you knew she was sick was probably already exposed, and for them your precautions might be too late. Nevertheless, it's best to try.

Another reason to keep a sick child away from others is to prevent that child from acquiring new germs from friends who might be in the early stages of something else. Let your child get rid of one disease before coming down with another.

You should not let your child put others at risk if you can prevent it. A child with rubella (German measles), for example, should be isolated until the danger of exposing a pregnant woman to rubella has passed. Rubella is usually a mild disease in a child, but an expectant mother who contracts it may give birth to a child with severe defects. A child with mumps should be kept away from teenage boys or men who have not had the disease. A bad case of mumps can cause a man to become sterile.

If you follow the prescribed schedule of inoculations (see *Immunizations,* pages 108–111), you will be less likely to have to worry about quarantine, because many contagious childhood diseases will simply pass your child by.

It is very difficult—if not impossible—to quarantine a child with a cold effectively. By the time you realize that your child has a cold, it is likely that he has already given it to any other children around. Toddlers seem to pass colds from one to the other and back again no matter what you do. (See *Colds,* pages 61–62.) As your child gets older and develops more immunity, she will have fewer colds.

# RASHES (OF A NEWBORN)

During the first week, many newborn babies develop a rash with little red bumps that look a bit like insect bites. Called "newborn rash," it causes no harm and may be ignored without concern. It will fade with time.

Between a month and six weeks of age, some babies develop a facial rash that looks somewhat like acne. Like newborn rash, infant acne is best dealt with by leaving it alone. It should fade within a month or so. You may notice some white dots on your baby's nose, forehead, or chin. These "whiteheads" are blocked pores, and they will clear up in time. Leave them alone. Resist the temptation to squeeze them.

Some babies have reddish-purple spots on the face and neck. These are called "stork bites." Do not worry about them; they will fade away as time passes.

The above-mentioned skin rashes are best ignored. They cause no harm and will take care of themselves with time. Diaper rash and heat rash (prickly heat), however, can be prevented and must be treated if they occur. (See *Diaper rash,* pages 78–89, and *Heat rash (prickly heat),* pages 100–101.)

# REFLEXES (OF A NEWBORN)

A baby has a number of reflexes at birth to help in adjustment to living outside the womb. One of the most important of these is the sucking reflex. When his lips are touched, a baby sucks. Touching the roof of the baby's mouth intensifies the sucking reflex. When you touch the side of a baby's face, she will turn in that direction and open the mouth to suck. That is called the rooting reflex. The sucking reflex and the rooting reflex work together to help a newborn feed at his mother's breast right from the start.

Another interesting reflex is called the moro reflex, or startle reflex. If a baby hears a sudden loud noise or is handled roughly, she may startle and throw both arms out quickly.

Chances are you will notice the newborn's grasp reflex right away. Offer a finger or similar object, and the baby will usually grasp it and hold on very tightly. The seeming strength of the grasp in a newborn is surprising.

# REYE'S SYNDROME

Reye's syndrome is a rare but serious and sometimes fatal disease that may follow a virus infection. Research has suggested a possible relationship between Reye's syndrome and use of aspirin in treating a child who has the flu. Even though very few children who take aspirin actually develop Reye's syndrome, most health-care providers are now extremely cautious about using aspirin to deal with a child's cold or flu symptoms. If your child seems to have the flu, consult your health-care provider. Don't administer doses of aspirin on your own.

Reye's syndrome is a very rare disease, and chances are you will never need to worry about it. Nevertheless, because Reye's syndrome can kill a child so quickly, parents should be aware of the symptoms so they know to get help immediately should the need arise. If your child has a viral infection (for example, influenza, a cold, or chicken pox), be alert to the following, especially during the recovery period:

- vomiting, especially if it is persistent
- lethargy (unusual lack of energy)
- strange or unusual behavior or personality change (a child who does not seem like herself)

Don't be afraid to call your health-care provider promptly if you are concerned about any or all of these symptoms. If you are unable to reach a medical professional immediately, take your child to the nearest emergency room. If the problem is Reye's syndrome, prompt treatment is essential. If the problem is not Reye's syndrome, no harm will have been done. It's better to be safe than sorry.

# ROUGH PLAY

Avoid the temptation to shake or toss your baby or toddler around, even in fun. Too much roughhousing can get out of hand, and even cause physical injury. Rough physical play and even strenuous tickling can cause anxiety that your child may be unable or afraid to communicate to you.

Do have fun playing with your child, but never forget that she is no match for you in size, strength, or ability to sort out teasing from reality. When the fooling around begins to border on violence, you've gone much too far.

(See also *Shaken baby syndrome,* pages 155–156, and *Teasing,* page 172.)

# SAFETY GATES

Safety gates can be used to close off places you don't want your mobile baby or toddler to explore. A gate in a doorway can help keep a child out of a room that is not childproof. If your house has more than one floor, you should have a gate at the top of the stairs and one at the bottom. Keep in mind, however, that a gate at the top of the stairs is not a guarantee. Most can be pushed or climbed over in some way.

Gates are not a substitute for supervision, and you should not assume that a gate will do the entire job of keeping your child where he belongs. A gate may reduce the chances of a problem at certain locations in your home, but you should keep in mind that the gate itself may present hazards of its own.

There are two basic types of gates. One, which opens and closes like an accordion, requires permanent installation. The other is kept in place by a pressure bar. A permanently installed gate is easier for an adult to open and close once it has been properly installed. The pressure-bar gates can be irritating to replace every time you want to go in or out of a room. Pressure-bar gates can be pushed out of place by an active child, and are not suited for the top of a staircase.

The accordion-type gates—permanently installed, or the type with a pressure bar— have been known to trap the head of a toddler trying to climb over, and cause serious injury or even death. These gates provide a foothold for a climbing child, so it is unwise to leave a child unattended and depend on the gate to do the entire job. The accordion-type folding play yards present the same hazard, and children should not be left in them without supervision. If not fastened tightly, these folding devices can fold up and pinch small hands and fingers.

For the gates requiring permanent installation, use the brackets and hardware provided. You must, however, be able to drill into wood studs to install the gate. It may not hold properly in wallboard or plaster. Pressure-bar gates are less secure. If you do use a pressure-bar gate, put it in the doorway with the pressure bar on the side to which the child does not have access.

Whichever type of gate you choose, be careful to purchase the correct size for the opening in which you use it. Take measurements with you when you buy. Keep in mind that a safety gate is only an aid, not a panacea. To ensure her safety, a mobile baby or toddler must still have an adult in the vicinity.

# SAFETY HARNESSES

A safety harness can be a valuable barrier between a mobile baby or toddler and an accident waiting to happen. Use a safety harness to keep your child secure in the high chair, the carriage or stroller, or anywhere else using one makes sense. If you have only one harness and try to use it for everything, there may be a day you fail to switch it from the feeding table to the stroller or vice versa. That is likely to be the day your child makes a head-first exit from where he is supposed to be. The cost of an extra harness or two still doesn't come close to the cost of one visit to the emergency room. It's best to have a harness for each piece of equipment your child uses regularly unless, of course, the item has a safety harness permanently attached.

When purchasing a safety harness, check the latest safety records for what you intend to buy. Make sure it is easy to use and adjust.

A safety harness with horse reins or a leash attached is very useful when you take an active toddler for a walk anywhere it would not be safe for the child to run about. With the harness, your child will have a bit of room for exploring, but you can rein her in before you reach the next street to cross, the gap in the fence near the nasty dog, or the glittering piece of broken glass that beckons a small hand to pick it up. Using the reins or leash is easier than trying to hold the hand of a toddler who is intent on darting this way or that.

Use a safety harness to keep your child safe in a situation where he could fall or pull away, even though you are right there. Do not use a harness to confine your child for any period of time while you are not watching. Never use a harness to attach your child to a tree or fence in the yard. When your child is out playing, you or another responsible caretaker should be out there too.

If your toddler has taken to leaving the crib at night, do not use a harness as a means to keep her in. Find a better way to deal with sleep problems. (See *Sleep problems,* pages 159–160.)

# SALT (SODIUM)

Sodium is a mineral that occurs naturally in many foods. It is also used in certain preservatives and flavor enhancers. Table salt is 40 percent sodium. A child needs a certain amount of sodium for normal growth and development, but a typical baby's diet (milk and baby food) contains more sodium than a child requires. An excess of sodium is not only unnecessary, but potentially harmful. Too much sodium in the diet may eventually contribute to the development of high blood pressure.

If you feed your child from the family table, remove his portion before adding extra salt. Cutting down on salt will be better for all of you. Experiment with alternative flavorings such as herbs or lemon. Look at the nutritional labels on canned or frozen foods and check the sodium content. Most processed foods have far more salt than they need. Commercial baby foods, however, are now manufactured with no salt added because they are better for your baby that way. Do not add salt to your baby's food to please your own taste. Keep in mind that your child does not find the bland taste of baby food as boring as you do. It's just as well if she does not acquire a taste for salty things.

# SEPARATION ANXIETY

During much of your child's second and third year, her life will involve conflict between the striving for independence and the fear of being separated from you. The typical toddler is quite ambivalent about his emerging independence—fighting for it one moment and turning full circle to clinging dependency the next. That can be very disconcerting to caregivers. It is not unusual for a toddler to cry vigorously when left in a play group or day-care center, even one where she is normally very content, and then an hour or two later to resist going home again.

Understand that fear of separation from you is an essential and inevitable part of your child's efforts to work out his independence as a person. There will be struggles no matter how predictable, secure, and supportive you are in dealing with this. Here are some suggestions to help you keep separation anxiety to a healthy minimum.

- If you are going to leave your child with a baby-sitter, be honest about it. Do not sneak out after bedtime and hope your child will sleep through your absence and not notice that you were gone. Avoid creating a situation in which a child might wake up to find someone else there in your place. It is better to leave when the child is awake and to reassure her that you will return.
- Be firm and matter of fact about leaving your child when it is necessary to do so. If you work outside the home and use a day-care facility, tell your child the truth. Don't say you will be in the next room or across the street if that's not where you will be. Don't promise to be back in a few minutes if you are going to be gone all day. Reassure your child that you will be back before supper, or after naptime, and so on. Then keep your word.
- Separation at bedtime is an important part of developing independence. Careful attention to predictable bedtime rituals can help your child feel secure. (See *Bedtime rituals,* page 27.) For a child who has trouble separating at bedtime, frequent-but-brief reassurances that you are in the house may be helpful.
- Be sensitive to well-intentioned but silly comments from acquaintances or strangers that might frighten your child. The neighbor or shopkeeper who says, "You're so cute I'd like to take you home with me" means no harm. Nevertheless, such remarks can thoroughly alarm a small child. Say firmly that your child is going home with you, and leave no doubt in the child's mind that you mean it.

# SEX EDUCATION AND SEXUALITY

Sooner or later, your child will ask questions about where babies come from and about the differences between girls and boys. How you handle those questions may have considerable influence on your child's feelings about sexuality and his sense of self as a sexual being. Here are some suggestions for dealing with this very sensitive and personal subject.

- Answer the questions asked, but do not provide more information than the child requires or can handle at that time. The toddler, for example, who asks if a baby really grows inside a mommy can be told, "Yes, there's a special place there for the baby to stay until it's time to be born." A lecture complete with diagrams on all the facts of human reproduction is not what the child needs or is seeking at that point. You have probably heard at least one version of the anecdote in which a parent launches into the long prepared speech on reproduction only to be interrupted by an impatient child saying, "But Caitlin came from Kansas."
- If your child asks, be sure to explain that her body is normal. The girl who wonders why her brother has a penis and she does not should be reassured that she is not defective. Tell her the way she is made will enable her to have a baby when she grows up. The boy who asks why he doesn't have breasts like his mother can be told that grown-up women have breasts so they can feed their babies. Men and boys have nipples and breasts that are flat because they don't need them to feed babies.
- Be honest with your child. Do not make up stories you will have to undo later. Babies are not purchased at department stores or hospitals. They are not found under cabbage leaves or brought by storks. Such tales serve no purpose.
- Use the correct words for body parts. The words *penis, vagina,* and *vulva* are not naughty words unless you make them so. Those labels should be used in as matter-of-fact a way as words like *toes, tummy,* or *knees.*
- Accept the fact that even very young children are sexual beings. Your baby or toddler will have a natural and healthy curiosity about her own body. Children soon learn that touching themselves feels good. Even if your upbringing has caused you to feel shameful or embarrassed about sexuality, try not to convey those discomforts to your child. That does not mean, however, that you should encourage or allow your child to masturbate in public, or to engage in exploratory play with other young children. This is an area of behavior in which limits are appropriate, and limits must be set. What is important is to set the limits in a way that does not make the child feel guilty or shameful about his body or feelings. (See *Masturbation,* page 121.)

# SEX ROLES AND STEREOTYPES _____

The sex-role stereotypes which have been part of our society for many generations die hard, even when conscious efforts are made to eliminate them. Whether or not they intend to do so, most parents do seem to treat boys and girls differently, although the differences may be subtle. As you rear your child, you have to be who you are and do what is comfortable for you as a family. You should try, however, to eliminate unnecessary and harmful sex-role stereotyping from your child's life as much as possible.

Boys and girls obviously do have some basic differences. What should not be different, however, is the opportunity provided for each child to develop fully as a person. No part of the wide range of opportunity to achieve or express oneself should be denied to a person simply on the basis of whether that person is male or female.

Boys should be encouraged to express their emotions and be gentle, tender, and kind. Girls can enjoy and participate in active play and romping about. Boys can play with dolls, and girls can play with model cars. Everyone can wear bright colors and nobody need wear only pink or only blue. Both boys and girls can dream of growing up to be doctors, firefighters, pilots, hockey or basketball players, horse trainers or jockeys, chefs, clothes designers, teachers, nurses, scientists, homemakers, artists, writers, or anything else they wish to be. Do not prejudge and force your child into a mold that meets your expectations rather than the child's wishes, needs, or talents.

In your efforts to avoid sex-role stereotyping, however, do not go overboard and force or forbid toys or clothes that traditionally have been applied to one gender or the other. If, for example, your little girl does not want to play with trucks or a tool set, she shouldn't have to. It is as appropriate for a girl to aspire to be a wife and mother as it is for her to hope to be a lawyer or doctor. Don't force baby dolls on a little boy who will have no part of them. Tender, nurturing feelings about small creatures can be developed in other ways. Do what works and is comfortable for you and your children.

# SHAKEN BABY SYNDROME

Gravely dangerous and sometimes deadly, shaken baby syndrome is a form of child abuse in which a parent or other caregiver shakes a baby or young child hard enough to cause injury. Shaking a child can cause the brain to move and strike the skull's hard inner surface, which can cause blood vessels to break and the brain to swell. The resulting loss of oxygen to the brain can cause serious injury including brain damage, seizures, paralysis, blindness, and even death.

There are approximately 1,500 cases of shaken baby syndrome nationwide each year, although increased awareness of the problem and some highly publicized individual cases seem to be bringing that number down. Nearly one third of the victims of shaken baby syndrome die. Caregivers who shake a baby typically do not intend to cause serious injury or kill the child. They simply lose control and shake the baby, often in exasperation to make her stop crying.

155

Many adults are unaware of how dangerous shaking a baby can be. Newly developed educational efforts include a video developed at the Children's Hospital of Buffalo, New York, by Dr. Mark S. Dias, a pediatric neurosurgeon. The video is shown to all parents before they leave that hospital with their newborns, and it is being adopted in numerous hospitals elsewhere. The video presents advice and counsel from health-care providers and three parents who talk about what shaking did to their babies. One baby is in a wheelchair, one breathes through a tracheotomy tube, and the third baby's tombstone is shown.

Information about shaken baby syndrome is available from the National Center on Shaken Baby Syndrome. Their Web site is www.dontshake.com, and their telephone number is 877-636-3727.

Now that you know what can happen if someone shakes a baby too hard, make sure that anyone who cares for your child—baby-sitter, relative, or friend—is aware of the potential consequences of shaking a baby.

# SHAMPOOS

It will be necessary to wash your child's hair from time to time, but it may not be easy. Water poured on the head frightens some children. Soap in the eyes only makes matters worse. Here are some suggestions.

- For a newborn (who probably does not have a lot of hair anyway), wash and rinse the scalp with a wet washcloth, just as you would wash the rest of the child's body. Use a mild soap or nonstinging shampoo.
- If your child is fearful of shampoos, don't make washing the hair part of the regular bath. If you do, you might end up with fears of baths and shampoos, not an easier shampoo.
- Don't pour water to wet the hair. As with a newborn, apply water and then shampoo with a wet washcloth. Use a nonstinging baby shampoo such as Johnson's Baby Shampoo. Use just enough water to get the job done, but not enough to create the sensation of running water. Rinse with a clean washcloth or sponge dipped again and again in clean water. That may cause fewer problems than pouring.
- Use a plastic headband or shampoo shield to keep water off the face. Using such a device may even make it possible to pour the water. If you don't have a shampoo shield, try a dry towel held over the child's eyes.
- Some children like a blow dryer; others are frightened by it. If your child does not like a dryer, towel-dry the hair and then comb and brush it. Use a wide-tooth comb. Be gentle with the tangles. If you do use a dryer, never use it while the child is sitting in a tub of water, even if you are holding it.
- For an older toddler, you might try playing beauty salon. Make an appointment for your child to have a shampoo. Set out all the equipment and make a big deal about it. You can also schedule a manicure for the same time, if needed.

Many children do not require any special efforts for successful hair washing. Some children even enjoy a shampoo. Start with a positive attitude, and perhaps the special suggestions listed will not even be necessary.

# SHOES AND SOCKS _____

Your baby can do without shoes, and will probably have an easier time balancing on her feet without them, until she is walking outside, when shoes would be needed to protect the feet from a world that sometimes is not nice for walking.

- Shoes should be large enough to give the feet room to develop. Too large is better than too small, but shoes should never be so large that the child curls his toes or contorts the foot to keep the shoes on.
- Have shoes professionally fitted in a reliable store, and check them for size at least every three months. Shoes must be the correct width and length. A new pair should have one-half to three-quarters of an inch of growing room beyond the longest toe.
- Shoes should be flexible rather than stiff with firm support. A child's foot must be able to move freely to develop strength, and stiff soles can cause a new walker to trip and fall.
- Do not keep a pair of shoes that no longer fits, even for special occasions. Comfortable everyday shoes are better for party wear than dressy shoes that are too tight. Don't count on a young child to tell you if shoes are too small. A toddler's feet are so flexible that they will crush to fit the space, and damage could be done without the child feeling pain.
- Flat soles with a nonskid surface to help keep a child from slipping and falling are a good choice. Avoid strangely shaped shoes, shoes with heels, and novelty items such as cowboy boots for a toddler. Dressy shoes for a toddler are an unnecessary expense, and your child probably would not get enough wear out of them to justify the purchase.
- Do not pass used shoes on to other children, even if the shoes look brand new. A young child's feet are so flexible that they mold to fit the shoes. Shoes that have been broken in by someone else's foot could cause a problem, even if they appear to be the correct size.
- Socks that are too small can cause harm just as tight shoes can. Make sure that your child's socks give the toes plenty of room. Cotton socks are a good choice because they let the feet breathe, but be careful not to shrink them in the laundry. Get rid of outgrown socks so you won't use them by mistake. If you buy several pairs of socks that look alike, you'll still find some that match when half of each pair disappears—as socks inevitably seem to do.

# SIBLING RIVALRY _____

As long as there have been brothers and sisters, there has been sibling rivalry. Some competition between siblings and feelings of resentment and jealousy should be anticipated, and should not be cause for serious concern. Try to treat all your children fairly and with understanding. Make efforts to see that sibling rivalry does not get out of hand and escalate into hostility.

# NEW BABY IN THE FAMILY

The arrival of a new baby can be an exciting and wonderful event. It can also be a source of jealousy and unhappiness for your toddler, who is not ready to yield her place to a new arrival.

- Let your toddler help you prepare for the new baby. Let him share in the shopping and getting the crib or room ready. It is unwise, however, to make the toddler give up his own crib at this time. Make a different sleeping arrangement for the baby—a bassinet for a while, for example—if you can.
- Prepare your toddler in advance for the fact that you will be going to the hospital or birth center to have the baby (unless, of course, you plan to deliver at home). Some facilities permit sibling visits to the nursery. Take advantage of that opportunity if it is available.
- The day you bring your new baby home, make an extra effort to pay special attention to your toddler. Think how difficult it must be for a child to sit unnoticed while everyone fusses over the new baby. Don't let that happen.
- Plan some time each day to do something personal and special with your toddler. Give her your undivided attention for a time. The time need not be long, but it must be something your child can count on. While the baby naps, for example, you could read a story, play a game, or make something. Have a conversation with your child. Listen to what she has to say.
- A toddler who sees how much attention a helpless newborn gets may try acting like a baby again. That is not uncommon, but you should not indulge your child's desires. An older sibling need not return to diapers or be permitted to suck at the breast. Do not reward or punish infantile behavior. Simply ignore it. Divert the older child's attention to something appropriate for his age. Call positive attention to things that make the older child different. Say, "Thank you for picking up your toys," for example, or, "Would you and Daddy like to have your juice in the new green mugs today?" or, "I like the way you picked out and put on your shirt."

# YOUR TODDLER AND OLDER CHILDREN

Do not make your toddler a burden for your older children. While older siblings might enjoy helping to care for a younger brother or sister, it is not fair to deprive an older child of her own childhood. Let an older child help you, but do not make care of a toddler a sibling's responsibility.

Be careful not to let your toddler do things that are suitable for an older child but not safe for a toddler. Be alert to the possibility that an older child might try to engage the toddler in unsuitable or dangerous activities. Keep your older child's toys out of a toddler's hands, both for safety reasons and because the older child should be able to enjoy some personal property without having it demolished by a two-year-old.

# SKIN CARE

For most babies and toddlers, ensuring adequate cleanliness and protection from the elements, especially sun, is all the skin care required. No special efforts or fussing are needed for most children. If there is some special characteristic or problem involving your child's skin, however, you should consult your health-care provider for advice.

(See also *Baths*, pages 21–24, *Diaper rash*, pages 78–79, *Eczema*, page 83, *Heat rash (prickly heat)*, pages 100–101, and *Sunburn*, pages 166–168.)

# SLEEP PROBLEMS

Sleep problems are not uncommon among babies and toddlers. How you handle those problems may well determine whether or not you end up with sleep problems too.

## PROBLEMS AT BEDTIME

Many children find winding down at the end of the day difficult. Add normal toddler separation anxiety to any reluctance to stop the day's activities, and you may have a sleep problem in the making. Here are some suggestions.

- An overtired or tense child is often more difficult to put to bed. An extra hour or so of activity for a child who tends to balk at bedtime is not usually the answer unless the child is clearly not tired. Further revving up is usually not a good idea. Avoid letting your child get overtired, even if that means providing an extra nap or earlier bedtime.
- Establish and pay careful attention to a routine of bedtime rituals. Predictable little routines—whichever ones you use—give the child a sense of security along with a clear indication of what you expect him to do in the immediate future. Bedtime should not involve surprises. Bedtime rituals, such as a story, enable you to give some special attention to your child while helping her to relax.
- Encourage the use of a comfort device, such as a cuddly toy. The child who has a favorite and huggable stuffed creature in the crib may feel less alone. Involve that cuddly creature in the bedtime rituals. If it is a teddy bear, for example, say good night to it and tuck it in.
- When the bedtime rituals are finished and the good nights said, you should leave the room. Reassure your child that you will be there if necessary, but that it is time for him to go to sleep.
- If your child cries or screams after you leave, reappear just long enough to say that you are still there but it is sleep time. Attend to any genuine needs such as changing a wet diaper or adding another blanket in a room that is too cool, but don't fall for the one-

more-drink-of-water game. Stay long enough for your child to see that you are available, but no longer. You may have to do this many times for several nights, but don't give up. Sooner or later your child will get the message that she is not being abandoned—after all, you do show up—but she also will learn that she will be left in bed because you will not permit otherwise. Be firm. The goal is a secure, comfortable child who realizes that bedtime is inevitable. This will not work if you weaken and let the child get up to play, or if you give in to her demands and stay there until sleep comes.

## WAKING AT NIGHT

If your child starts waking up at night, try to identify and remedy the reason. Is he cold or wet, for example? Is the room overly noisy? Has there been some unusual tension during the day? Sometimes the cause of night waking will not be easy to find. Changing a diaper is simple; figuring out what is going on in a small person's mind and feelings may not be so easy, but try.

A nightmare can waken and greatly distress a young child. If a nightmare wakes your child, provide support and reassuring comfort. (See *Nightmares,* page 128.)

The more rapidly you attend to a child's needs when she wakes in the night, the sooner there is a chance you all can get back to sleep. If the child refuses to let you go, employ the same brief appearance schedule suggested for dealing with bedtime problems. Show your face, tell your child that it's time to sleep, and leave. Do that as often as necessary. Letting the child cry it out is almost never a satisfactory solution, but remaining there until the child finally sleeps will start a habit that may be hard to break.

## EARLY RISING

If your child wakes long before you think it is time to start the day, a quick diaper change or visit to the potty may make him comfortable enough to settle down for a while longer. A supply of safe toys may keep a child occupied while you get a little more sleep. If you have an older child, perhaps she could be enticed to make early morning a togetherness time with your toddler. If the older child is able, she could read a favorite story to the toddler. That would be good for both of them.

## CLIMBING OUT OF THE CRIB

When your child learns to leave the crib without your help, you must make provisions for his safety during and after the exit. Lower the crib side so there will be less distance to fall. You may need to try a mattress on the floor. Childproof the room. Use a gate in the doorway if you wish, but respond to a child at the gate before he tries to climb over it. If your night wanderer manages to get to your room, put him gently but firmly back where he belongs.

(See *Bedtime rituals,* page 27, and *Cribs,* pages 69–70.)

# SMOKING

Parents who smoke typically do not intend to harm their children. Nevertheless, the adverse effects on the children begin before birth and continue as long as the children are exposed to secondhand smoke and even longer, because some of the damage caused by smoking cannot be reversed.

Smoking by parents during the prenatal time is associated with low infant birth weight. Babies of smokers are at risk for being less well developed at birth, are more vulnerable to respiratory problems and diseases of early infancy, and are more likely to die in infancy than babies who are not exposed to secondhand smoke. Children who grow up in smoking households have significantly less lung capacity than those who grow up in clean air.

Having parents who smoke significantly increases a baby's risk of dying from sudden infant death syndrome (crib death). Exposure to secondhand smoke increases a child's risk of developing asthma. Children with asthma who are exposed to secondhand smoke have an increased risk of dying from asthma-related problems.

Exposure to secondhand smoke is now recognized as a serious pediatric health problem. A young child cannot choose to avoid the secondhand smoke that is inflicted on him by surrounding adults. Children need to be protected, therefore, from secondhand smoke in public places such as restaurants as well as in homes and vehicles. The no-smoking rule must apply to all—guests, relatives, friends, and other caregivers as well as parents.

Parents who smoke not only compromise the health of their children, but also set a bad example. Children of smokers are more likely to smoke when they grow up. Careless smoking is a major cause of fires in the home, and that is another risk to a child's safety. Research suggests that harmful ingredients in secondhand smoke—even in what you think may be a well ventilated area can persist indoors for many hours. Smoking while a child is in another room, therefore, and then bringing the child back into the room is not sufficient protection for the child.

If you are a smoker and are unable to stop despite the compelling reasons to do so, your health-care provider may be able to direct you to the help you need.

(See *Asthma*, pages 11–12, *Fire*, pages 93–94, and *Sudden infant death syndrome (SIDS)*, page 165.)

# SOLID FOODS

Breast milk or formula is sufficient nutrition for your baby's first six months. Do not rush to introduce solid foods to your baby, no matter what you may hear about the potential benefits of doing so. Ignore the advice of the acquaintance who tells you that her grandchildren all slept through the night from the fourth week on because their mother weighed them down with cereal. A baby's digestive system is too immature during the first few months to digest fully the nutrients in solid foods. Breast milk is the perfect food at that time; formula is the next best.

Your baby's health-care provider can help you decide when to start your child on solid foods. When it is time to begin feeding your child solid foods, start with one food. Many parents first offer a single-grain cereal such as rice or barley cereal. Others find, however, that a smooth fruit, such as commercially prepared baby applesauce, is easier for the child to swallow at first, so they introduce the fruit a week before the first cereal bite. Either way is fine.

Introduce no more than one new food per week. That way you can be sure it agrees with your child before you add something new to the menu. Follow a week of strained applesauce or strained banana, for example, with a week of the fruit with rice or barley cereal added. Mix the cereal with expressed breast milk or formula to a mushy (not quite liquid) consistency. Take the amount of strained fruit you plan to use out of the jar with a clean spoon, and store the rest in the refrigerator for up to two more days. Do not feed directly from the jar, because bacteria in the child's saliva can cause the contents to spoil.

Start with about a teaspoonful of the food on day one. Add another teaspoonful on day two. Increase the amount gradually, a teaspoonful at a time each day throughout the week. Your child will indicate when it is enough.

## HOW TO FEED

During the early days of solid foods, your child will still be getting most of her nourishment from breast milk or formula. Start with a few minutes on one breast or with a part of a bottle. A very hungry child is a poor candidate for learning to take food from a spoon. After a bit of milk, try some spoon feeding before completing the rest of the meal with breast or bottle. If you give all the milk before offering the spoon, the child will be too comfortable to bother. The solid portion of the meal should be in the middle.

A spoon with a tiny bowl is best for the first feedings. Do not force. Taking nourishment from a spoon is an entirely new experience for a child who is used to eating by sucking. Hold the spoon at the edge of the child's mouth and let the child suck a bit of the food in. That may help you get started. Expect that much of what goes in at first will come out without being swallowed. Keep your sense of humor and patience as you rescue the meal from the child's chin a spoonful at a time, and try again.

When you are feeding your child and he grabs the spoon, it is time for a two-spoon meal—one spoon for you and one spoon for him. That way you will get some of the food into his mouth as he learns to manipulate the spoon.

## FEEDING SCHEDULE

When you begin solid foods, begin with either breakfast or supper, whichever works best for you. Add the other meal after a day or two, and work up to three meals a day. For the first month or so, stick to cereal and fruit. Then, for the midday meal add vegetables, following the one new food per week rule. Begin with yellow vegetables (carrots or sweet potatoes, for example), which are easier to digest, and then add green vegetables. When the child has settled into vegetables, add strained meat or mixtures such as vegetables with lamb or beef, if you wish. There are no hard-and-fast rules. Your health-care provider might have additional suggestions.

## FROM BABY FOOD TO FINGER FOOD

At some time near the end of your child's first year, after you have introduced lumps into the strained foods, your child will be ready to start finger foods. A long, thin piece of toast, a lump of cooked carrot or boiled potato, a string bean, or a slice of beet are possible choices. The first experiences with finger foods will probably be more like play than eating, but most children soon get the idea. Encourage your child to feed herself with these items. Let your child develop her own style of self-feeding. There will be plenty of time for table manners later.

# SPANKING

Should you spank or hit your child? Physical punishment will not ensure that your child learns the specific lesson you have in mind. It may, however, convey the undesirable message that hitting people is acceptable behavior.

A baby or toddler is unlikely to be capable of making the cause-and-effect connection between something she has just done and the spanking that follows. Even if you feel you are dishing out a well-deserved dose of discipline, chances are that spanking will not achieve the long-term results you intend. (See *Discipline*, pages 80–81, and *Punishment*, page 148.) That does not mean that you should permit your child to be naughty or to do whatever he pleases. There are simply better and more effective ways to manage a child's behavior than by using physical force.

At one time or another, even the most even-tempered and well-meaning parent may strike a child—either as a result of accumulated exasperation or in spontaneous response to a specific situation. As long as that is not a frequent occurrence, don't spend time feeling guilty about it. A rare swat on the backside with the hand is hardly cause for concern if it is done as an attention getter and is not done in anger.

If you need to take a child's hand to stop her from throwing a toy at the family dog or the television set, do so without adding hitting to your action. Never slap your child across the face. Do not strike your child repeatedly or with an object; that crosses the line into beating, which is abusive.

If you find that striking your child or losing your temper with him is becoming routine, consider professional guidance to help you find more satisfactory ways of coping.

# STROLLERS

Strollers are available in several levels of sturdiness and quality, with a wide price range to match. The one you buy should suit your particular needs and lifestyle. Bigger and more costly is not necessarily better. The best way to make a good choice for your family is to shop carefully and compare various models until you find what you need.

Try before you buy. Make sure that your choice is easy to unfold, fold, and carry. It should have a strong safety restraint to contain an active child. Make sure that the model you choose locks securely in the open position so that it will not collapse and cause harm when you are wheeling your child.

Swivel wheels, at least in the front, make the stroller easier to steer. Push and steer the stroller in the store before you buy. Is it comfortable for you to use? Is it deep enough for your child to be safe? Is the lining safely secured, without decorative features that could break loose and become a hazard?

Do the brakes work easily and well? Will they hold adequately? (Even so, never leave the stroller unattended with a child in it.) If you plan to use the stroller to take your child with you shopping, is there sufficient storage space for groceries or other purchases? Hanging bags on the handles is not a good idea, because the stroller could tip over. If you expect to be out a lot in bad weather, consider a stroller with a protective enclosure that fastens on and zips up to protect your child from the elements.

Some strollers have multiple functions. One type, for example, can be used with a rear-facing car restraint/carrier for an infant, and later without the carrier for a toddler who can sit comfortably unassisted. Depending on the particular model and your needs, a multiple-use device may or may not be a good choice. Ask a lot of questions before you buy.

An umbrella stroller is a very useful item for babies six months and older. When you are not wheeling your child in it, you can fold it up to fit in a closet, corner, trunk, cargo area, floor of a vehicle, or over your arm (like an umbrella), ready at the next moment of need.

Whatever you choose, you should check out the safety record of that particular model. Consult the Consumer Product Safety Commission's up-to-date recall list. That is especially true if you are considering buying or borrowing a secondhand stroller.

Early in 2001, for example, there was a recall of about 650,000 car restraint/carrier combination strollers after nearly seven hundred complaints about the stroller collapsing or the carrier portion breaking loose. The 250 injuries reported included a broken elbow, three concussions, and two skull fractures, as well as minor injuries. The particular models involved in the recall were on sale from 1996 until March of 2001. The strollers have since been redesigned, and the company offered a free repair kit to parents who had purchased the risky models. Be careful that you don't end up with a potentially dangerous stroller that was not well designed or properly repaired to make it safe.

# STUTTERING OR STAMMERING

As a child's speech is developing, some hesitations, repetition of sounds, or even long pauses because the right word isn't there should be considered normal. Fluency takes time to develop, and few preschool children will speak perfectly and smoothly. The greater the fuss you make about the way your child speaks, the greater the chance you will cause a problem where there might not have been one. Efforts to prevent stuttering and stammering—well intentioned as those efforts might be—often reinforce the child's tendency toward speech problems, and insure that problems will continue.

There are likely to be occasions when your child wants to say something but the words, unable to keep up with the thoughts, stumble or tumble out not quite right. Try to listen and respond to the context of what your child is saying, not the specific techniques of forming and putting the words together. Do not continually correct your child's efforts to communicate. Be careful not to make him self-conscious about speech. If you are concerned about your child's speech development, consult your health-care provider for advice. Chances are time, patience, understanding, and a conscious effort on your part not to pressure your child will be all the remedy that's needed. If there is a problem requiring further assistance, the health-care provider can refer you to a qualified speech therapist.

# SUDDEN INFANT DEATH SYNDROME (SIDS)

Sudden infant death syndrome (SIDS), sometimes referred to as crib death, is the sudden and unexpected death of an apparently well or almost-well infant whose death remains unexplained even after an autopsy. Although the chances are small that you would ever be faced with the problem directly, there are some facts you should know.

Recent research has shown that sleep position can affect the chances of a baby falling victim to SIDS. Although many generations of parents were taught to put their babies to sleep on their stomachs, it is now known that a baby should *not* be allowed to sleep on her stomach. The risk of crib death is greatly reduced by the simple act of placing a baby on her back to sleep. (See *"Back to sleep,"* page 20.) Make sure that anyone who cares for your child knows that she is to be placed on her back for nap or bedtime. It is especially important to communicate that fact to older relatives or caregivers who might be unaware of the new research.

Infants who are exposed to secondhand cigarette smoke have an increased risk of sudden infant death syndrome. Although there is much that is not known about SIDS, you can help make your baby safer. Do not allow anyone to smoke in your home. (See *Smoking*, page 161.)

Most crib deaths occur among infants two to four months of age. Few infants over six months are involved. Some "near-miss" babies narrowly escape SIDS because someone just happened to be right there when the baby stopped breathing. If you notice your baby stop breathing and turn blue for no apparent reason, begin mouth-to-mouth rescue breathing immediately. (See *Breathing emergency*, pages 42–43.) Tactile stimulation— holding and touching the baby—may also help.

Report any such "near misses" to your baby's health-care provider. An infant at risk of SIDS can be placed on a monitor to alert you to any interruption of breathing or heartbeat. Most victims of SIDS, however, give no advance warning of a problem. The parents of such a child must understand that their sad loss does not imply guilt on their part.

# SUGAR

Most children consume far more sugar than is good for them. Even if parents make an effort to avoid the obvious sources of sugar, the typical American diet contains many sweet substances that are not so readily identifiable. It is not just candy or sweet desserts that contain sugar; you may find sugar in products ranging from toothpaste to ketchup and peanut butter. Children's chewable vitamins and a number of breakfast cereals aimed directly at the child market contain sugar as a major ingredient.

Excess sugar should be avoided in your child's diet. Sugar can contribute to tooth decay, obesity, and the potential for diabetes. For some children, excessive sugar consumption seems to be related to hyperactivity. Too much sugar in the diet can take the place of other necessary nutrients. (See *Nutrition,* pages 130–137.)

For most children it is not necessary to eliminate sugar from the diet completely, and you would probably find it difficult to do so even if you wanted to. Awareness of the many ways sugar is used in today's foods will enable you to plan your child's diet sensibly so that an excess of sugar can be avoided. (See *Candy and sweets,* page 44.)

- When you first introduce solid foods to your child, avoid any temptation to add a little sugar to make things "taste better." Allow your child to become accustomed to the natural taste of foods.
- Read labels carefully. Not all sugar is called "sugar." Watch for ingredients that end in *-ose,* such as fructose or dextrose; they are sugars too. Honey, molasses, maple syrup, and corn syrup are also sugars. Brown sugar is still sugar; it has molasses in it.
- When you read product labels, remember that ingredients are listed in order of importance in the item. Be alert for and try to avoid products in which sugar plays a major role.
- Stay away from presweetened cereals, sugared vitamins, and highly sweetened drinks such as Kool-Aid. Many of these contain artificial colors as well as too much sugar.
- Do not fall into the trap of using candy or desserts as behavior-management devices. Using sweets as bribes gives them even more appeal than they normally would have.

# SUNBURN

Direct exposure to the sun for any extended period of time can be a serious problem for babies and toddlers, whose tender skin is especially sensitive to the ultraviolet rays that cause sunburn. It is now known that a child who has one or more severe sunburns, or repeated mild sunburns, may later be more prone to skin problems such as premature aging and skin cancer.

How long you can permit your child to remain in the sun depends, of course, on the season, the time of day, where you live, and what that day's weather is like. Three minutes of midday summer sun on a hot day might be too much. An hour of late afternoon sunshine on a spring or fall day might be pleasant and harmless. Use common sense, extra caution, and sunscreen when planning sunny outings for your child. Note that babies under six months of age cannot use sunscreen.

## SUNBURN PREVENTION

- Keep in mind that a sunburn does not really show or hurt until the damage is done. By the time your child complains or the skin looks red, it's too late.
- A baby or toddler is likely to be more sensitive to the sun than you are. Fair-skinned children (and adults) are usually more sensitive than those with darker skin.

- Areas of the skin that are rarely exposed to sun and air (the diaper area, for example) are more likely to burn than parts of the body that are not kept covered all the time. Remember that before you let your toddler romp around the yard or the beach without clothes.
- If you go to the beach or anywhere you will be spending a lot of time in the sun, keep your child comfortably covered to avoid sunburn. Use a shirt with long sleeves, long pants, and a hat with a wide brim all around. No matter how stylish, a baseball cap worn backward does not protect the nose and face. If there is no natural shade available, a beach umbrella is a must.
- Infants are especially vulnerable. A child under a year should not be allowed to sunbathe even with sunscreen. Consult your health-care provider about using sunscreen on a baby, and always keep the child covered.
- For toddlers and older children, apply sunscreen about thirty minutes before exposure. Renew it frequently. Even waterproof sunscreen tends to wash off if the child is in the water or perspires heavily. In strong sun, it may be wise to use sunscreen even under clothing such as a T-shirt, which may let some of the rays in.
- Choose sunscreen with a sun protection factor (SPF) of at least 15. If you have any questions about what you should be using, ask your child's health-care provider.
- Be alert to situations in which sunburn could occur even when it might seem less likely. Winter sun, especially reflecting off snow, can be a serious problem. Some ultraviolet rays can get through even on cloudy days. Don't let the sun going behind a cloud lull you into a false sense of security. Use a window shade in the car for a long ride on sunny days.

## TREATMENT FOR SUNBURN

Prevention is the best treatment for sunburn. If it is already too late for prevention, here are some suggestions.

• Put your child in a cool (not icy or cold) bath as quickly as possible. Apply cool water compresses several times a day to the most painful parts. If a cool bath is not available, wrap your child in a cool, wet towel or shirt.
• An Aveeno oatmeal bath can soothe sunburned skin. You can buy Aveeno in most pharmacies. Follow the directions. A cool Epsom salt bath might also help.
• Calamine lotion is soothing. Apply it generously.
• Vitamin E oil is expensive, but some people find it to aid in healing.
• To avoid further irritation, have the child wear very soft, loose-fitting clothing. Stay out of the sun completely until your child's skin is healed.

If your child appears badly burned or seems to be very uncomfortable, consult your health-care provider promptly. Call for medical help immediately if the child has nausea, chills, or fever.

# SWADDLING

Tightly wrapping, or swaddling, your new baby may help her to feel secure as well as warm. Some babies seem to sleep more soundly and for longer periods of time if they are swaddled.

Here is one way to wrap your baby securely in a square receiving blanket. First fold one corner of the blanket halfway toward the middle. Place the baby's head on that folded corner. Next bring the opposite corner up over the baby's feet. Then wrap the other two corners over the baby, one over the other.

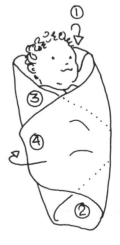

# SWALLOWED OBJECTS

Mobile babies and toddlers tend to put things in their mouths, which is why small objects should be kept safely out of reach. No matter how careful you are, however, there may be an occasion when your child has swallowed something you wish she hadn't. In most cases, if a swallowed object reaches the stomach, the object will pass right on through the digestive system without a problem. (See *Choking*, pages 58–59, for dealing with objects that are inhaled.)

If the swallowed object is something that might get stuck and cause harm, call your health-care provider.

# SWIMMING

In some places there are swimming programs available for infants and toddlers. Many young children seem to enjoy these programs. Make sure that the pool you are using has warm water and be careful that your child does not get chilled.

If the idea of infant swimming classes does not appeal to you, don't bother. You have not failed as a parent if your three-year-old still doesn't swim, although swimming is a pleasurable, healthful, and useful skill which at some point should be included in your child's education. If there are no good swimming programs for very young children in your area, it is best not to force the issue. A bad early experience in the water can set your child back and cause fears that would be difficult to overcome.

Even if your baby or toddler does learn to swim, the acquisition of that skill does not eliminate or even diminish the need for supervision in water activities. An unattended baby could drown in the bathtub even if he knows how to swim. Swimming skill is no guarantee of safety for young children playing unsupervised near a body of water or at poolside.

# TALKING

You need not consciously or deliberately teach your child to talk. In fact, you probably couldn't even if you wanted to. Learning to talk has its own built-in timetable. For most children, speech develops at its own pace and in its own way. While there are no special "talking lessons" you could or should sit down to teach your child, there are things you can do to facilitate and support her oral language development.

Listening and comprehending are essential steps a child must take in learning to talk. One of the best things you can do for your child's oral language learning is to give him lots of conversation to listen to. Talk to your child, and in the presence of your child. Providing examples of ongoing conversation is far more useful than trying to teach the child to say certain words or phrases as you would train a parrot.

Provide opportunity for your child to learn the meaning of words and phrases. Label things and point them out as you say what they are. Describe events as they are happening, so that the child can see the connection between words and what is going on.

Your child's language will develop best in a pleasant and supportive social context. If you are pleased with your child's early language efforts, he or she is likely to keep on trying. If, on the other hand, you keep correcting the child and try to insist that articulation be clear and syntax correct, you will probably end up with more tension than talking. (See *Baby talk,* page 18. For specific suggestions and activities as your child learns to talk, see pages 116–120.)

# TANTRUMS

Tantrums are not uncommon among children between the ages of one and three, so don't be surprised if your toddler has a tantrum from time to time. A tantrum is a way for a toddler, who does not yet possess all the language she needs to communicate, to express anger and deal with frustration. A child trying to become independent who is baffled or frustrated may respond by lying down and kicking, screaming and banging on the floor, or by tearing around in an uncontrolled rage.

Some children, particularly bright and very active ones, may get a bit carried away with their efforts to achieve independence. They know what they want and they become fiercely angry when they can't get it. Although tantrums are a normal toddler response to being frustrated, that does not mean you have to encourage them as a means of self expression. It's best to handle tantrums in a way that will minimize their frequency and their ill effects.

## COPING WITH A TANTRUM

The exact strategy for coping with your child's tantrums will, of course, depend on how your child reacts. Use what works best for you.

- Do not bother trying to talk sense to a toddler who is in the middle of a tantrum. Reason and rage do not operate simultaneously.
- Keep your child from getting hurt or from hurting anyone else during a tantrum. You may need to protect things from your rampaging child. Either move the child or move objects from her path.
- Do not hit, spank, or use physical force to fight back or try to stop the tantrum. Remember that a child in a tantrum is not being deliberately naughty, but is temporarily out of control.
- Ignoring the tantrum works well in many situations. That is especially true if an audience seems to intensify your child's tantrum behavior. Make sure the child is safe, stay out of the way, and let the tantrum run its course.
- If you are unable or unwilling to ignore your child's tantrum, here's another approach. Hold the child gently on the floor to keep him safe. Your presence, along with kind, gentle firmness, can be reassuring and comforting when the rage starts to decrease. You may, instead of holding the child on the floor, hold him in your arms if you are able to do so. This works for many children, but not for all.

- A few children become even more violent when touched or held during a tantrum. If your child is one of these, don't fight back with physical force. Clear the path, stay out of the way, and be ready to move in quickly when the tantrum subsides.
- If the tantrum is happening in a public place (the playground, an aisle in a supermarket, or a restaurant, for example) remove the child from the situation as quickly as possible so you can deal with the tantrum in your own way. Just leave. You can finish your shopping (or whatever) later. Ignore unsolicited input from strangers on the scene.
- Do not reward the tantrum, but do not punish it either. A child should score no points for stopping a tantrum, but should not lose any for having had one, either. When the tantrum is over, pick up exactly where you left off.
- As soon as the tantrum starts to subside, get on with whatever activity makes sense at the time. Try to get the child actively involved in doing something—a story, a nap, a game, a walk outside, or a snack—it doesn't really matter as long as what you do is neither a reward nor a punishment for the tantrum. Whatever follows should be a rapid return to normal routine.

## PREVENTING FUTURE TANTRUMS

Although there is no foolproof way to ensure that your child never has any more tantrums, there are steps you can take to minimize their occurrence. It's important not to give in to whatever caused a tantrum. If it was a forbidden sweet your child wanted, for example, don't produce one at the tantrum's end. If refusal to put on shoes was the tantrum trigger, don't give in and permit a barefoot afternoon. If demand for a product you didn't want started a tantrum in the supermarket, don't buy the item just to keep the peace. If you yield in hopes of ending a tantrum quickly, your child will learn that she can use temper to manipulate you.

Children are more likely to have tantrums when tired. If fatigue seems to contribute to your child's tantrum behavior, try to prevent it. If an extra nap isn't possible, at least try to avoid situations that are likely to add additional frustration to the child's tiredness. Other discomforts may also contribute to the likelihood of a tantrum. A comfortable child—not too warm or too cold, not hungry, not insecure or anxious—is less likely to have a tantrum than a child who is stressed.

Try to divert your child from a situation that is likely to cause a tantrum. That does not mean you should give in to a child's whims and inappropriate demands. It does mean, however, that you should be clever enough to present your demands and requests in a way that does not set up a power play. Make a game out of getting dressed, for example, instead of provoking conflict by demanding that your child sit still for the shoes.

Above all, be tactful and courteous to your child. Never respond to a tantrum by descending to toddler emotional level, no matter how tempting such an approach might seem in the heat of the moment. There will be many times you will need to make your child do something he does not want to do. Try to leave your child a way to get out of an impossible situation without losing face. Be as nice as you can be. Remember that you are the mature and wise one in the relationship. (See *Contrariness*, pages 65–66, and *Discipline*, pages 80–81.)

# TEASING

Teasing a baby or toddler is not an appropriate form of entertainment for either of you, although it may seem fairly harmless at the time. A young child is not an able match for an adult or even an older child. Do not allow older children to tease your child.

Don't use teasing, ridicule, or sarcasm as a form of discipline. Remember that a young child tends to take everything at face value. A literal-minded youngster may not be able to distinguish between a teasing remark said in jest and one that is intended to be carried out. Who knows what a child really thinks and feels, for example, when a parent says something like, "Do that again and I'll kill you." There is no need to add anxiety or unhappiness to the child's situation. (See *Discipline,* pages 80–81, and *Rough play,* pages 150–151.)

# TEETHING

Teething causes considerable discomfort for some babies and may be accompanied by drooling, irritability, and a tendency to put any sort of object into the mouth. Teething may go on virtually unnoticed for other babies, and you'll hardly know it's happening until a click on the spoon tells you your child has her first tooth.

The diagram on page 173 shows the usual order and approximate timing of the arrival of a child's baby teeth. Keep in mind, however, that these times may vary quite a bit from one child to another. A baby who gets teeth early is not necessarily bright or more advanced in other ways, and late teething is not an indication of backwardness.

The first teeth are generally cut with a minimum of distress. If it is just the first teeth your child is getting, problems such as digestive upset, diarrhea, or fever are likely to be unrelated to teething, and may be a sign of some other illness. If your baby seems sick, consult your health-care provider. Don't blame the symptoms on teething and hope they will go away.

The first and second molars are likely to cause the most teething discomfort. Your child might be irritable, cranky, or even downright miserable for some time while these teeth are coming in. Here are some suggestions to ease the discomforts of teething for your child.

- Cold eases gum pain. Give your child an ice cube wrapped in a handkerchief or tied into a clean baby sock. Freeze some juice in a paper cup until it's mushy and let your child sip it or take it with a spoon.
- A hard rubber teething ring or toy for chewing may provide some relief, or at least some diversion from the discomfort. A gel-filled teething ring that you can cool in the refrigerator provides something cold and comforting to chew on.
- Massage the child's sore gums with your finger. That may help, and it indicates to your child that you understand about the hurting and that you care.
- A popular and effective old-time remedy for teething pain is to rub a bit of brandy or whiskey on the child's sore gums. If you are comfortable with the idea, try it.
- Don't administer pain relievers such as acetaminophen, baby aspirin, or fever drops unless your child's health-care provider specifically instructs you to do so. She may suggest a topical pain reliever such as Orajel.

172

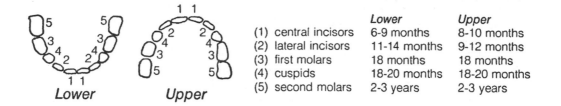

| | | Lower | Upper |
|---|---|---|---|
| (1) | central incisors | 6-9 months | 8-10 months |
| (2) | lateral incisors | 11-14 months | 9-12 months |
| (3) | first molars | 18 months | 18 months |
| (4) | cuspids | 18-20 months | 18-20 months |
| (5) | second molars | 2-3 years | 2-3 years |

If your child seems to be in a lot of pain, check carefully to make sure that there is not another problem. An obviously troubled child who keeps touching the side of his face, for example, may be suffering from an earache rather than new teeth. If you have concerns, call your child's health-care provider for advice. (See *Dental care (professional)*, pages 77–78.)

# TELEVISION

Most children watch far too much television in today's world. Many preschool children spend a substantial portion of their waking hours in front of the television set. What does the daily dose of television do to or for children? How can you use television wisely as entertainment and an educational tool without allowing it to be the dominant force in your child's life? You can and must be in control. Here are some things to consider.

## SOME TV PLUSSES

- Television has the potential to expose children to a wide variety of interesting people, places, and things that they might never have the opportunity to experience in person.
- Television can help increase a child's vocabulary by exposing the child to new words and their meanings in context.
- Some (but not all) children's programming may teach useful skills or send appropriate messages to preschool children. Some youngsters do, for example, learn letters and number concepts from *Sesame Street. Mr. Rogers' Neighborhood* (available in reruns since the host's retirement) provides social lessons and information in a calm, low key tone. You might find the program boring, but a very young child is likely to find it interesting as well as reassuring. Mr. Rogers (or similar programming) should not be used as a substitute for your conversations with your own child, however.
- Television can attract and maintain a child's attention. The time an active toddler spends watching TV may give caregivers a chance to accomplish other essential tasks.
- If you select the programs carefully, television has the potential to provide suitable role models and interesting experiences for young children.

## SOME TV MINUSES

- Television requires nothing of the child other than sitting in front of it. The child passively receives what the screen presents and need not respond actively in any way. Too much television may actually lead to a tendency to process information superficially and could hinder a child's intellectual development.
- Television has a mesmerizing effect. The powerful and ever-changing images may be overwhelming for some very young children.
- Many television programs, from entertainment shows to news broadcasts, contain levels of violence that are unsuitable for children.
- Advertising on television creates unnecessary and artificial demands for numerous products, leaving you with the ongoing task of teaching your toddler he cannot have everything he sees or wants.
- Television takes valuable time that could be better spent looking at books, playing with suitable toys, being outside in the fresh air, or interacting with other people.
- Although television may add to a young child's list of known vocabulary words, it may also cut down on personal interactions essential to the development of language as a tool for communication.
- Although television can provide suitable role models for children, it frequently does not. Television often shows sex-role and minority-group stereotypes and unrealistic depictions of various occupations.

## USING TELEVISION WISELY

- You must control your child's television viewing. Don't leave program choices to a V-chip, a baby-sitter, or to your child. Carefully monitor the content of the programs your child watches.
- Control the amount of time your child spends watching television. Make your own decision about how much is too much, but keep in mind that less is probably better. You should be the custodian of the remote. If you decide to eliminate television from your toddler's life, you will have done no harm, and will have more time for other things.
- Talk with your child about what she has seen on television. Encourage active responding and application of appropriate learnings to other activities.
- Do not leave the television on continuously. Turn it on for specific programs and then turn it off. Do not keep the TV on as background noise for the rest of family life.
- Do not let your child sit too close to the set, and make sure the volume is not too loud.
- Do not routinely use television as an electronic baby-sitter. There may be times when it would be useful to keep your toddler engaged while you do something nearby that you must do. Just don't make a regular habit of it.
- Be especially careful to minimize the violence your child is exposed to on the television screen. You must pay careful attention, because program descriptions are not always accurate.
- Give your child lots of other things to do. A child who is busy with interesting activities does not need to sit passively in front of a television set.

# TEMPERATURE (OF INDOOR ENVIRONMENT) _____

Don't keep your child in overheated rooms or wrapped up in too many layers of clothing. Some conscientious parents mistakenly believe that it is necessary to keep a child's room especially warm. Your baby or toddler will do nicely, however, at whatever temperature you normally keep your home. If you need a sweater to be comfortable, your child probably needs one too. As a general rule, however, a child does not need more layers of clothing than you do, so don't put an extra sweater on the child just to be on the safe side. Parents often overdress their children and that practice, although well meaning, is unhealthy.

Let your own comfort and common sense be a guide. Don't be misled by the temperature of your child's hands. A young child's hands customarily feel cool. If you keep putting additional layers of clothing on the child in an effort to warm up the hands, you will have an uncomfortable and very warm child indeed.


# TEMPERATURE (TAKING CHILD'S) _____

If you suspect that your child might have a fever, the only reliable way to be sure is to take his temperature. Feeling the forehead will not give you an accurate indication if fever is present. You should have a rectal thermometer (the kind with the short, round, bulbous end) readily available in your medicine cabinet or first-aid kit, because you never know when you might need it. Mercury is now known to pose health risks; make sure your thermometer uses a mercury substitute or is digital. Never put a thermometer in the mouth of a child under five. Here's how to take your child's temperature.

## RECTAL METHOD

The rectal method is the most accurate and, once you get used to it, actually quite easy.

1. Shake the thermometer down to make sure that the mercury substitute is well below the normal mark. Just hold the thermometer (not over a table or other hard surface) by the high temperature end and snap your wrist sharply a few times.
2. Lubricate the bulb of the thermometer with a dab of petroleum jelly (such as Vaseline).
3. Hold the child facedown on your lap or on a convenient and safe surface. Spread the buttocks slightly and insert the thermometer into the anal opening about an inch. If you meet resistance, don't force. Try again gently. Don't let go of the child or the thermometer at any time. If you are having trouble holding your child still, you may be able to get a fairly accurate reading in a minute, although at least two and preferably three minutes would be better.

4. Remove the thermometer and read the temperature. Write it down so you remember the number accurately. Be sure that you know how to read the thermometer correctly before you need to use it. If you are uncertain, don't be afraid or embarrassed to ask your health-care provider for help.

## AXILLARY METHOD

The axillary (armpit) method is not quite as accurate as the rectal method, but it does have the advantage of allowing you to take the child's temperature when she is asleep if that is necessary. Use the same thermometer you would use for the rectal method.

1. Shake the thermometer down.
2. Place the thermometer in the child's armpit and hold the arm gently to his side. Make sure that the tip of the thermometer is touching the child's skin and that no clothing gets in the way.
3. Wait at least three minutes. Remove the thermometer from the armpit. Read and record the temperature.

## OTHER METHODS

Oral thermometers are unsuitable for children under five. The ear thermometer, which is fairly costly (about $50), is easy to use but not accurate. One recent study indicated that the ear thermometer missed about half of low-grade fevers and nearly one fourth of fevers over 102.2 degrees F. Some health-care providers, furthermore, advise against using ear thermometer for babies because an infant's small ear canal may lead to an inaccurate reading.

Another type of thermometer is a forehead scanner, which is stroked over the child's forehead to determine a reading. Not only is the device very expensive (about $80), but it is not particularly accurate. As the technology improves, that might change. Ask your health-care provider if there are any new developments in devices for taking your child's temperature. The rectal method, however, remains the method of choice for accuracy.

Whichever method you use to take your child's temperature, you should be consistent from one time to the next. When you report a reading to your child's health-care provider, be sure to identify the method used.

# TERRIBLE TWOS _____

Even before your toddler gets there, you'll probably hear warnings about the "terrible twos." Be careful, however, not to let such talk turn into a self-fulfilling prophecy. While life with a two-year-old is likely to have its terrible moments from time to time, there will be many pleasant and wonderful times that just don't seem to get enough attention. People who point out how delightful and exciting two-year-olds can be are about as frequent as newspaper headlines that proclaim good news. Nevertheless, many things about being two can be terrific rather than terrible.

An excellent book for parents of a toddler is *Making the "Terrible" Twos Terrific!* by John Rosemond (Andrews and McMeel, Kansas City: 1993). This book provides common-sense suggestions and structure for living with a two-year-old based on the developmental characteristics of the age.

While the typical two-year-old may well provide you with contrariness, tantrums, dawdling, or troublesome curiosity, she can also cause delight with responsiveness, love, language, and new accomplishments. Make an effort to notice and enjoy all the good things, because someday not too far off you'll probably be wondering where all the time has gone and why it passed so fast. (See *Contrariness*, pages 65–66, *Curiosity*, page 72, *Dawdling*, page 73, *Discipline*, pages 80–81, and *Tantrums*, pages 170–171.)

# THRUSH

Thrush is a fungus infection that babies sometimes get inside the mouth. Thrush is sometimes related to the use of antibiotics, but not always. Thrush is the same fungus (monilia) that often causes a woman to have vaginal infections during pregnancy.

Symptoms of thrush in your baby's mouth are white flaky spots that look like curdled milk. These spots do not wash off the way milk curds do, however, and the spots may be tender or painful and may even bleed.

Consult your health-care provider if you suspect that your baby might have thrush. Prescribed medication may be appropriate. If you are breast-feeding, be sure to keep your nipples clean. Ask your care provider if medication is recommended for you as well as for your baby. Sterilize any rubber nipples or pacifiers that your baby is using.

# THUMB-SUCKING

Some children suck a thumb, finger, or fist to satisfy comfort needs. The thumb is a built-in, safe, and portable pacifier that is always there when the child needs it. It is always under the child's control. A child who sucks his thumb does so because the practice is pleasurable and comforting. When the need is no longer there, the sucking will stop.

If your child sucks her thumb, it's best to ignore it. The bigger deal you make of it, the more likely you are to prolong the practice. Parents who resort to bribes, threats, punishment, ridicule, or substances that taste nasty are actually giving thumb-sucking far more attention and importance than it deserves.

If you set up combat with your child over thumb-sucking, you will create unnecessary tensions that may increase the inclination to use the thumb as a comfort device. Provide a secure and loving environment, and leave thumb-sucking alone. Chances are the habit will diminish and disappear when the time is right. (See *Comfort habits*, pages 63–64.)

# TOILET TRAINING AND LEARNING

Few child-rearing topics engender as much talk, fuss, tension, and overthinking as toilet training. What can and should be just another step in a child's development often becomes a source of anxiety and failure for both child and parents. There is no need to let that happen.

Toilet training is what the caregivers do; toilet learning is the child's accomplishment. True toilet learning cannot occur until a child is able and willing. The child must recognize the need to go, hold the urine or bowel movement until she is on the toilet or potty, and then release it. Most children are not ready—either physiologically or psychologically—to accomplish those steps until at least the middle of their second year.

Most children, regardless of when toilet training efforts are begun, are able to stay relatively dry and clean by the age of two-and-a-half to three years. Earlier starts at training do not typically lead to earlier successes, but do drag the process out much longer and provide more opportunity for conflict.

## READINESS FOR TOILET LEARNING

It is best to begin your child's toilet training when he is ready to learn. Readiness usually occurs some time between eighteen and thirty months of age. Here are some signs that a child is ready.

- When she regularly wakes up dry in the morning or after a nap, and stays dry for two or more hours between diaper changes during the day, she is probably ready.
- A child who is ready to use the toilet tells you when he is about to go. Before that readiness, most children are able to tell you that they are in the process of going.
- A child who asks to be changed or who attempts to change her own diaper is ready to begin learning to use the toilet.

- A child who asks to use the toilet or shows some interest in the process is indicating readiness.

When your child shows these signs of readiness, it is time to begin teaching him how to use the toilet. Be careful not to wait so long that the period of optimum readiness passes by. If you don't teach your child when the signs of readiness are noted, she might lose interest. If that happens, training will not be as easy as it might have been when enthusiasm and eagerness were working with you.

## TOILET EQUIPMENT

A small potty chair that the child can get on and off of without help is best. A few children fear the height of a seat attached to an adult toilet, and some are frightened by the noise of a flushing toilet. Even if your child has no such fears, a toddler-size potty toilet is easier to manage. Remove the deflector designed to keep a little boy's urine in the pot to avoid injury. The sooner a little boy learns to urinate standing up, the better. The pot should be easy to remove and to empty. Many children take pride in completing this final step of using the small toilet successfully.

Don't spend money on a potty chair that plays a tune or rings a bell when the urine or bowel movement is deposited in the bowl. The novelty of such an item quickly wears off, and may even distract the child from the task at hand. Also, some clever children quickly discover that a glass of juice or a small toy thrown into the pot does just as well as the intended products.

Toddlers usually find rolls of toilet tissue to be great fun. The roll will last longer if it is out of reach of the child's potty chair. Let your child take one handful of toilet tissue before sitting down. For bowel movements, a disposable wipe will be easier for the child to use. Remember to teach a little girl to wipe from front to back so that germs from the bowel movement are not introduced into the vagina.

## WHEN YOUR CHILD IS READY

When your child wakes up dry, the potty chair should be the next stop. Suggest using the potty when you think it's time. If the child does not want to, don't force the issue. Be pleased at the successes and do not make a big fuss over the inevitable failures. Simply say, "Next time try to put the peepee [or whatever term you use] in the little toilet over there." If you make clear what the child is supposed to do, and provide encouragement and support, chances are the child will learn to use the toilet quite readily. If you make a big deal or battle out of toilet training, you will increase the likelihood of a long-term problem.

While your child is learning to use the toilet or potty, make it as easy for him to succeed as possible. During the day in the house, you might find pull-up disposable pants to be helpful. You can't expect a toddler to negotiate the removal of a diaper in time to go. A bare bottom or underpants will work too, if you can handle the inevitable accidents. Praise your child for trying. Continue to use diapers at night and during naps if necessary. Do what makes the most sense to you; there is no one right way.

## AN ALTERNATIVE APPROACH

If you think you would prefer more direction in toilet training your child, try reading *Toilet Training in Less Than a Day* by Nathan H. Azrin and Richard M. Foxx, Ph.D. (Pocket Books, New York: 1974). This structured behavior-modification approach to training your child to use the toilet is very effective if used as directed.

Do not be misled by the "less than a day" claim in the title. You still have to wait until your child is ready before using this technique, and many children continue to have accidents even after learning what they are to do. Nevertheless, the book can help you communicate to your child what is expected, and the step-by-step guidelines leave little to the imagination.

If you do decide to try this approach, consider using edible or tangible rewards other than candy to reinforce the desired toileting behavior. Candy will work, but it is unwise to build the experience of sweets into your child's expectations. By doing that you may introduce a new problem, even though you accomplish the toilet training.

# TONSILS

Tonsils are masses of lymphoid tissue on each side of the throat that act as a filter to trap disease-causing germs. In misguided efforts to prevent sore throats and upper respiratory problems, tonsils used to be routinely removed if they became enlarged. That is no longer done. It is now recognized that the tonsils are an important part of the body's defense mechanism against infection.

Most young children have enlarged tonsils. In a child, however, enlarged tonsils are not necessarily the sign of a problem but are more likely to be an indication that the tonsils are actively working at their job. In current practice, removal of the tonsils in a child under five is almost never indicated. Even tonsils scarred by infection are likely to have some capacity to perform their function.

Consult your health-care provider for advice if your child frequently seems to have a sore throat with swollen and sore tonsils. A throat culture may be done to see if the germs are bacterial in nature. If so, an antibiotic will be prescribed. Try to make your child as comfortable as possible. Fluids, especially cold ones, may help. If your house tends to be dry, add moisture to the air. (See *Vaporizers,* page 186.) Fortunately, sore throats involving the tonsils tend to become less frequent as a child gets older.

# TOOTH CARE (DAILY)

Daily care of the teeth should begin early, even before the first teeth have actually come in. Start with cleaning the gums to promote good oral health and to get your baby used to that kind of attention. At least twice a day after a feeding, gently wipe the baby's gums with a clean, wet cloth. One of the most important things you can do for your child's oral health is not to let her fall asleep with a bottle of milk or juice in her mouth. Naptime and bedtime bottles are a direct path to tooth decay.

As soon as a tooth comes in, it is time to start brushing. At first you will have to do the job. Brush the tooth or teeth gently with a soft-bristled brush. Do not use toothpaste at first. When the child has six or more teeth, it's time to add a little toothpaste to the process. Choose a fluoridated toothpaste but avoid a tartar-control paste, which could be abrasive and is also unnecessary for a very young child. Brush at least twice a day. If it is impossible to brush after a meal, the child should take a little bit of water to rinse the remaining food off the teeth.

Soon your child will try to imitate you and take over the brushing efforts. Encourage him to do so, but you will still have to help to make sure the job is done well. When there are two adjacent back teeth, introduce flossing once a day. That is a task for you, because a toddler will be unable to manipulate the floss and do the job. It's easiest to floss your child's teeth from behind. Let him stand in front of you facing away, while you reach around and floss. If you sit, the child can lean his head back into your lap.

Be sure to set a good example for your child. She will be more likely to take tooth care seriously if you brush your teeth regularly. Beginning by age three, regular visits to a dentist are a good idea. (See *Dental care (professional)*, pages 77–78.)

# TOY SAFETY

When choosing a toy for your child's use, use your best judgment to decide whether or not that toy is safe. The recall of an unsafe toy may eventually remove that item from the marketplace, but that typically does not happen until after children have been injured or killed. Use common sense along with the following guidelines from the U.S. Consumer Products Safety Commission.

- Do not give a baby or toddler toys intended for older children. What may be quite safe for a third grader could be very dangerous for a two-year-old.
- Be alert for things that could be swallowed. Avoid tiny toys, or toys with parts your child could remove.
- Don't let your toddler play with sharp or pointed objects such as knives, scissors, or knitting needles. Beware of seemingly safe toys that could be dismantled to reveal sharp features.
- Electrical toys that require plugging in are not safe for young children. Make sure that any battery-operated toy is specifically designed for toddler use before turning your child loose with it.
- Toys that shoot things (darts, arrows, rockets, etc.) are never safe for young children. Even those with so-called "safety" rubber tips could seriously damage a child's eye. Such tips, furthermore, can often be removed to create additional hazards.
- Avoid toys with sharp edges. Even if an item doesn't start out with sharp edges, make sure it is strong enough not to be broken into sharp-edged pieces.
- Keep things with strings away from babies and toddlers. Never let a toddler take a pull toy to bed.
- Avoid toys such as cap pistols or guns that make extremely loud noises. Such items can damage a child's hearing as well as irritate caregivers and encourage violent play.

- Beware of toys and trinkets distributed by fast-food outlets along with meals packed for children. They may be poorly made with parts that can break and cause harm. Tens of millions of these toys have been recalled in the last few years. Even if there is a warning that the toy is intended only for children over three, your toddler could have the toy in one hand and a piece of fast food in the other before you could stop her. It is best not to get your toddler started on the fast-food habit or any connection between eating and free toys.

Do not store your child's toys in a toy box or trunk with a lid. Such storage containers have been known to trap young children and cause serious injury, or even death. Even if the container is not large enough to contain the child, the lid could close on small fingers and smash them. Open cardboard containers covered with contact paper are an attractive, safe, and economical choice.

# TOYS

Toys are a child's tools for learning as well as for entertainment. Young children learn by doing—touching, manipulating, and playing with things. While it's important to make toys available to your child, it is not necessary to spend a lot of money to do so.

Everyday objects around the house and yard are likely to be more interesting and appealing in the long run than elaborate or expensive purchased playthings. The same toddler who rapidly tires of the costly doll that does everything—walk, talk, drink, wet, and wave bye-bye—may willingly spend hour after hour with a few old pots, pans, and spoons, creating lovely dirt and leaf dinners for you and imaginary playmates. Use your imagination and allow your child to do the same.

Here are some guidelines for buying toys.

- Toys for a baby or toddler should be sturdy, safe, and washable. Even if you think your child is mature for his age, don't risk providing a toy designed for older children.
- Choose toys that encourage a child to be creative and imaginative. Avoid complicated items that do the entire job with little or no input from the child.
- Study the item itself carefully before you buy. Don't be fooled by the packaging. A toy labeled "educational" may not be.
- Buy toys you will allow your child to actually use. If you can't stand noise, for example, don't purchase your child a drum set and then get annoyed when he beats away. Don't buy a wheeled riding toy if the only place it could be used is in the living room, where you won't permit it.
- To avoid creating stereotyped sex roles for your toddler, be sure to include some toys that traditionally have been associated with children of the opposite sex. Try tools or a model sports car for a girl, for example, and small cleaning implements and a doll for a boy.

# TRAVEL

Travel with a baby or toddler can be a challenge, but with careful planning it can also be fun. If your intended travels will take you to hotels, it is best to plan ahead and make reservations in advance.

When you make reservations, be sure to find out what will be available for your child. Reserve a crib in advance, and inquire about the safety standards. For a toddler, find out what meal services are available and whether or not a high chair will be provided. Be persistent when making your reservations, and get confirmation of your requests in writing if there is time.

## TRAVEL DOCUMENTS

For international travel, even a newborn will need a passport. As of July 2001, it is required that both parents give written consent before a passport is issued for a child. Previously a child could obtain a passport upon application of only one parent, but the new rules were implemented to reduce cases in which a parent in a custody dispute could leave the country with the child without the other parent knowing about it.

For a listing of documents required to obtain a passport for a child, you can telephone 900-225-5674 or use a computer to go to www.travel.state.gov. Information about what is necessary for a passport may also be available at your local post office or county clerk's office if there is no passport office near you.

It would also be prudent to carry with you a copy of the child's birth certificate. A toddler should always have identification on her person in addition to what you carry. If only one parent is traveling, some destinations may require notarized written permission from the other parent. If one or both parents and/or the child use different surnames, documentation of the relationship might be required in some instances. FamilyTravelForum.com is a contemporary resource that can help you sort out what you would need. Domestic travel is less complicated, but suitable identification for all is appropriate.

## AIR TRAVEL

Make your reservations as early as possible. Depending on your knowledge and personal comfort level with air travel, you may make your own reservations via computer, deal directly with the airline by telephone, or use a travel agent. Reserve your seats when you book your flight. Look at a seating chart for the aircraft scheduled for use on your flight, or consult the airline or your travel agent for help in finding the available row that is best suited for travel with an infant or toddler.

On domestic flights, children under two typically fly free, but they then sit on an adult's lap. On international flights there is usually a charge of 10 percent of the adult fare. Don't count on having an empty seat next to you for your child; these days many planes are flying full or nearly full. If you want the child to have his own seat, you must pay for it.

If you can afford to do so, buying a ticket for a young child is the safest way to fly. Bring a car seat that is federally approved both for vehicles and for air travel. An infant is safest on a plane seat belted into a rear-facing restraint. Although the chances of injury or death in a plane are statistically very small, lap baby passengers have been injured when severe turbulence causes the parent to lose hold. Unrestrained children have been killed in what otherwise might have been a survivable crash.

Most airlines will preboard passengers traveling with small children. If you are traveling with an infant, boarding early makes sense because it gives you time to get you and your baby settled. If you are traveling with an active toddler, however, it is probably better to decline the invitation to get on the plane early. As long as your seats are confirmed, most families find it better to remain outside the plane as long as possible. Preboarding could add thirty to forty-five minutes to the time you would have to keep your toddler in her seat on the airplane.

Pack an easy-to-open, lightweight carry-on flight bag with everything you think you will need en route. Bring extras of key items as a precaution in case your flight is seriously delayed and you cannot get off. You will need bottles for an unweaned baby if you are not breast-feeding; take one bottle of water if you are breast-feeding. If your child is taking solid foods but is not ready for an airline meal, you will need baby food (now available in plastic jars). Bring a generous supply of disposable diapers and wipes. Some airlines have these on board, but don't count on it. One complete change of clothes for your child is also a wise precaution. Here are some suggestions for keeping your child comfortable and, in the case of a toddler, busy during the flight.

- During takeoff and landing, let your child suck. The swallowing will help keep his ears comfortable as the pressure changes. If you prefer not to breast-feed at this time, use the bottle of water. For an older child who has outgrown bottles, this is one time to permit gum chewing or sucking on a sweet.
- If you have paid for a seat for a toddler or an older child, find out what the special children's menu is before you accept it in place of the regular airline meal. A sodium-laden hot dog or a leathery hamburger might not be as wise a choice as the chicken or deli bag everyone else is getting. For a baby still on formula, carry at least a two-day supply with you, especially on international flights, to see you through in case your luggage goes astray.
- For a toddler or older child, bring a bag of things to keep her entertained. Include crayons and a coloring book, small but safe toys, and games. Gift-wrap a series of small surprises that you can use to pass the time and to reward the child for good behavior. Plan a surprise for every twenty to thirty minutes or so. Tell your child that there will be another one if he plays nicely for that time. If you wrap the surprise in a clever way, the unwrapping can consume a lot of time. Some of the surprises might be appropriate munchies such as crackers or fruit.
- No matter how tempting it might be, do not let a mobile baby crawl in the aisle or permit a toddler to wander around during the flight. Even a small bit of turbulence could cause a mishap. It is not acceptable, furthermore, to allow your child to bother other passengers who may or may not find the antics entertaining. Keep your child under control at all times, even though it might not be easy.

## BUS TRAVEL

Although typically less expensive, bus travel for a long distance is likely to be the hardest on you and your child. Avoid it if you can, but if you must travel by bus, be prepared. Bring everything you will need for your child. Pack it in a small, easy-to-handle bag. Especially if the bus is crowded, you will not have room to maneuver. If you are lucky, the droning noise of the bus will keep your child drowsy or sleeping for some of the time.

Be prepared to keep your baby on your lap for the entire trip unless you have paid for two seats. On a bus, there is really nowhere you can go. Practice changing your child's diaper discreetly right on your lap. A bus bathroom is very small and usually unsuitable for tending to an infant or toddler.

For a mobile baby or toddler, pack a surprise bag just as you would for train or plane travel. Make sure the items are safe, but small enough to be played with in a very confined area, because that is all the space you will have.

If your child is inclined toward motion sickness, the bus is probably a poor choice for transportation. If you must travel by bus, ask your child's health-care provider for advice on medication to prevent motion sickness. (See *Motion sickness,* pages 125–126.) Make sure you have a travel-sickness bag handy in case the prevention does not work.

## CAR TRAVEL

The major advantage to long-distance travel in your family vehicle is that it is under your control. You can stop when you wish, or go on a little longer if the trip is going well. If you have forgotten something you need for your child, you can stop somewhere along the way and try to purchase a replacement. To keep a toddler happily occupied in the vehicle, use a bag of gift-wrapped surprises as suggested for planes, trains, or buses.

Be sure your child is securely fastened in a properly installed, approved child restraint every time the vehicle is moving. Make no exceptions. Do not, for example, allow a tired child to lie down on the backseat or in an SUV's cargo area. If your child is inclined to get carsick, follow the suggestions on pages 125–126.

## TRAIN TRAVEL

Long-distance travel by train can be manageable with an infant or toddler if you plan ahead and pack carefully. Some families do enjoy train travel, which does have the advantage of views other than clouds passing by the windows, but a long trip on a train with an active child can be wearying.

Bring everything you will need to care for your child en route. Once you are under way, you will not be able to purchase any child-care items. If you have a lot of luggage with you, pack the things you need for things like diaper changes, feedings, or snacks in a small bag that you can manage with one hand. Try to limit your family's luggage to what you and any other adults or older children can manage without additional help. Don't count on being able to find a porter or baggage cart when you need to.

Do not sit in a car where smoking is permitted. If you reserve seats in advance, make sure you do not have to walk through a smoking car to get to the dining car, snack bar, or restroom. If you bring an umbrella stroller, you can walk your child up and down the aisle. The restrooms designed for the handicapped are spacious enough for you to wheel the stroller in with you. Even if you regularly use cloth diapers, disposables are a must for traveling.

As on a plane, keep your mobile baby or toddler in sight and under control at all times. It is dangerous to allow a child to roam unattended in the aisle.

# UNDERWEIGHT CHILDREN

If you make appropriate foods available to your baby or toddler, chances are he will eat what is necessary as long as you don't make a big deal about mealtime. Do not attempt to force specific foods on a reluctant eater. Young children have strong survival instincts and will not deliberately starve themselves.

If you think your child's weight is not increasing at a rate to keep up with her height, discuss your concerns with your child's health-care provider. Do not make major changes in your child's diet without suitable advice from a professional. A lean build may well be natural for your child, in which case you should leave well enough alone. Long gone are the days when plumpness in a young child was considered a sign of good health and caring parents.

If the child's lack of weight gain is caused by illness, in contrast to a naturally slim build, there are likely to be other symptoms of a problem. If you are concerned, consult a medical professional. (See *Nutrition,* pages 130–137.)

# VAPORIZERS

Overheated dry air can be irritating to the mucous membranes of the nose and throat, and perhaps make children more vulnerable to cold viruses. Using a vaporizer or humidifier to add moisture to the air can help provide a more healthful environment. In air that is moist rather than too dry, a person with a cold or breathing distress is likely to be more comfortable.

It is safer for a mobile baby or toddler to use a cold-mist humidifier rather than a steam vaporizer. If tipped over, a steam vaporizer could cause serious scalding. If your toddler is able to climb out of the crib, don't count on her—even if sick—to stay away from the steam. A cold-mist humidifier puts moisture into the air without the potential hazard of scalding. Pans of water on the radiator will not provide enough moisture to make a significant difference, and containers of boiling water are not safe anywhere near a mobile baby or toddler, so if your child tends to suffer from colds or other respiratory problems, invest in a cold-mist humidifier. You can find one in your local hardware store or pharmacy.

# VIOLENCE _____

We should make every effort to protect our children from exposure to violence wherever we may find it—in personal interactions, toys, the Internet, or on television. You probably will find it impossible to entirely eliminate the examples of violence from your child's environment. Nevertheless, you can take steps to teach your toddler that violent behavior and unbridled aggression are not acceptable.

There is a correlation between the aggressive behavior of children and viewing violence on television. You should monitor your toddler's television fare very closely, therefore, to eliminate those shows in which violence abounds. Do not assume that a show is acceptable simply because it is aimed at a kiddie audience on Saturday morning. Certain children's cartoons may be among the worst offenders. Many toddlers are unable to differentiate between clobbering a playmate in real life and the actions they see on the screen.

Perhaps even more difficult these days than turning off a violent cartoon show is handling the violence on the evening news. Real people committing real acts of violence against other real people seems to have become a daily staple of our society. Children shooting children has reached epidemic level. How can you spare young children from such examples? A young child does not need to watch the evening news. You do not want him to get the idea that violence in society is acceptable or inevitable. Skip the violence on TV, reality based or so-called entertainment.

Toys of violence do not belong in a young child's collection. For many children, playing with toy guns significantly increases antisocial and aggressive behavior. The typical toddler has no need for such stimulation. Although many children will point their fingers and say, "Bang, bang!" or fashion their own toy guns out of sticks, that is not quite the same as using an object designed to resemble a real weapon. Let your child indulge in fantasy gunplay if you wish, but don't give it your overt approval and encouragement by providing the props.

The best way to discourage violent play is to keep toy weapons away from her without making a big deal of it. A child under three is too young to comprehend lengthy explanations, so skip the lectures and make sure your child has lots of other activities. When your child is old enough to draw a firm line between fantasy and reality, you may choose to permit certain toys and activities that were previously unsuitable for a child unable to make such distinctions.

# VISION (PROBLEMS) _____

If you suspect that your baby or toddler has vision problems, discuss your concerns with your health-care provider. It is important to identify any difficulties as soon as possible so that corrective measures can be taken. Referral to an eye specialist who deals with young children may be appropriate. As you observe your child's visual behavior, here are some questions to think about.

- When you look at your child's eyes, do they appear to be working together, or does one or both turn in or out and remain that way for any period of time?
- Does your baby or toddler seem to be visually responsive? Does he look at things and make some eye movements that suggest that the things are being seen?
- Does your mobile baby or toddler frequently bump into large objects or pieces of furniture while moving around?
- Does your child hold objects very close to look at them? When she tries to pick up a small object, does the hand often miss the object? Does there seem to be a lack of co-ordination between eyes and hand movement?
- Does your child regularly appear to favor one eye over the other when looking at something? Does he frequently rub his eyes? Does your child blink, squint, or frown excessively? Does she often close one eye?

# VITAMIN SUPPLEMENTS

Many families and their health-care providers believe that a vitamin supplement is an added safeguard to ensure that your child gets the necessary vitamins even on days when he is exercising toddler individuality about what to eat.

- Use liquid vitamins for a baby or toddler who cannot or will not deal with tablets. The best way to administer them is to use the measuring dropper provided to drop the pre-scribed dose right on the child's tongue. Many children like the taste. An alternative is to mix the drops in a tiny amount of juice. Use a small amount of juice to make sure the child will finish it.
- If you plan to use chewable vitamins for your toddler or older child, choose carefully. Most children's chewable vitamins contain large amounts of sugar, which harms chil-dren's teeth. Some contain ingredients that may be linked to hyperactivity or other behavioral problems. Avoid products with artificial coloring, artificial flavorings, un-necessary preservatives, and excessive sweeteners. You will do better to buy vitamins without the unnecessary extras and mash up a tablet into a spoonful of fruit.
- Do not refer to vitamins or any other tablets as "candy." Children who think vitamins are candy might be tempted to help themselves when you are not looking. That could be dangerous. Vitamins should have a child-resistant cap, and they should be stored out of your child's reach.
- Even if you take megadoses of vitamins and believe that practice to be personally help-ful, it is unwise to dose your child in that way. Children are more susceptible to harm from a vitamin overdose than an adult would be. There is no evidence, furthermore, that large doses of vitamins have any specific benefits for a young child. Stick to the normal daily dose suggested by your child's health-care provider.

# VOMITING (NEWBORN)

Spitting up is a normal happening for a newborn. Vomiting, however, is not the same as spitting up, and it is important for you to be aware of the difference. When a new baby spits up, the milk just gently comes back out the baby's mouth. She may not even be aware that this has happened.

Vomiting, in contrast to spitting up, is the forceful emptying out of the stomach. The contents are vigorously pushed out of the baby's mouth. Vomiting so forceful that what comes out lands a foot or more away from the baby's mouth is called "projectile vomiting." That may be an indication of a serious digestive problem or allergy.

Simple spitting up may be a mess, but it is typical of a newborn and it is not a health problem. Occasional vomiting if a baby is otherwise healthy is not a cause for concern. Projectile vomiting or ordinary vomiting that is more often than occasional should be reported to your health-care provider.

# VOMITING (OLDER BABY OR TODDLER)

There are several possible causes of vomiting in a young child—illness such as a viral infection of the stomach, fright or upset, pain, injury, or an overdose of dinner. If your usually healthy child vomits after eating too much at a birthday party, chalk it up to an excess of goodies and excitement. If, however, your child vomits and you can't trace the cause to something relatively harmless, here are some questions to consider.

- Does the child appear ill? Is he acting strange?
- Is there a fever? If so, how high is it?
- Is the vomiting accompanied by diarrhea?
- Is she vomiting with great force (projectile vomiting) rather than simply throwing up?
- Does the vomiting persist? Has he thrown up more than twice in a day?
- Does the child seem dehydrated? Is there a lack of saliva or tears? Is she passing less urine than usual?
- Does the child seem to have stomach pain? (It may be difficult to tell for sure with a child who is too young to explain exactly where it hurts.)
- Has the child fallen on his head? Is he pale or drowsy?

If the answer to one or more of the above questions is yes, then you should consult your child's health-care provider. The problem may just be a stomach virus that will run its course with no lasting harm. The vomiting, however, could be a symptom of a more serious problem. The sooner you find out what to do, the better.

## TREATMENT

If you have contacted your health-care provider, follow specifically any directions given to you at that time. If the cause of the vomiting is a mild stomach virus or a case of too much to eat, here are some suggestions to follow.

• Give the child's stomach a chance to rest. It is unlikely that she will want to eat or drink anything anyway, but make sure that food is not available for a while.
• If there has been no vomiting for two or three hours, you can try to start replacing lost fluids. Offer a small quantity (begin with a teaspoonful) of clear liquid such as water, juice, a sports drink, or flat ginger ale. If the child can keep that down for ten minutes, give a little more. Continue to supply small quantities of liquid as long as the child can keep it down. The key to doing this successfully is to give small quantities at frequent intervals. Do not overload the system with too much at once.
• A day of clear liquids can be followed by a day of light foods such as dry toast, cereal without milk, Jell-O, rice, applesauce, or bananas. Avoid milk, meat, or eggs for another day or two.

When your child handles the light foods well, gradually ease back to a normal diet. Don't do it all in one meal.

# WALKERS

A walker is a wheeled device that suspends a baby in an upright position with her feet touching the floor. A walker is not necessary, either for teaching a child to walk or for managing a mobile baby. In fact, some children may actually learn real walking less quickly because they are able to get around so rapidly in a walker.

A walker can make a prewalking baby extremely mobile. This can be both fun for the child and dangerous. Whether or not to use a walker is a personal choice. If you do allow your child to use one, keep safety in mind.

• When the wheels of a walker meet the edge of a carpet, a doorstop, or some other impediment to forward motion, the walker and the child may tip over. Choose a walker with a wide wheel base that is less likely to tip. It should only be used on smooth surfaces. If you choose a model that stops if one wheel is not on a level surface, so much the better.
• Walkers and stairs or steps are a potentially deadly combination. Gates at stairs are essential, as is constant attention from a supervising adult. A child who catapults down a flight of stairs in a walker could be seriously injured—perhaps even more seriously than he might have been had the fall occurred without being in a walker.
• Never allow your child to use a walker near a swimming pool. Sidewalks and curbs are also dangers that should be avoided.
• Minor cuts, bruises, and pinched fingers have long been a hazard of walker use. More recently, walkers have been redesigned to minimize the chances of a child's fingers getting trapped in the device. Check the safety record of the walker you choose.

A walker is not a confinement device like a playpen or play yard. It cannot be used to keep a child out of trouble. In fact, a walker may transport the child to potential trouble and even cause a few problems on its own. Do not leave your child unsupervised in a walker, even for a minute.

# WALKING

While many babies are able to walk on their own by the age of fifteen months or so, some who are perfectly normal take a while longer to get started. Walking is not something you need to teach a developing child. It will occur when the time is right. Some babies manage to take their first steps without any assistance at all, but many benefit from encouragement and support. Although you should not pressure your child to walk, it is a good idea to be helpful when he is ready to take that first step.

Before walking unaided without holding on to something, most children try upright locomotion while hanging on to something that can support them—a piece of furniture or the side of a crib or playpen, for example. When your child is standing well and seems ready to take a step or two without holding on, you can help. Sit on the floor just about within reach of where your child is standing. Hold out your arms and encourage her to take that first step. Be patient, and one of those times the step will happen.

# WATER (TO DRINK)

Offer water to your baby or toddler at least twice a day, more often in hot weather. Use a bottle if the child is not yet weaned. Use a cup or a glass (plastic is safest) if she can handle it. Many toddlers enjoy using a straw, although some have difficulty grasping that concept.

Sometimes a baby who seems to be demanding a feeding is not hungry, but is really thirsty instead. Offer water, and if your child is thirsty he will probably drink it. Water is a much better choice for a thirsty child than sodas or fruit drinks, which contain sweeteners and artificial flavorings or color. If your child is very thirsty, water is a better choice even than milk, which fills and adds calories without truly quenching thirst.

Right from the start, get your child used to taking water when thirsty. That will help build in a healthful habit that will be good for the rest of her life. If the safety of your water supply is questionable, consider bottled water for drinking.

# WEANING (FROM THE BOTTLE)

You can wean your child from the bottle completely and relatively abruptly at a time of your choosing, or you can let the child gradually wean himself as he wishes. There are advantages and disadvantages to each approach. Regardless of which one you choose, remember that evening bottles that end up being taken to bed increase the chances of tooth decay, so this should not be allowed.

## WEANING AT THE CHILD'S PACE

A child obtains comfort and pleasure as well as nourishment from sucking. Having the bottle available places it under her control. Use of the bottle may diminish the need for thumb-sucking as a comfort device. Using a bottle helps ensure that the child will get enough milk in his daily diet, and an evening bottle may make relaxing before bedtime easier. (Do not, however, allow the child to take a bottle to bed.)

For some children, a gradual transition from bottle to no bottle is less likely to cause upset than abrupt weaning.

## WEANING AT A DEFINITE TIME

Some children become increasingly attached to and dependent on the bottle as time goes on. If left to her own devices, a child might not give up the bottle with complete willingness.

Children who drink bottles well into the second year may consume more milk than they need which, in turn, can lead to excess weight. Once a mobile child discovers that a bottle is portable, the bottle may take on a new attractiveness and the child independently carts it about. Early weaning can eliminate the opportunity for that discovery.

Consider the pros and cons of weaning methods and choose whichever approach you think will work best for your child and your family's lifestyle. If you wish to be relaxed about weaning and let your child use the bottle as a comfort device for as long as he wishes, that is your choice. If, on the other hand, you prefer to eliminate the bother of bottles and get your child completely to the cup as fast as feasible, that is fine too. Keep in mind, however, that your child may turn to other comfort devices when the bottle is no longer available.

## DRINKING FROM A CUP

Whether you wean your child completely at a particular time or let the process occur naturally over weeks or months, you will still have to teach your child to drink from a cup. Here are some suggestions.

- A lightweight plastic cup is safest. At first, it probably will be easier for your child to manage a cup with two handles.
- Begin by putting just a swallow or two of milk or formula in the bottom of the cup. That will prevent the child from taking too much at once, and will leave less available for the inevitable spill.
- You will have to help your child hold and maneuver the cup at first until she figures out what to do with it. Gently guide her hand to get started.
- Some children find using a straw to be an excellent transition from sucking a bottle to sipping from a cup. Others, however, don't seem to have a clue about how a straw works. The short straws that bend are easiest for a child to use if he is going to make one work.
- If you give juice and water only from a cup right from the start, and never put either of those drinks in a bottle, your child will have a head start on the weaning process.

- If you always hold your child during bottle-feeding and never let her carry the bottle around, chances are that complete weaning will happen fairly rapidly. If, on the other hand, your child learns to bring the bottle with her, chances are that the bottle use will persist somewhat longer.

## TRAINING CUPS

A training cup is a plastic cup with a lid and little spout with holes in it. The purpose of a training cup is to help prevent spills while easing the transition from bottle or breast to cup. Some children use the device effectively, as intended. Others, however, discover quite quickly that turning the cup upside down results in lovely little streams of milk pouring out. If a training cup does not work as intended for your child, you could try a nonspill cup (with a valve in the lid), or simply discard the lid altogether and use it as a regular cup later.

# WEANING (FROM THE BREAST) _____

Weaning from the breast is done best for both mother and child if it is done gradually. Depending on when you wean your breast-fed child and how long you intend the process to take, you can either switch the child to a bottle or directly to taking milk or formula from a cup.

When you wean your child from the breast should be a personal decision and choice. It is really no one else's business, although friends, family members, and even complete strangers may express an opinion on the matter.

If you are breast-feeding your baby, it is recommended that you do so for at least a year. There may be circumstances such as work outside the home, for example, that might make this difficult. If you continue to breast-feed your child well into toddlerhood, make sure that you are meeting the child's needs, not simply your own. (See *Breast-feeding*, pages 37–41.)

If you must wean your child from the breast before he is six months old, you probably will want to use bottles as an intermediate step. For a child who is already taking solid foods from a spoon and juice or water from a cup, you may wish to skip the bottle stage entirely. If you omit bottles, you will probably have to stop nursing more gradually in order to meet your child's continuing sucking needs until they naturally diminish.

To begin weaning your child from the breast, begin by giving up one feeding during the day. Most mothers find that it is easiest to give up the midday feeding. Substitute milk or formula in a bottle or cup, according to your plan, for the breast milk at that feeding. If your child is already taking solid foods, give a little milk before the solid part of the meal and the rest afterward. After you have stopped giving a regular feeding from the breast, your milk supply will naturally decrease. If your breasts are uncomfortably full, express a small amount of milk to ease the discomfort, but not enough to stimulate additional milk production.

When you have successfully eliminated one daily feeding for two or three weeks, and you and your child have adjusted to the new schedule, eliminate another feeding. Whether you retain the evening feeding at the breast or keep nursing at breakfast time is up to you. Many mothers find that keeping on with the evening feeding helps a child relax at bedtime, but you should do what makes sense to you. Give up whichever feeding you think your child will miss the least. After you have reduced your nursing schedule to once daily, this feeding too will diminish and disappear completely and naturally.

As your child nurses less, your breasts will produce less and less milk until weaning is complete. There is no one correct way to wean a child from the breast. Follow your instincts and do what works comfortably for both of you.

# X RAYS

If your child requires an X ray, try to remain with her if possible. The procedure can be quite frightening. Explain that an X ray is just a picture of part of the body taken with a special camera. Preparation in advance can be helpful, but if the reason for the X ray is an emergency, you would not have the luxury of time to prepare. Most medical facilities will permit you to remain with your child during emergency treatment if at all possible. Indicate firmly your desire and intention to remain with your child.

Avoid routine X rays that are not essential for diagnosis of a problem. A lead shield should be used to protect your child's genitals when another body part needs an X ray. If the technician seems to be overlooking that safety precaution, be sure to speak up.

# YARD SALES

In many neighborhoods, yard sales are an excellent source of bargain merchandise. One family's discard may turn out to be another family's newfound treasure. Be careful, however, of using yard sales as a source of certain essential items such as car seats or cribs for your newborn baby or toddler.

Before you purchase any item that may have safety implications for your child, it's important to make certain that the item fully meets up-to-date standards. A vintage crib, for example, may look lovely but contain features now known to be dangerous. A car restraint, even if it appears to be in fine condition, may have been in an accident and, as a result, may no longer be able to offer the full protection your child deserves.

There may also be sanitary considerations involved in purchasing used items from strangers. Who knows where that darling teddy bear may have been, and what its furry surface may harbor.

If you enjoy shopping at yard sales or flea markets, it's fine to continue doing so. Just be especially careful to think through each potential purchase and make sure what you buy does not place your child at risk. (See *Automobile safety,* pages 12–16, *Cribs,* pages 69–70, *Furniture,* page 96, and *Toys,* page 182.)

# YEAST INFECTION

If your child has a diaper rash that seems to go beyond the ordinary diaper rash, you might want to check with the doctor to see if the rash indicates a yeast infection. As any woman who has ever had a yeast infection knows well, the discomfort from such a problem can be virtually unbearable.

If the color of the rash looks like uncooked hamburger, there are pinkish spots near the red area, and the rash has invaded the creases of the groin, you might be dealing with a yeast infection rather than routine diaper rash. Yeast infections frequently accompany the taking of antibiotics, but that connection is not the only cause of such a problem. If you suspect that your baby has a yeast infection, consult your health-care provider. A yeast infection can be treated with an antifungal cream, certain types of which may be purchased over the counter. It's best, however, to find out exactly which product your doctor recommends.

(See also the sections on *Changing diapers,* pages 53–54, *Diaper rash,* pages 78–79, and *Thrush,* page 177.)

# ZINC OXIDE OINTMENT

Zinc oxide ointment, which is a major ingredient of brand-name diaper rash remedies such as Desitin, is an effective and inexpensive treatment for diaper rash. Little jars or tubes of zinc oxide ointment are readily available without prescription in your local supermarket or pharmacy. For additional suggestions for prevention and treatment of diaper rash, see *Diaper rash,* pages 78–79.

# ZOOS

Visiting a zoo can be an exciting experience for a young child. Remember, however, that wild animals are wild animals, even in captivity. Keep your child under control at all times. Do not let any member of your family—child or adult—climb over guardrails for a close-up picture, no matter how tempting that scene might be. Hold on tightly to your child as he stands in front of the guardrails.

In the children's section of the zoo, where children and tame animals are allowed to mingle, remember that a toddler's good judgment probably does not keep up with her curiosity. You may need to protect the animals and your child from each other. Another concern about a visit to a children's zoo, petting zoo, or farm is cleanliness and the potential for bacterial infection. Be sure that your child washes his hands thoroughly after touching the animals and before putting them to his mouth or taking food.

An afternoon at the zoo can be fun as long as you keep it safe and recognize your child's limitations. For your own comfort as well as your child's, a backpack or stroller is a must. Even a strong toddler is likely to get tired of walking long before she is tired of looking.